Women in the First Capitalist Society

Women in the First Capitalist Society

Experiences in Seventeenth-Century England

Margaret George

University of Illinois Press
Urbana and Chicago

Publication of this work was supported in part
by a grant from Northern Illinois University.

This book is printed on acid-free paper.

For Jessica
Precious Companion

Contents

PART 5

Of Learned Ladies and Silent Signposts

Acknowledgments

I wish to thank Elizabeth Fox-Genovese for her careful reading of a raw manuscript, and for critically invaluable suggestions. My thanks go as well to Bridget Hill, who provided an evaluation of the study which was both challenging and supportive. My longtime friend and colleague Marvin Rosen has my gratitude for insightful and encouraging comments on my work. And but for Charles H. George's skeptical prodding the project might not have been started.

I am indebted especially to the resources and reference staffs of the Bodleian Library, the British Library and the Public Record Office, and the Newberry Library, Chicago.

I thank Carole Appel of the University of Illinois Press for her efforts in guiding the manuscript toward publication. I greatly appreciate the contributions of Carol Bolton Betts of the Press, who gave the manuscript not only support but meticulous copyediting. Finally, I am grateful to Karen Blaser and Cheryl Fuller, of Northern Illinois University, whose responsibility it was to manage the typing and retyping.

Introduction: The Fixed Foundation

This is a book shaped by seventeenth-century women. That it is dominated by biographical anecdote is recognition of forceful personalities, the well-known Lucy Hutchinson, the notorious Elizabeth Celliers, the obscure Susanna Eyres. The gentlewoman, mistresses, and goodwives would have it no other way.

For a rather long time in my research the weight of the evidence pushed a mode of presentation in another direction. I had come to the study of the experiences of women from 'gentle' to the 'middling sort' in the seventeenth century because, convinced of this as the classic period of the establishment of capitalism in England, I wanted to see them in the midst of the revolutionary activity which Marx of the *Manifesto* called "bourgeois." And in this early research necessarily concentrated upon the achievements of social change, if not losing sight of women altogether, I was perceiving them as indistinct and passive figures.

Manifestly, women were not the prime agents in a society being transformed by the emerging structures of agrarian capitalism. They were not the actors and planners in "the accumulation of capital in trade and usury, the expansion of commodity markets in towns and villages, the blasting of rural social structures to 'free' peasant labor, and . . . the explosive acceleration of imperial investments and the creation of a world market."[1] It was not their initiative which was dealing "a deathblow to the age-old conception of society as a hierarchy of interdependent orders," replacing it with "a notion of society as a series of independent and necessarily antagonistic classes,"[2] and wrenchingly rearranging social relations "among yeomen, journeymen, merchants, peers of the realm, and the mass of the 'laboring poor.' "[3]

Resoundingly in the contemporary sources it was the start of what the eighteenth century would celebrate as the Age of Man. Thomas Hobbes so recognized the individualistic acquisitive male in his environment that he took the competition for power and profits as the eternal basis of human "nature," and if his perceptions of brutal individualism upset the old-fashioned they made him the most relevant social theorist of his time. Essayists and dramatists obsessively portrayed the same male initiators. Protestant preachers thunderously denounced them, through the first half of the century, at least. Gerrard Winstanley, special in holding a transitory—historical, revolutionary—view of the dominant actors, isolated them in the enclosing landlords of Surrey (and their minions now of the "murdering" law and the "tithing" priesthood) who had "put mankind upon buying and selling of the earth and her fruits," and who as declared owners of private property had shut "poor commoners" from digging and planting on the wastelands of St. George's Hill.[4]

The male revolutionaries whose designs were transforming society and social relationships were not merely obstructing my view of women; they were the mediators through whom I felt compelled to go to get the proper and exact view. They were rethinkers as well as redoers, dazzling in their mania for definition and redefinition, whether of the constitution of the state, the sources of wealth, power, and social hierarchies, the mechanics of the universe, or the 'nature' of women. This was the compelling point: the male sources were telling me what Woman should be and do in their sketching of an image/ideal that would only begin to blur in western middle-class culture in the twentieth century; and they were insisting that all women—all *their* women—exactly pattern themselves upon the model.

Consider, for example, the literary free-for-all, the "popular controversy"[5] about women which went on from the late sixteenth century: the public tip of rumbling readjustment of marriage and familial structures to the needs of the emerging society of individual property owners. The male participants created an absorbing furor: in pamphlets and poems, solemn tracts and porno-doggerels, with moral earnestness or furious misogyny or bawdy commercialism discussing female character, behavior, and appearance; and, pro or con on the subject of the daughters of Eve, positing a remarkably uniform ideal which with diligent effort their women might approximate. It was woman-as-wife they were recasting, trimming her for but one career in that reformed and Protestant marriage viewed as holy in the sight of God, fundamental to the orderly society of men, and essential to the well-being and peace of mind/body of the respectably busy man. Chanted the poets, "God to each *Man* a private *Woman* gave / That in that centre his desires might stint / That he a comfort like himself might have / And that on her *His Like* he might imprint."[6]

Could the paste-up portrait be made more clear than in the urgent eulogy of "the good Burgomaster's wife . . . who ever met her Husband at the Portell with a gentle word in her mouth; a sweet smile on her lippe; a merry looke on her cherry cheeke; a paire of slippers in one hand: and in the other, a . . . Towell to rubbe him after his travaile"?[7]

Similarly, the great Protestant preachers are impossible to miss and hard to get by in their female-shaping. The point has been made that the English clergy were not the "makers of capitalist civilization," indeed that to review their sermons "is to be confronted with absolutely negative information about the new class forming."[8] In their age of iron and fire the preachers were horrified by the impulses of secular self-interest, of "possessive individualism"; their social vision was a Christian community of the male heads of nuclear families, streamlined Old Testament patriarchs who walked narrowly in the way of the Lord in unmediated responsibility for themselves, and for the piety and obedience of their women, children, and servants. Still, their differences with the most worldly bourgeois were imperceptible in their insistence upon the family as the "little Church" and the "little Commonwealth," and upon the woman within it as chaste, comforting, and submissive. Thus the sermons on "domesticall duties," which, as the famous Dr. William Gouge of Blackfriars said, were "first uttered out of the pulpit," conceived of her "no sooner" a woman "but presently a Wife"; she was content in her subordination, indeed yielded a "voluntary subjection" to the husband who was her "King," her "Priest," and her "Prophet," who had not only "robed" her of her "virginitie" but had as well "possession and use of her will."[9]

Even in dismissing women, men were both fascinating and distracting, a point brilliantly illuminated in Brian Easlea's book *Witch Hunting, Magic and the New Philosophy.* Easlea's protagonists, male achievers of the "privileged classes" in late seventeenth-century mechanical philosophy, applied science, and the "Appropriation of Nature," defined themselves by their distance, actually difference, from women—or, precisely, from their restatement of the Judaic-Christian image of women. The female, they said, was "matter"; man was "mind." Women, by definition mentally inferior, tied to their reproductive function and sexually obsessed, insatiable in their "carnal" desires, were the reminder of a fading past; they were the embodiment of the forces of nature, which had for so long mystified and tormented men, and which were now being subjected to the cool penetration and control of the male intellect. Easlea provides an arresting array of the promises of the practioners of the New Philosophy, their vows of the conquest and subjugation of "Dame Nature" by "masculine" science. Francis Bacon issued the invitation "to inaugurate the 'truly masculine birth of time.' " His disciples seized the theme: Nature was "a Mistress" who would yield to "the forward, and the Bold"; her suitors had advanced from her "antechamber to her inner closet," had "all most broken her Seale, and exposed her naked to the World"; the scientist had "powers which may be called creative . . . which have enabled him . . . by his experiments to interrogate nature with power, not simply as a scholar, passive and seeking only to understand her operations, but rather as a master, active with his own instruments."[10] "It would rather appear," remarks Easlea, "that after a long historical development a class of men had emerged in western Europe who would sever ties with 'mother earth' in pursuit of a compulsive drive to prove their masculinity and virility. The means was to be ever-developing technological appropriation of a passive earth so that men might achieve, in Francis Bacon's momentous words, 'the effecting of all things possible.' "[11]

As with Easlea's, other recent studies reinforced my focus, the direction of my attention. In the monographic literature are fine-lined sketches of the doers, the actual "makers" of bourgeois civilization: gentlemen and yeomen turning land into capital—and customary tenants into wage-earners; coal industrialists, textile merchants, shipbuilders, brewers, glass or paper or pottery manufacturers, all flexing their ambitions in expanding national and international markets; parliamentarians, gentlemen, professionals, or businessmen, asserting the political sovereignty of themselves and their propertied constituents.[12] Close examination allows us to see them as well as the individual members of "civil society," as contrasted to the old "lineage society," each the head of a household, increasingly in "defensive isolation," and "entrenched with his family in the fortress of his property."[13]

Studies of the family, then, the family being adapted to the requirements of the individual constituents of "civil society," provide more vivid images of men acting, relating, purposing, transforming. They were erasing the old encompassing sense of family as kinship group, reducing and redefining 'family' to what had traditionally been but a nuclear "sub-unit."[14] They were 'spiritualizing' the family into the "little Church," its members prepared for Puritan godliness by the rigorous discipline of the husband and father.[15] They were building a polity on the family as the basic political cell, the heads of families, "free-men," taxpayers, voters, responsible to the state for the civil obedience of their dependents.[16] They were restricting the family, individualizing and personalizing it, assuming it as the extension of self and property.[17]

Further, in their privatization of property and production, which separated both from "the patriarchal social household,"[18] seventeenth-century men were organizing the family enterprise, managing its members in their contributions to the "domestic economy."[19] Thus, as in the list of requirements of a late sixteenth-century diarist, a man needed a wife for companionship as well as for assistance in the "care and looking after children," the "care of household matters," and the maintenance and increase of "substance."[20] (Of course, the preachers and essayists were shaping the 'good woman' to her domestic responsibilities as well as to voluntary submissiveness, enjoining her to be hardworking, thrifty, and skilled in her family tasks.)[21] And gradually, unevenly, according to their enterprises, their growth and prospering, they separated production and the family, again redefining the family base, this time as the place of retreat and rest for themselves and of the nurturing of their heirs, its domestic routines the specific content of 'woman's world.' It was a transition perfectly caught by Daniel Defoe in a book published in 1726: Defoe thought it an "injustice" to the wives of some tradesmen "such as linen and woolen drapers, mercers, booksellers, goldsmiths, and all sorts of dealers by commission, and the like," that they had been "shut out," ordered by their husbands not to "meddle" or "be seen" in their shops; what a few tradesmen started others followed, said Defoe, because they would "not have their trades or shops thought less masculine or less considerable than others. . . ."[22]

Now I am not complaining, nor saying that this concentration upon the immensely informative and often entertaining evidence of male activity and thought was a dead end, or even an endless detour. My objective—knowledge of women, 'gentle' to the 'middling sort'—remained unchanged. It is just that wherever I turned for female experience, in the "fortress" of the family, in working relationships and activities (with, as argued by the historian Alice Clark, diminished status, in the loss of the 'rough equality' with husbands in the precapitalist past?),[23] in educational achievement (more loss, a decline from the "golden" Tudor times?),[24] I was invited to watch the makers of bourgeois civilization 'making bourgeois woman.' Unquestionably the men were shaping my inquiry, and directing a presentation of women as objects, as though ready-framed in good English oak.

My encounter with Lucy Hutchinson, whose autobiography fills chapter 1 of this book, was critical in wonderful ways, and particularly satisfying in this: she, rather than the male managers, gave me proper direction. Mrs. Hutchinson did not need mediators. Her unsolicited testimony related squarely to the measuring, cutting, and trimming of revolutionary social designers. She made it quite plain that she did not resent being 'spiritualized' or diminished by dominant males, that as a late product herself of Tudor-courtier educational privilege, and a Puritan to boot, she was indifferent to being left behind by the scientific masters of nature. Simply, or rather consciously, seriously, she created *herself* in the men's world and with the materials handed her; to put it another way, in reproducing in her own terms the hardening definition of the female role she embellished and strengthened it. The obvious is nonetheless striking: as much as any man Lucy Hutchinson was a maker of bourgeois culture.

Lucy Hutchinson's autobiography turned me from contemplating framed figures, or from counting wax-like shapes in Defoe's tradesmen's upstairs parlors.[25] I decided to select and concentrate upon the garrulous and the sharply visible, women with staying power and flesh on their identities who, like Mrs. Hutchinson, could simultaneously reveal both themselves and the dynamic whole of what Hobsbawm called "the first complete bourgeois revolution."[26]

Thereafter the chapters grew because of the richness of the sources, their quality the remarkable sign of the new, seventeenth-century female self-conscious self-involvement.[27] Perhaps the sections on women in the Civil War fit clumsily. The evidence is frustrating: plentiful enough to justify a certainty that urban women of all classes were up to their ears in home, street or tavern talk, and action; sadly lacking in individual appearances.[28] But I could not ignore the critical subject of women's experiences of the crashing conflict in the English revolution, of their angle of vision of the issues involved, the stakes being gambled. Women were politically impotent, legally 'as if dead.' That was one bit of ancient tradition still unquestionable, requiring only repolishing by husbands gathering courage to kill their king. Yet women registered their civic existence, compelled by the cataclysmic events and the new currents of public assertiveness to edge, warily, apologetically, toward the forbidden arenas. These are narrative chapters: here, they say, are ways in which wives of rich Londoners peered into the male preserve of national politics; here is evidence of the painfully angled view of political power of Leveller women, their lessons learned in continuous presence in the rear echelons of the popular revolutionary army.

The bulk of this book is of individual stories, from autobiographies, diaries, letters, chosen for their fullness and selected too to give a range of adult female experience. I was not put off by male-crafted tales of women. The wonderful jumble of the Thomason Tracts is filled with them, some sensationalized, commercialized, to the rim of fantasy, but verifiable in court records, state papers, or county archives and family chapels. They are quite usable when listened to with exquisite care. The various personalities, revealing themselves and their society, seemed to me almost eerily familiar. Saintly Shaw, loud-suffering Thornton and possessive Freke, the scheming Theodosia and the selfless Brilliana, Cellier the professional and Susanna the survivor—they might be characters in bourgeois novels from the late eighteenth century.

I finish with Celia Fiennes; she is at the opposite end of the book, opposite end of the transforming age, from Lucy Hutchinson. The last words are shared by early, isolated feminists: already in this fast-moving century lonely voices were anticipating Mary Wollstonecraft, complaining bitterly of the contrast between male freedom and opportunity and women's restricted domestic assignment.[29] But the less reflective Fiennes seemed the appropriate witness, spokeswoman for a majority of serious-minded, middle-class women in the rooting culture. She accepted the circumscribed 'woman's world' in male-defined society as natural and unchangeable; her projects were designed, very successfully,[30] to be both useful and personally satisfying without violating its limits.

I have kept the seventeenth-century spelling, punctuation, and capitalization. Not only would it have been absurd to change it; the written language is a story in itself of the gap between the achieving males and the left-behind females. How contrarily striking it is that while the male intellect, developing in mounting and marvelous complexity, expressed itself in ever more formal 'modern' English, women continued to say their homely thoughts in a riot of phonetic individuality.

NOTES

1. Charles H. George, "The Making of the English Bourgeoisie," *Science & Society*, Winter 1971: 389.
2. Ibid.
3. *The Agrarian History of England and Wales*, ed. Joan Thirsk, 4: 465.
4. For the mirror image of the new society in Winstanley's pamphlets, see *The Works of Gerrard Winstanley*, ed. George M. Sabine (New York, 1965).
5. The phrase is from Louis B. Wright, *Middle-Class Culture in Elizabethan England* (Ithaca, 1935), chapter 13.
6. *A Wife Now the Widow of Sir Thomas Overburye. Being a most exquisite and singular Poem of the choice of a Wife* (London, 1614).
7. Richard Braithwaite, *Ar't asleepe Husband* (London, 1640), p. 108.

8. George, "Making of the English Bourgeoisie," pp. 405-6; also, C. H. and Katherine George, *The Protestant Mind of the English Revolution* (Princeton, 1961), chapter 4, and passim.

9. William Gouge, *Of Domesticall Duties* (London, 1622), Preface; Matthew Griffith, *Bethel: or a forme for families* (London, 1633), p. 232; Gouge, *Of Domesticall Duties*, pp. 26, 345-48; Robert Cleaver, *A Godly Form of Householde Government* (London, 1598), p. 167.

10. Brian Easlea, *Witch Hunting, Magic and the New Philosophy* (Sussex, 1980), pp. 246-48.

11. Ibid., p. 248; see too, Carolyn Merchant, *The Death of Nature: Women, Ecology, and the Scientific Revolution* (New York, 1980).

12. A tiny, eclectic sample: L. A. Clarkson, *The Pre-Industrial Economy in England* (London, 1971); Mildred Campbell, *The English Yeoman* (New Haven, 1942); Eric Kerridge, *The Agricultural Revolution* (London, 1967) and *The Farmers of Old England* (London, 1973); *Changes in the Countryside: Essays on Rural England, 1500-1900*, ed. M. S. A. Fox and R. A. Butlin (London, 1979); W. G. Moskins, *The Midland Peasant* (London, 1957); R. G. Wilson, *Gentlemen Merchants* (Manchester, 1971); Ralph Davis, *English Overseas Trade, 1500-1700* (London, 1973); Christopher Hill, *God's Englishman* (New York, 1970) and *Intellectual Origins of the English Revolution* (Oxford, 1965); *Puritans and Revolutionaries: Essays in Seventeenth Century History Presented to Christopher Hill*, ed. Donald Pennington and Keith Thomas (Oxford, 1978).

13. Mervyn James, *Family, Lineage and Civil Society* (Oxford, 1974), p. 189.

14. Lawrence Stone, *The Family, Sex and Marriage in England, 1500-1800* (New York, 1977), p. 4.

15. See chapter 13, "The Spiritualization of the Household," in Christopher Hill, *Society and Puritanism in Pre-Revolutionary England* (New York, 1964).

16. See Elizabeth Fox-Genovese, "Placing Women in Women's History," *New Left Review*, Summer 1982: 19 and passim, for a fine discussion of, and full bibliography on, these points. The reader will note my interest in the theme of Fox-Genovese's article.

17. Alan Macfarlane, *The Origins of English Individualism* (Oxford, 1978); Keith Wrightson, *English Society, 1580-1680* (New Brunswick, N.J., 1982); Roberta Hamilton, *The Liberation of Women: A Study of Patriarchy and Capitalism* (London, 1978); Cicely Howell, *Land, Family and Inheritance in Transition* (Cambridge, 1983); *Family and Inheritance*, ed. Jack Goody, Joan Thirsk, and E. P. Thompson (Cambridge, 1976). For a recent study which insists on the continuity of "familial forms, functions and ideals," see Ralph A. Houlbrooke, *The English Family, 1450-1700* (London, 1984), p. 16.

18. Elizabeth Fox-Genovese and Eugene D. Genovese, *Fruits of Merchant Capitalism* (Oxford, 1983), p. 301.

19. Ibid., chapter 11, for a discussion of "The Ideological Bases of Domestic Economy."

20. From the Rogers Diary, in *Two Elizabethan Puritan Diaries*, ed. M. M. Knappen (Gloucester, Mass., 1966), p. 74.

21. This occurs in all of the preachers' "domestic conduct" tracts, from Thomas Becon, *The Boke of Matrimony* (1560), to Matthew Griffith's *Bethel* (1633). An early classic from a secular instructor was Richard Braithwaite's *The English Gentlewoman* (London, 1631).

22. Daniel Defoe, *The Complete English Tradesman* (London, 1726), p. 355. The excellent reporter Defoe gives a glimpse of women's wills here in the early eighteenth century: as "ladies now manage," he says, they "scorn to be seen in the compting-house, much less behind the counter; despise the knowledge of their husband's business, and act as if they were ashamed of being tradesmens wives, and never intended to be tradesmens widows" (Ibid., p. 348).

23. I am referring, of course, to the argument of Alice Clark, *Working Life of Women in the 17th Century* (London, 1919 and 1968), in which she was sure that capitalist reorganization of production—relevantly, the obsolescence of "Family Industry"—had rapidly lowered women's value and therefore social esteem, brought the "decline" in their "social and economic position" which is "so noticeable in the seventeenth century" (Ibid., pp. 300-303). Certainly, "Clark exaggerated the extent of the decline of productive domestic partnership during this period" (R. A. Houlbrooke, *The English Family*, p. 8). And it is true that her work has led some historians "to romanticize life in precapitalist—and especially preindustrial—societies," as pointed out in Fox-Genovese, "Placing Women in Women's History," p. 21. But as it did Alice Clark, the quality of the critical attention paid to women in seventeenth-century English sources continues to impress me. My hypothesis, evident in the foregoing pages, is that women were not set back, but left back, by the great leap forward of men. In moving so far so fast, men were measuring themselves against the female, the latter defined as static, ignorant, "carnal." That that definition came so readily to mind makes it impossible, obviously, to romanticize women's esteem in the precapitalist past. For some judicious uses of Alice Clark's work, see Sheila Robotham, *Hidden From History* (New York, 1976), Introduction; and Simon Shepherd, *Amazons and Warrior Women* (New York, 1981), chapter 4.

24. The questions continue about the content, the social spread, and the legacy of humanist advocacy of learning for women. See Pearl Hogrefe, *Tudor Women: Commoners and Queens* (Ames, Iowa, 1975); for a cautionary study, Retha M. Warnicke, *Women of the English Renaissance and Reformation* (Westport, Conn., 1983).

25. More Defoe commentary: "The tradesman is foolishly vain of making his wife a gentlewoman, and forsooth he will have her sit above in the parlour, receive visits, drink Tea, and entertain her neighbors" (*Complete Tradesman*, p. 355).

26. Eric Hobsbawm, "The Crisis of the 17th Century," *Past and Present* 6 (November 1954): 63.

27. For the kinds of sources available to historians before the seventeenth century, see *Women in English Society, 1500-1800*, ed. Mary Prior (London, 1985); and *Women in the Middle Ages and the Renaissance*, ed. Mary Beth Rose (Syracuse, 1986). In the latter we are told that in the "late" seventeenth century English women "begin" to write "secular" autobiography (p. 245).

28. Historians are not exactly swamped with such material, in any case. Clarendon, in his *History of the Rebellion*, mentions the women's petitions, as we shall see. S. A. Gardiner, *History of the Great Civil War*, gives them in volume 1: 218-21. Valerie Pearl, *London and the Outbreak of the Puritan Revolution* (Oxford, 1961), includes all the evidence, and Anthony Fletcher, *The Outbreak of the English Civil War* (New York, 1981), none of it.

29. See Hilda L. Smith, *Reason's Disciples: Seventeenth-Century English Feminists* (Urbana, Ill., 1982).

30. To anticipate an objection: Celia Fiennes was upper-middle-class, in seventeenth-century rank, upper class; she could do what she did so successfully because she was a privileged spinster from solid gentry wealth and power.

PART 1

Witnessing Supremely

1

Lucy Hutchinson, Keynote Speaker

née Apsley

Lucy Hutchinson's biography of her husband is a source known to every student of the English Revolution. She wrote it in a large manuscript of over four hundred pages, with the homely title "The Life of John Hutchinson, of Owthorpe, in the County of Nottinghamshire, Esquire." Most of it dealt with Hutchinson's activities between 1642 and his death in 1664; a Protestant turned Puritan country gentleman, he was successively colonel in the parliamentary armies, governor of the castle and town of Nottingham, M.P. for and sheriff of Nottinghamshire, a judge in the trial of Charles I, member of the Commonwealth Council of State, and finally prisoner and regicide casualty of the Restoration government of Charles II.

The manuscript is intriguing as an evocative account of episodes in the civil wars, and as simply first-rate biography. Colonel Hutchinson was not a crucially important parliamentary leader—Christopher Hill observed that he was "interesting as a Puritan, and of some significance as a republican"[1]—but his record in holding the divided citizens of Nottingham to the defense of the county against the royalist forces, his solitary decisions to kill the king in 1649 or to oppose Cromwell in 1651, his last yearning for a regicide's fate, all of these are wonderful pieces of the drama of the age.

Of further interest: Lucy Hutchinson's manuscript, justification, vindication, apotheosis of her husband, was addressed "To My Children," and apparently intended only for private reading; its acidulous comments on the character and behavior of prominent people, and its unrelenting hatred of the royalist side, written in the punitive atmosphere of the 1660s, would make that prudent. At any rate, the manuscript was kept privately in the possession of subsequent generations of Hutchinsons. By the mid-eighteenth century it was a tempting secret to various outsiders (the eminent historian Catherine Macaulay tried unsuccessfully to pry it from the family drawers) until a new heir, the Reverend Julius Hutchinson, edited a censored version for publication in 1806. Despite the clergyman's cautions of Colonel Hutchinson's "predilection for a republican government," and unrepentance as a regicide, the book went through three editions between 1806 and 1810.[2] From the time of that first rush of attention (curiously from a British generation troubled domestically in its wars with Napoleonic France) the *Memoirs of the Life of John Hutchinson* has had the various fresh and full editions that stand in rows on library shelves.

In this appreciation of John Hutchinson's life his biographer has not been ignored. No danger of that: Lucy Hutchinson's presence is inescapable. Obviously the notes she kept of John's contentious years as governor of Nottingham Castle emerged from her discussions with him, but the bulky manuscript which became the *Life* was her product, the testament to the whole of their lives. Christopher Hill, in his short article on the Hutchinsons, asserted: "And what a testament! It is one of the great biographies of the English language, probably the greatest written by that date . . . certainly the best by a woman."[3] That is a high accolade to Lucy Hutchinson's intelligence, initiative, devotion.

Given the circumstances, no one contemplates her alone, as an autonomous individual; necessarily, it seems, she is defined within the married state, the distaff side of (and again the phrase is Hill's) the "perfect Puritan marriage."[4] To be sure, she set that perception herself: except in a "Fragment" of autobiographical writing about a child named Lucy Apsley, she never presented herself other than "Mrs. Hutchinson." In the *Life* she fixed her identity; she was John's "very faithfull mirror, reflecting truly, though but dimmely, his owne glories upon him. . . ."[5]

Even on her own terms Mrs. Hutchinson was too modest. In being a mirror for husband John she required of herself the mirroring of his/her entire world: a historical background of the Reformation in Europe and England; a summary of a hundred years of English government and party (Protestant) politics; an account of the civil wars thorough enough to give even the uninformed a basic understanding. Here, as an example of Mrs. Hutchinson's command of her material, is her analysis of how the label "Puritane" became "fixt" in the reign of James I upon "whatever was odious or dreadfull to the king":

> . . . if any durst dispute his impositions in the worship of God, he was presently reckon'd among the seditious and disturbers of the publick peace, and accordingly persecuted. If any were griev'd at the dishonor of the kingdome, or the griping of the poore, or the unjust oppressions of the subject, by a thousand wayes invented to maintaine the riotts of the courtiers and the swarms of needy Scotts the king had brought in

like locusts to devoure the plenty of this land, he was a Puritane. If any, out of mere morallity and civill honesty, discountenanc'd the abominations of those dayes, he was a Puritane, however, he conform'd to their superstitious worship. If any shew'd favour to any godly honest person, kept them company, reliev'd them in want, or protected them against violent or unjust oppression, he was a Puritane. If any gentleman in his country maintain'd the good lawes of the land, or stood up for any publick interest of his country, for good order or government, he was a Puritane; and in short, all that crost the interest of the needie Courtiers, the proud encroaching priests, the theevish projectors, the lewd nobillity and gentrie, whoever was zealous for God's glory or worship, could not endure blasphemous oathes, ribald conversation, prophane scoffes, sabbath breach, derision of the word of God, and the like; whoever could endure a sermon, modest habitt or conversation, or aniething that was good, all these were Puritanes; and if Puritanes, then enemies to the king and his government, seditious factious hipocrites, ambitious disturbers of the publick peace. . . . Such false logick did the children of darknesse use to argue with against the hated children of light. . . .[6]

Yet Mrs. Hutchinson had deficiencies as a biographer. Hill identified the obvious one: the *Life*, he remarked, was "not a subtle psychological study, such as one might have expected from a Puritan," having "none of the insights of *Grace Abounding* or Fox's Journal."[7] True, the *Life* is not a subtle psychological study of John Hutchinson. But then Mrs. Hutchinson told us why it was not. Her avowed intention was to "celebrate the glories of a saint." She declared John in vivid image a Moses figure, "prepar'd to be a leader of God's people out of bondage . . . to deliver his country, groaning under spiritual and civill bondage." As she began writing she was tense with fear that she would "disgrace his name with a poore monument"; his "vertues come very much sullied out of my hands," she lamented, and "indeed he that would commemorate his heroique glorie should have a soule equally greate to conceive and express that which my dejection and inferior spiritt cannot performe."[8] Mrs. Hutchinson was never less than clear: in preserving the memory of John's "holy" life she was tracing genesis and nurturing, conflict and overcoming, martyrdom and transcendence.

An easy assumption might be that Mrs. Hutchinson thus gave her readers not John but a flawless man she made up. Too easy: her narrative is so good and so convincingly honest that a very real male personality emerges. The point is that Mrs. Hutchinson *thought* her husband flawless, that the circumstances of her life and the bent of her intellect and emotions compelled her to think him flawless.

The interesting psychological study, obviously, is Lucy Hutchinson, "Puritan" woman, bourgeois wife. The *Life* of Colonel John is autobiography, and to paraphrase Hill, what an autobiography!

The "Fragment" about Lucy Apsley, which was included as a special piece in the Reverend Julius Hutchinson's publication of the *Life*, is undated and unfinished, in fact breaks off in mid-sentence, as though Lucy Hutchinson had been impatient, or embarrassed, with the project. Presumably it was the work of the widow of the 1660s, her life as she felt it essentially over (in her forties) and she with empty hours to assess it: who was Lucy Apsley/Hutchinson, and what was the meaning of her existence?

Mrs. Hutchinson had no way of knowing how many other women sat in their closets writing secret memoirs and diaries. Nor do we. How many in this England of four or five million souls? One thousand? One hundred? Twenty? But it is safe to say that Lucy Hutchinson was very special, and that *she* knew she was special and took pride in it. "All this and more is true," she confided to her notebook, "but I so much dislike the manner of relating it that I will make another assay."[9] Writing was her gift, and it was a difficult, demanding, satisfying skill and distinction.

The Calvinist consciousness, though, veered away from the selfish implications of that truth. A special gift had to exist for a higher purpose than self-fulfillment: pride in one's self was a sinful delusion which must be snuffed out in recognition and acceptance of the unfathomable superior intelligence. Thus Lucy Apsley/Hutchinson was, manifestly, one of God's Elect, and as such had been granted "general and particular providences" and "special indulgences," which were "talents" intrusted to her only for the "emproovement for God's glory." Chosen from birth and blessed with special gifts, her obligation was precisely to mirror her age: "I was brought forth," she said, to be a "witnesse of God's wonderfull workings in the earth." Even those words might have suggested a seed of the devil pride: "I cannot reflect," Mrs. Hutchinson added, "without deepe humiliation for the small emproovement I have made of so rich a stock. . . ."[10]

A seventeenth-century formula in autobiography was to thank God for being born then, and in England. The words typically were wooden; a woman almost exactly Mrs. Hutchinson's contemporary gives thanks to the Lord for "bringing me into a land where the Gospel flourished. . . . For giving me that great blessing of religious Parents, that tooke a tender and religious care of me from my youth. . . ."[11] By contrast, Lucy Hutchinson made the ritual phrases come alive. Chief among the "many mercies" granted to her through God's goodness was to be born in England: her "lott" it was "to fall in a good ground . . . a pleasant pasture where the well-springs of life flow to all that desire to drinke of them," where "Better lawes and a happier constitution of government" never existed, with its safeguards for "popular liberty" and its kings "well hedg'd in." And as "crowne of all their glories," in "pietie and devotion" God had made the English "one of the truly noble nations in the Christian world"; out of the "wast common of the world" God had "enclosed all people here . . . to serve him with a pure and undefiled worship."[12]

The significant time of her birth, 1620, God's assignment to her of existence in the second century of the Protestant Reformation, Mrs. Hutchinson expressed in a shining passage: ". . . . my coming into the world . . . was not in the midnight of poperie, nor in the dawne of the gospell's restored day, when light and shades were blended and almost undistinguisht, but when the Sun of Truth was exalted in his progresse and hastening towards a meridian glory. It was indeed early in the morning, God being pleased to allow me the privelledge of beholding the admirable growth of gospell light in my dayes; and oh! that my soule may never forget to blesse and prayse his name for the wonders of power and goodnesse, wisdome and truth, which have bene manifested in this my time."[13]

Mrs. Hutchinson developed at length the particular blessing bestowed upon her in her parents. Her father was Sir Allen Apsley, "leiftenant of the Tower of London" during her childhood. He was a younger son of a "gentleman of competent estate" in Sussex, who had made his name and fortune through connections at the court of Queen Elizabeth, judicious marriages with rich widows, and a knighthood from James I. Her mother was his third wife; she was a daughter of Sir John St. John of Wiltshire, and a gentlewoman who had early rejected the "superstitious service" of the Anglican Church to devote a lifetime to the "Geneva discipline." However, except for a passing mention of thankfulness for "the rank that was given me in my generation," the distinction of her gentry/courtier pedigree was not Mrs. Hutchinson's point. Rather it was that both parents deliberately encouraged her precocious intellectual growth. The father was one of the young Lucy's "particular providences" in that he designed the education of the bright first daughter of his third marriage, "would have" her learn Latin, and was pleased that she "outstript" her brothers who were in school. The mother performed her part by being a selfless model of Calvinist woman and wife, and by agreeing that her daughter's religious education took priority over competence with needle and harpsichord.[14]

Thus little Lucy Apsley was allowed to feel herself a special person. With her parents' indulgence she spent her youth reading serious literature, and listening to sermons, and in that typical achievement of the quick Puritan child repeating them "exactly" from memory. She preferred to be with "elder company," the adults of "a great deale of witt" who frequented her father's house. She heard "serious discourses" there, and, a reminder that Sir Allen Apsley was a courtier bred by Elizabethans, light amusements as well: "I was not at the time," Mrs. Hutchinson recalled, "convinc'd of the vanity of conversation which was not scandalously wicked. I thought it no sin to learne or hear wittie songs and amorous sonnetts or poems, and twenty things of that kind, wherein I was so apt that I became the confident in all the loves that were managed among my mother's young weomen, and there was none of them but had many lovers. . . ."[15]

The historians' near-unanimous interpretation of the evidence is that in the England of the sixteenth and seventeenth centuries parent-child relations were distant and cold. An extreme position is that in early modern England most women and men showed "all the overt symptoms of parental deprivation," psychological "wounds" from neglect or brutality; the certain uncertainty of life itself, the universal routine of tight swaddling, the upper-class practices of sending infants to wet nurses and ten- and twelve-year-old daughters and sons to be coolly 'trained' in the house of other families (like the Lady Apsley's "young weomen"), the harsh imperative to break the wills of children, these resulted, say some historians, in a society-wide "psychic numbing."[16] However, it is interesting to find in Mrs. Hutchinson's autobiographical musings unmistakable relationships supposedly inseparable from the nuclear 'warmth' of the later, 'truly' bourgeois family. The uncompleted sentence with which the "Fragment" ends is this bit of self-exposure: "Five years after me my mother had a daughter that she nurst at her owne brest, and was infinitely fond of above all the rest, and I being of too serious a temper was not pleasing to my. . . ."[17] Her father, Mrs. Hutchinson wrote, "was severe in the regulating of his famely, especially would not endure the least immodest behaviour or dresse in any woman under his roofe" (this probably his daughter's way of indicating the Puritan ex-courtier's aversion to the Court of James I, that "nursery of lust and intemperance" which had turned "every greate house in the country" into a "sty of uncleannesse").[18] But in that severe Puritan environment no one seems to have tried to break Lucy Apsley's will. She was not traded off with another upper-class household for female conditioning; she was not locked into single-track preparation for the role of gentry wife. Apparently she was permitted to grow to a proud, willful, self-centered—albeit religiously absorbed—adolescence.

Only the "Fragment" was written in the first person. When Lucy Apsley appeared again in the *Life* (leaving large gaps, for one any personal reaction to the death of her father in 1630), she was a character just entering John Hutchinson's experience. It was 1636-37, and Lucy "scarcely past" childhood, an unhappy girl, isolated and at odds with her mother. She was "perplext in mind" that she displeased her parent by refusing "many offers" of marriage "advantageous enough," the latest from a gentleman of the St. John home-base of Wiltshire which her mother was negotiating to the "Treaty" stage. To no avail: Lucy would not, could not marry "such as she could find no inclination to." She "shun'd men," and had few friends. She was known as reserved and studious, was the target of the "witty spite" of other young women who ridiculed the "negligence of her dresse and habitt and all womanish ornaments."[19]

The season was summer and the place the town of Richmond, "where the prince's Court was," and where for the privileged young there "was a very good company and recreations." Lady Apsley had a house there, though her elder daughter did not play the belle's part in the local entertainments. By chance a young man named John Hutchinson was visiting briefly, awaiting the more healthful fall months to begin a tour of France; he was son and heir of Sir Thomas Hutchinson of Nottinghamshire, and a twenty-year-old drop-out from Lincoln's Inn who had found the study of law "unpleasant and contrary to his genius." By further chance, John Hutchinson heard performed at a party a sonnet that impressed him, composed, he was told, by a woman. Intrigued, "fancying something of rationallity in the sonnet beyond the customary reach of a shee witt," John Hutchinson inquired the name of the author. She was, of course, Lucy Apsley; his informant told him that though she was "the nicest creature in the world of suffering her perfections to be knowne," she avoided "the converse of men as the plague," lived only "in the enjoyment of herself," and had not "the humanity to communicate that happiness to any of [the male] sex." Himself introverted and intellectual, Hutchinson was captivated: "Well," said he, "but I will be acquainted with her"; indeed the story of her "reserv'd humour" attracted him "more than all elce he had heard, and fill'd him now with thoughts how he should attaine the sight and knowledge of her."[20]

Only "blind mortals," narrator Mrs. Hutchinson observed, "call the most wonderful operations of the greate God the common accidents of humane life"; they "either forget or believe not" that God takes "a care and account of their smallest concernments, even the haires of their heads." That is to say, Lucy Apsley perceived the meaning of her short life—the bookish peculiarities of her childhood, the stubbornness and disobedience of her youthful self—in meeting John Hutchinson, in knowing his admiration and love. A "secrett working" which he said he felt too, calling it a "secret power," had designed her for him, surely a most wonderful operation of the great God.[21]

The two were married in 1638, "the third day of July . . . being teusday," at St. Andrew's Church in London, where then in Holborne in "a place call'd Bartlett's Court" they lived with her mother. The Lady Apsley must have swallowed her annoyances. Her daughter was wedded advantageously enough to her young gentleman of good family, sound principles, and excellent connections (John's father, Sir Thomas, was a moderate but sturdy Puritan and parliamentarian, his mother of the noble family of Biron). And despite the recent unpleasantness there was in her no rebellion, no reservations about marriage. The "Geneva discipline" had had its shaping way: daughter Lucy was concentrated now on being as fine a Christian wife as the eulogized models in the clerics' "Domesticall" sermons she had memorized as a child.[22]

In Mrs. Hutchinson's telling she and John began marriage as though on display for Protestant instructional literature, as though behind them on their shelves were the open and well-marked works of the Reverends Perkins, Cleaver, or Gouge. If any areas of tension arose between them Mrs. Hutchinson did not consider them important contributions to John's biography. Both delighted in their "holy and blessed" union. They were passionately in love—of this the ministers would not have disapproved: "sweet kisses and imbracements," the latter taught, enriched and lightened the home.[23] They were quickly on their way to being a family, that "little Church" and "little Commonwealth": Mrs. Hutchinson miscarried in four months, and bore twin sons the next year (at John's death in 1664 eight children had survived; Mrs. Hutchinson had at least one other miscarriage). And both assumed their roles within the Christian matrimonial hierarchy with such obvious ease that a headstrong, self-involved young person named Lucy Apsley might never have been.

John Hutchinson was by that "ordinance" of God "setled even in the order of nature," as the clerics put it, "master," the "chiefe head of the familie" and "he which hath authoritie over his wife." Such was immediately his position because Mrs. Hutchinson made it so. This was the conditional with which the ministers were so acutely concerned. No "pride and ambition" stiffened her against "yeelding subjection" to her husband, against fashioning her "minde and her will" to "voluntary" submission: happily, raptly even, she created John king, priest, and prophet, to govern, pray with, teach, and instruct her.[24]

Her extraordinarily detailed explanation of this marital arrangement emerged from Mrs. Hutchinson's assertion of the principled, by definition superior, quality of John's love. He had for his wife, she wrote, "as strong and violent affections" as "any man had," loved her better than his life, "with unexpressible tendernesse and kindnesse." But, "never was there a passion more ardent and lesse idolatrous." Despite his "love and esteeme of her," Mrs. Hutchinson continued, John yet "consider'd honour, religion and duty above her." He never allowed in himself the "dotage" which would blind him to "her imperfections." Indeed, his love was a creative force which "augmented his care to blott out all those spots" he marked in her, through which he "polisht and gave forme to what he found with all the roughnesse of the quarrie about it." Mrs. Hutchinson made the metaphor explicit: John was "Pigmalion," who sculpted his wife with such skill that "he soone made her more equall to him than he found her." And since he had in her "a compliant subject to his owne wise government" he had "as much satisfaction as he gave, and never had occasion to number his marriage among his infelicities."[25]

Immediately following these revelations are sentences which Mrs. Hutchinson might have written as her own epitaph. Thus early in their marriage she had become John's "faithful mirror, reflecting truly, though but dimmely, his own glories upon him, so long as he was present; but she, that was nothing before his inspection gave her a faire figure, when he was remoov'd was only fill'd with a darke mist, and never could againe take in any delightfull object, nor returne any shining representation. The greatest excellence she had was the power of apprehending and the vertue of loving his. Soe, as his shaddow, she waited on him everywhere, till he was taken into that region of light which admitts of none, and then she vanisht into nothing."[26]

That a woman who so deified a man should have proceeded to construct a splendidly lively biography is a major triumph. That Mrs. Hutchinson managed it is high mark of her historian's intelligence and honesty, and attributable as well to what must have been to her a 'natural' selection of format and technique. In the narrative of the core of John's story, as parliamentary partisan, army officer, regicide, and martyr, he remains fixed on his pedestal, unselfconsciously a saint, pure in thought and behavior (just once did he slip, as we shall see, in a strangely contradictory episode). Meanwhile Mrs. Hutchinson is his peculiar mirror. She who is nothing is lit only by his presence; there she shines in his light and 'knows' his glory. And precisely because of her inferiority she can interpret his life, and see it fully in the context of a gross materiality; further, as narrator and editor she can interject a running commentary of very human opinions, naming and judging the foolish, the base, and the wicked. Perhaps the technique was not inevitably nor accidentally chosen. Perhaps in the "Fragment" about herself Mrs. Hutchinson had said exactly this: she perceived it the task, in her world-view the God-given task, of the gifted woman to be earth-bound interpreter of the transcendent male.

Thus *The Life of Colonel Hutchinson* dips up and down, soaring with the saintly John, descending with the earthier perceptions of his wife. To start with, it may be that John "lov'd her soule and her honor more than her outside," that "her honor and her vertue were his mistresses" (and these like "Pigmalion's images of his owne making").[27] But young Lucy Apsley had melted at the first sight of him, had been "surpriz'd with some unusually liking in her soule" for his "haire, eies, shape, and countenance," sufficient "to begett love in any one. . . ." In her lonely widowhood Mrs. Hutchinson lingered over that physical memory: John's "stature, of a slender and exactly well-proportion'd shape in all parts, his complexion fair, his hayre of a light browne, very thick sett in his youth, softer than the finest silke, curling into loose great rings att the ends, his eies of a lively grey, well-shaped and full of life and vigour, graced with many becoming motions; his visage thinne, his mouth well made, and his lipps very ruddy and graceful, all though the nether chap shut over the upper, yett it was in such a manner as was not unbecomming; his teeth were even and white as the purest ivory, his chin was something long, and the mold of his face, his forehead was not very high, his nose was rays'd and sharpe, but withall he had the most amiable countenance, which carried in it something of magnanimity and majesty mixt with sweetnesse. . . . His skin was smooth and white, his legs and feet excellently well made. He was quick in his pace and turnes, nimble and active and gracefull in all his motions. . . ."[28]

John was as "pious and obedient" a son as ever father had, surely better, Mrs. Hutchinson intimated, than Sir Thomas Hutchinson deserved. When the latter died, an M.P. in London in 1643, he left a will which "gave all his personal estate and all that was unsettled at Mr. Hutchinson's marriage to his second wife and her children." John was deprived of his full inheritance, and at a most difficult time for him: he was governor of Nottingham Castle in 1643 and supporting out of pocket a large portion of the food, supplies, and pay of the parliamentary garrison (when the wars ended he was thousands of pounds in debt); moreover, both his parliamentary critics and royalist enemies bruited about the story that Sir Thomas, who was much esteemed in the country by both sides as a peace-seeking gentleman (Mrs. Hutchinson plainly thought him a fence-sitter), had disinherited his eldest son as sign of displeasure with the latter's "engagement" in the parliamentary Cause. From her vantage as biographer Mrs. Hutchinson related two reactions. Without reproach or resentment John had accepted the transfer of part of his estate to stepbrothers, had expressed only his "tender love" and sorrow for the loss of his parent. She, on the other hand, still disliked that second family of Hutchinsons, and left plentiful clues as to her feelings about Sir Thomas giving "away all that was in his power to give from him" and exposing his first son in a time of extreme vulnerability to financial distress and the insults of his enemies.[29]

Certainly John Hutchinson never lacked enemies. They surrounded him in Nottinghamshire, he who after characteristic hesitation in early 1642—he had been pondering the conflicts between king and Commons, and waiting for God's sign of his duty—had assumed military post in selfless commitment to the parliamentary Cause. He was almost alone among the county nobility and gentry, all "passionately the King's," and was thus branded by those of his own class (even his Biron cousins) as traitor. When he entered as commissioned governor of the brooding castle above it the town of Nottingham was royalist: of seven aldermen only one "own'd Parliament"; the majority of the population smoldered as though under foreign occupation, ever ready to welcome roaming bands of royalist troops. And then, hardest to bear, even the Nottingham supporters of Parliament detested the governor: the supposedly "godly" of the middle-class townspeople distrusted him because he was a gentleman (they thought it "scarce possible for anyone to continue a gentleman and firme to a godly interest"), and because he had been imposed upon them from London; they disliked him probably because he was so young (twenty-seven) and inexperienced, because he took no notice of what were long-standing contentious divisions among them, because (though one must read between the lines of Mrs. Hutchinson's account for this insight) he was arbitrary, stiff-necked, and self-righteous. The details of the governor's relations with the town committee appointed to assist him in its defense are simply horrendous: constant bickering, backbiting, infighting, slandering, plotting; the burgers so intent on their factional disputes and individual ambitions that it seems a miracle they held against the internal fifth column and Prince Rupert's slashing cavalry. Committeemen ignored or countermanded Hutchinson's orders, sent town troops out or kept them home in complete defiance of his planned tactics and strategies. The situation became so poisoned that a clique within the committee posted a fabricated accusation to London, charging the governor with intent to turn over the castle to the royalists.[30]

John Hutchinson persevered among his tormentors with poise, self-discipline, and Christian forbearance. He could get angry; in fact, he once struck one prominent townsman who was more concerned for property than principles in his commitment to the Cause. But, said Mrs. Hutchinson, though he never "disguiz'd hate or aversion" it was aimed not at "any party or person, but to their sins." He "lov'd even his bitterest enemies," and "mourn'd for them"; it was only "their wickednesse his righteous soule abhorr'd." For those who injured him he gave "recompence with favours instead of revenge," rendering "benefitts" rather than "vengeance," so that "at last his own friends would tell him, if they could in justice and conscience forsake him they would become his adversaries, for that was the next way to engage him to obligations."[31]

To forgive may have been divine but Mrs. Hutchinson did not require of herself that saintly behavior. (Just once, in relating John's problems with the parliamentary townspeople, did she utter a criticism of him: "If he were defective in any part of justice," she wrote, it was in his "clemency," his inability to punish his enemies.) How she hated them, the sly Nottingham persecutors who had tried to "mump" the governor. Their like "infested and disturb'd" almost all parliamentary garrisons, she wrote, so that many "worthy gentlemen" were "wearied out of their commands"; they were "factious little people," a "meane sort of people." For whatever the late satisfaction, she took a measure of vengeance in the razor prose of the *Life*. A Charles White of the county was a man "of meane birth and low fortunes," who "yet had kept company with the underling gentry of his neighbourhood"; he was of the "most factious, ambitious, vaineglorious, envious, and mallitious nature that is imaginable . . . the greatest dissembler, flatterer, traitor and hipocrite that ever was. . . ." Huntingdon Plumptre was a "Doctor of Phisick" in Nottingham, and a "horrible Atheist," of "such an intollerable pride that he brook'd no superiours"; he had "some witt," and "tooke the boldness to exercise it in the abuse of all the gentlemen wherever he came, and only scap'd beating because he was unworthy of it, for to uphold this greate pride he had neither courage nor quality." James Chadwick, a colonel in the army and a member of the town committee, was a fellow who had "scrap'd trenchers" in great houses in his youth, and from his "meane education and poverty" arrived "at a degree unfitt for him"; he was crafty enough to keep up "his credit with the godly," cutting his hair in the plain 'roundhead' style and pretending "sanctity," but he was a true "Judas," who "would kisse the man he had in his heart to kill, . . . was so exquisite a villaine that he destroy'd those designes he might have thriven by, with overlaying them with fresh knaveries." Gilbert Millington, a member too of the committee and M.P. for Nottingham, one whom the governor thought his friend and supporter, was drawn into the "confederacy" of town plotters when they "hir'd" him with promises of sharing in sequested royalist estates, "spoyles" and "good booty to his meane famely"; Millington was central in the conspiracy to oust John in order, Mrs. Hutchinson said, to put in a Millington son as governor of the Castle. These "wretched men" so lacking in "publick spiritednesse" predictably "fell away" from all "sobriety and honest morall conversation"; they met in "Taverns and Brothells, till at the last Millington and White were so ensnar'd that they married a couple of Alehouse wenches, to their open shame and the conviction of the whole country of the vaine lives they led." They became a "reflection upon the Parliament itselfe," Mrs. Hutchinson concluded, "when Millington, a man of sixty, professing religion, and having but lately buried a religious matronly gentlewoman, should goe to an alehouse to take a flirtish girle of sixteen. . . ."[32]

Mrs. Hutchinson did not explicitly number among John's virtues an awakened egalitarianism from his commitment to the Cause, she who had such satisfaction in remembering that even his enemies felt "awe in his presence." But her narrative made it perfectly clear that the beleaguered governor of Nottingham valued the "truely" honest and godly "middling" men of the town, the people of lesser rank and property, in religious-political labeling the Independents or "Separatists." Invariably the governor "favour'd and protected" the Independents against the town elite who as "Presbyterians" dominated both church and committee; he deemed them "honest, obedient and peacefull," even thought they "seperated from the publick Assemblies." Indeed Hutchinson's sympathy with the Independents was one of the most furious issues between him and the committee clique: the nasty Charles White lashed him for his defense of a "company of Puritanical prickear'd rascalls." And later, from 1647, by then plain Colonel Hutchinson had "a greate intimacy" with the Levellers, "good hearted people," Mrs. Hutchinson called them, who never "endeavour'd the levelling of all estates and qualities," as their upper-class persecutors charged, but only demanded that "common justice" belong equally "to the poorest as well as the mighty." Out of political necessity though they may have been, John's social views apparently stretched in the struggles of the English revolution.[33]

But Mrs. Hutchinson remained the steadfast transmittor of their gentry snobbism. In her view godliness, honesty, morality, patriotism, and absolute loyalty to the Cause went naturally (though of course not inevitably, given the "nobillity" who seemed to be "licenc'd in all vice") with wealth and social position; thus she was almost as surprised as pleased to observe these qualities in the 'meaner' sort of people. The one trustworthy alderman in Nottingham was "a very honest, bold man, but had no more than a Burger's discretion; he was yett very well assisted by his wife, a woman of greate zeal and courage, and more understanding than weomen of her rank usually have." A member of the inner staff of the castle was called Mister even though he "could not be reckon'd among the gentry"; Mrs. Hutchinson thought him nevertheless a "stout and an understanding man, plaine and blunt, but withall godly, faithfull to his country and honest to all men." She found it contradictory, too, that a Mr. Widmerpoole stood firm in the Cause though he had by some incompetence dissipated a "small fortune," had "declin'd all the splendor of an old house . . . into the way of the middle men of the country"; it was warming to know that he had "yet" a "perfect honest heart to God, his country and his friend" (that is, his friend Governor Hutchinson). Closer to expectation was Mr. Salsbury, at first the efficient and loyal secretary to the governor's council; after being named treasurer as well, "being poore" he "proov'd ambitious and froward" and "fell into some temptation."[34]

To Mrs. Hutchinson the sublime center of John's character was his intellectual individualism, his solitary integrity, traits she liked to ground in his gentry genealogy. A family of "good repute" and "auncient inheritance," the Hutchinsons had long been "fixt" in the county: once their "first achievements" had "elevated" them above "the vulgar" they had spurned ugly competition for position and power; though they "successively matcht into all the most eminent and noble famelies" none until Sir Thomas, John's father, had "advanc'd beyond an Esquire," mark of the "unambitious genius of the famely rather than their want of meritt." John's qualities were foreshadowed in his father's approval in the 1630s of the "oppressed saints and honest people of those times," a sympathy quiet but yet open enough that he was "branded" by his neighbors with the epithet of "Puritanisme." Still, though he had "stinted not his expence" with John's education at Cambridge to arm him against "popish superstitious practices" and "Arminian principles," Sir Thomas desired that his son, and all his children, individually find a way in religion and politics that they might "discerne things with their owne eies, and not with his."[35]

Carefully raised and wisely instructed, John Hutchinson was a man who thought problems through, slowly, deliberately, rationally, before taking his stand. It was only after his marriage, in his early twenties, that he explored the works of Calvin on "that greate poynt of Predestination," exhaustively informing himself in this "first place" of "God's absolute decrees." Thus he became a Puritan, not in emotional crisis of conversion, but after a two-year search and resultant conviction. Once formed his conviction was fixed for life: the knowledge that he was "elected" for salvation by God, "so farre," Mrs. Hutchinson wrote, "from producing a carelessnesse of life in him, a thing usually objected against this faith . . . excited him to a more strict and holy walking in thankefullnesse to God, who had bene pleas'd to chuse him out of the corrupted masse of lost mankind to fixe his love upon him. . . ."[36]

And though he had now become joined in faith with "the religious and holy persons in the land" John Hutchinson did not hurry to political commitment in 1640-41. Only slowly did the "noyse of warre and tumult" filter into his secluded domesticity at Owthorpe, or rather he controlled its penetration as he "applied himselfe" to understanding "the things then in dispute," as he read "all the publick papers" and "private treatises" on the quarrels between king and parliament. He was still so absorbed in this research in early 1642 that he refused the urging of his kinsman Henry Ireton to be a member of the parliamentary commission for the county. Such were quintessentially his methods: he had to be "abundantly inform'd in his understanding, and conscience of the righteousnesse of the Parliament's cause in poynt of civill right"; and he would move only when he perceived his individual call, the sign of a divine assignment for him alone.[37]

The *Life* being John's story, "his wife" is almost entirely a shadowy figure in the background. In the few scenes in which the narrator is forced to bring her into the light Mrs. Hutchinson appears intellectually tentative, impulsive and emotional. For one example, there was an intriguing little tale of her insecurities about biblical interpretation and church doctrine. At some point in 1643-44, in the midst of the governor's difficulties with the Nottingham Presbyterians, Mrs. Hutchinson read several Independent tracts against infant baptism.

She was pregnant at the time and the matter was thus personally compelling. She carefully compared the Anabaptists' arguments with scriptural references to baptism, with the result that she "found not what to say against the truths" asserted in the Independents' position: she convinced herself, in short, of "the misapplication" over the Christian centuries of the "Ordinance" of baptism to infants. But as she was "young and modest," and loathe to "defend a singular opinion of her owne," she consulted, indeed turned over the problem to her husband. John "diligently" retraced her studies and could find no more justification for "Pedobaptisme" than had she; he went further in directly questioning "all the ministers" of the town. Finally he made up their mind: satisfied that the sole defense of the practice was "the tradition of the Church from the Primitive times," the Hutchinsons decided to leave the new baby unbaptized (to the great scandal of the ministers and the Presbyterians, though the couple continued to worship in the "publick" Assembly).[38]

At least once Mrs. Hutchinson did a plainly stupid thing. It was mid-1642, the war just started, and Nottinghamshire, where the king had first set up the standard which declared military solution to his impasse with the Commons, was controlled by the armies of Charles and his nephew, Prince Rupert. Marked as a Parliament sympathizer by his neighbors (though still awaiting his call to action), John Hutchinson found it prudent to go briefly to the safety of the Puritan stronghold of Northamptonshire, leaving his wife in the company of his younger brother, George. She was visited by a royalist captain who had known her family—a friend of her brother, also an officer in the king's army—and who now twitted her about John's deserting her in such dangerous circumstances. Stung, "peeck'd," Mrs. Hutchinson retorted that her husband was in fact with her, and as proof called in and introduced young George by his brother's name. The upshot of this unfunny farce was that poor George was arrested and taken away; only with difficulty and delay, and the "interposition" of royalist kin, Lord Viscount Grandison, "a cousin germane of Mrs. Hutchinson's," and his "cousin Birons," was he released.[39]

Mrs. Hutchinson told this story with John as its focus as an early episode of his isolation in his royalist home county: that is to say, she did not even acknowledge her own thoughtless behavior, let alone excuse it on some grounds of youth or inexperience. But after all, what had she to apologize for, when she had made so clear that in her marriage she was the 'mere' woman God had created her? Nor did she reveal any sense of contrition in relating the events of eighteen years later in the most critical, the most perilous moment of John's revolutionary career, when she not only 'acted the woman' but drew him down from his pinnacle, for a moment, to her womanly weakness and capitulation. In the terms of the open hagiography that the *Life of John Hutchinson* had become by then she did a terrible thing: she who was John's mirror-self played the craven temptress, distracting him from his destiny. Surely it is interesting that as narrator and author Mrs. Hutchinson did not dwell upon that; her moving hand blamed only the wicked, the "children of darkness" who had destroyed the glorious Cause which had "so generously attempted, and had almost effected, England's perfect liberty."[40]

It was 1660; the Cromwellian experiment had crumbled with his death, and the Stuart heir called Charles II was restored to the throne. The great men of the land tumbled over one another to disown and obliterate the structures of the Commonwealth and republicanism. Royalists and Presbyterians alike "fell a thirsting," Mrs. Hutchinson wrote, "urging that God's blessings could not be upon the land till justice had cleans'd it from the late king's blood." The men who had sat in judgment upon Charles I and had signed his death warrant were ordered to London, Hutchinson of course among them. Seven were "nominated" for "exemplary justice"—they would be tried, hung, drawn and quartered—and the rest to be interrogated, with probable penalties of loss of estates and civil rights. For various reasons there was hope that John would be one of the lucky of the latter: he had broken publicly with the "usurper" Cromwell and from 1651 had lived privately in Owthorpe; he had just been elected to the restored Long Parliament, a confirmation of his stand against the "tirannicall" policies of the Cromwellian Protectorate; and, not least, he had powerful relatives close to the king to intercede for him, who advised him, in fact, that to keep his property he had only to appear before royal or parliamentary committees, recant properly, name a few names, and pledge his fealty to the new monarch.[41]

Ever honest and wonderfully clear Mrs. Hutchinson described the ripping tension within the 'perfect puritan marriage' as husband and wife fumbled with the choices presented them by the Restoration. There is no reason to doubt her implication that for the first time she and John concealed their thoughts, lied to one another, while she took to subterfuge, in her marital morality a formerly unthinkable disobedience. John tried to shut her out of his problem: to keep her "quiet," she said, he told her "that no man would loose or suffer by this change." But Mrs. Hutchinson was beyond soothing words: "att this beginning [she] was awakened, and saw that he was ambitious of being a publick sacrifice." And so "herein only her whole life, [she]

resolv'd to disobey him . . . for she sayd she would not live to see him
a prisoner. . . ."[42]

Lucy Hutchinson assumed command of the situation. Somehow she
convinced John to stay out of London, "to secret himself with a friend."
And then she forged a letter to the Speaker of the House of Commons,
"writt her husband's name to the letter, and ventur'd to send it in,
being us'd sometimes to write the letters he dictated, and her character not much different from his." It was a desperate letter, pleading
and obsequious. In his wife's composition John Hutchinson told the
Commons that his "penitent sorrow" was "above utterance," that a
"deep and sorrowful sence" pressed his soul "for the unfortunate
guilt that lies upon it." He was made to say that like thousands of
others "in those unhappy dayes" he had been "seduc'd," had fallen
into the Cromwellians' "pernicious snares," not through "avarice, or
ambition," but in "ill-guided judgement." And he had left them, "even
before Cromwell broke up the remaining part of the House"; he had
"sett Cromwell's honors and his friendship" at "defiance," had never
accepted "aniething from him, to make or joyne in any address to
him, or so much as to give him one civill visitt." His "repentance"
grew as he watched the Lord Protector-Usurper, and swelled to an
"earnest desire" to "returne to that loyall subjection to the right
Prince" from whom he had been "so horridly misled." His supposed
peroration had him "humbly begging" that the Commons "pluck"
him from the "horns" of the king's sacrificial "alter," and allow him
freedom on his word while his case was deliberated. In propitiation
he would then make the rest of his life a "perpetual dedication to his
Matie's service. . . ."[43]

These expedient tactics worked, buttressed by Lucy Hutchinson's
lobbying among friends and relatives. Her brother, Sir Allen Apsley,
high in the royal councils, was her particular ally; he "us'd some
artifice," that is, traded in distinctly unholy deals (so soon was sainthood out of fashion) to save Colonel Hutchinson. John was a suspect
still. Sir Edward Hyde, Lord Clarendon, by being next to the king the
most powerful man in England, distrusted him, and his old enemies
in Nottinghamshire were sharpening their knives, but though he was
ejected from the House of Commons and forbidden to hold public
office during his life he was free and in possession of his (debt-en-
cumbered) Owthorpe estate. Meanwhile "the other poore gentlemen," regicides like Hutchinson, were "trapan'd," deceived by the
initial court promises of clemency, the "whole cause it selfe" was
being "betrey'd and condemn'd," and the doomed seven were being
prepared for their hideous end on the scaffold.[44]

And for a little longer the roles of the Hutchinsons, husband and wife, were reversed. John was in a torment of indecision about his "deliverance." Lucy Hutchinson was stunned at his ambivalence: she who had "thought she had never deserv'd so well of him as in the endeavours and labours she had exercis'd to bring him off" had instead "never displeas'd him more in her life." He was in turn angry, guilty, relieved (there were those eight children to be considered). His wife "perswaded" him to be "contented," and in his uncertainty he was quieted by the strength of her arguments. He was "by her convinc'd that God's eminent appearance seem'd to have singled him out for preservation." Not only did he acquiesce in that apocalyptic vision, but made it his own: "And he would often say the Lord had not thus eminently preserv'd him for nothing, but that he was yett kept for some eminent service or suffering in this cause; although having bene freely pardon'd by the present powers, he resolv'd not to doe aniething against the King, but thought himselfe oblieg'd to sitt still and wish his prosperity in all things that were not destructive to the interest of Christ and his members on earth."[45]

Had John Hutchinson remained an emasculated saint the *Life* would never have been written. In retirement at Owthorpe he brooded upon "all that was past," and upon the Cause that was now judged treason, "rebellion and murther"; and he prayed God "to enlighten him and shew him his sin if ignorance or misunderstanding had led him into error." And he knew that he regretted nothing: "the more he examin'd the cause from the first, the more he became confirm'd in it . . . and [this] made him rejoyce in all he had done in the Lord's cause." When demanded as a witness in London he would not testify against those pinioned by the triumphant Restoration, would not be used by court, judges, and "that vile Trayter [General Monck] who had sold the men that trusted him."[46] With the regicide prisoners he "believ'd himselfe to stand att the Barre"; "while he saw others suffer, he suffer'd with them in his mind. . . ."[47] His behavior was provocative, and noted as such by the court: Mrs. Hutchinson quoted Lord Clarendon telling her brother, "in a great rage and passion, 'O Nall . . . what have you done? You have sav'd a man that would be ready, if he had opertunity, to mischiefe us as much as ever he did.' "[48]

John was arrested in 1663, on the groundless suspicion of a nervous court that he was complicit in a northern uprising for the Cause of the godly republic. He was imprisoned first in the Tower of London, then in Sandown Castle in Kent, a "lamentable old ruin'd place," dour, cold, and wind-blasted. Though she labored again with court connections to get him at least a measure of rudimentary comfort

Mrs. Hutchinson yielded to his martyrdom, exalted even in her pain and bitterness that he "was not at all dismay'd, but wonderfully pleas'd with all these things . . . this captivity [which] was the happiest release in the world to him." He sickened in Sandown Castle, of poisoning, Mrs. Hutchinson thought, and "continued in a feaverish distemper"; but always he was able to "ravish" and "refine" his "soule" with biblical reading. His condition improved intermittently, and it was in one of these lulls that Mrs. Hutchinson returned to Owthorpe to see to affairs there and bring back necessities. She was absent when he declined. Asked how he did in his last days—a daughter and his brother George were with him—he answered, "Incomparably well, and full of faith." The attending doctor, whom Mrs. Hutchinson noted had been a "pretender" to religion when it "was in fashion," marveled at John's serenity and hope, at his certainty that "There's none but Christ, none but Christ, in whom I have unspeakable joy. . . ." He left word that his wife was to bury him at Owthorpe, and added this admonition against unseemly grief: "Lett her . . . as she is above other weomen, shew her selfe in this occasion a good christian, and above the pitch of ordinary weomen."[49]

Lucy Hutchinson will be a silent presence in the chapters ahead. Could contemporary women comprehend the subterranean rumblings and revolutionary explosions transforming societies in the seventeenth century? Absolutely; think of Lucy Hutchinson. Could women, as formal female education became ever more functional,[50] that is, preparation for domestic vocation and/or 'good' marriage, be historians, analysts, and articulators of social relations and events?[51] Certainly; remember Lucy Hutchinson. In the fullness of her life she had so many accomplishments: precocious poet and classicist, translator in her "vainly curious youth" of books of Lucretius later abhorrent to her for their "atheisms and impieties";[52] doctor, nurse, and chemist for the fighters in Nottingham Castle; political lobbyist and surrogate attorney; estate manager and sole support for the several small Hutchinsons who survived their father; and to her end the Puritan pedagogue, author of theological treatises, one "Addressed to her Daughter."[53]

But once more, or finally, it is *Mrs.* Hutchinson, the matchless model of the married lady, who should be kept in mind. So above the pitch of ordinary women she is no 'typical' reference point of the bourgeois wife. Rather, she was the *best*. The obvious is worth stressing: Mrs. Hutchinson's fervent Protestantism was the fundament of her self-made qualities; in submission to God she created an earthly dialectic of lordship and subordination (in shorthand, no Lucy, no

John). The preachers were right in their incessant pounding at the theme: the good wife was a truly Christian wife. That was unquestioned fact to Mrs. Hutchinson, who observed other women with cold, judgmental objectivity. Those who were impaled on her scathing lines were by clear implication 'pretenders' to religion, and therefore incapable of godly marital duties and attitudes. One wonders if with her keen mind she might have appreciated the work so well done that following generations of the formerly godly could quite nicely substitute for "God's Will" an obedience to tradition and Mrs. Grundy.

NOTES

1. Christopher Hill, "Colonel John Hutchinson, 1615-1664: A Tercentenary Tribute," *Transactions of the Thoroton Society of Nottinghamshire*, 1965, p. 85.

2. *Memoirs of the Life of Colonel Hutchinson, Governor of Nottingham Castle and Town. Written by his Widow Lucy* (London, 1892), ed. The Rev. Julius Hutchinson, Preface, p. xii.

3. Hill, "Colonel John Hutchinson," p. 86.

4. Ibid., p. 85.

5. Hereafter I have used the recent scholarly edition: Lucy Hutchinson, *Memoirs of the Life of Colonel Hutchinson, with the fragment of an autobiography of Mrs. Hutchinson*, ed. James Sutherland (London, 1973), p. 32.

6. Ibid., pp. 43-44.

7. Hill, "Colonel John Hutchinson," p. 86.

8. Hutchinson, *Life*, pp. 2, 35-36, 1, 12.

9. Ibid., p. 14.

10. Ibid., p. 278.

11. *Memoranda of Mrs. Elizabeth Aldersey, wife to Thomas Lee of Darnhall, Esq., afterwards Second Wife of General Venables* (Lancaster, 1870-71), Chatham Society, 4: 9.

12. Hutchinson, *Life*, pp. 279-81.

13. Ibid., p. 282.

14. Ibid., pp. 282-88.

15. Ibid., pp. 288-89.

16. Lawrence Stone, *The Family, Sex and Marriage* (New York, 1977), p. 101.

17. Hutchinson, *Life*, p. 289.

18. Ibid., pp. 286, 42.

19. Ibid., pp. 31-32.

20. Ibid., pp. 29-30.

21. Ibid., pp. 278, 31.

22. Ibid., pp. 33.

23. Robert Cleaver, *Householde Government* (London, 1598), p. 148.

24. See above, Introduction, p. 3: again, William Gouge, *Domesticall Duties*, pp. 345-48.

25. Hutchinson, *Life*, pp. 32-33.

26. Ibid.

27. Ibid., pp. 10, 33.

28. Ibid., pp. 31, 3.

29. Ibid., pp. 90-92.

30. Ibid., pp. 61, 70, 89, and passim.

31. Ibid., pp. 85, 142.

32. Ibid., pp. 142, 133, 158, 69, 70-71, 71-72, 137, 146.

33. Ibid., pp. 156, 131, 146, 85, 179.

34. Ibid., pp. 179, 70, 73.

35. Ibid., pp. 15, 17, 34.

36. Ibid., pp. 34-35.

37. Ibid., p. 53.

38. Ibid., p. 169.

39. Ibid., pp. 65-66.

40. Ibid., p. 17.

41. Ibid., pp. 227, 209.

42. Ibid., pp. 229.

43. Ibid., pp. 290-91.

44. Ibid., p. 234.

45. Ibid.

46. Ibid., p. 235.

47. Ibid., pp. 235, 234.

48. Ibid., p. 236.

49. Ibid., pp. 255, 271.

50. See Rosemary O'Day, *Education and Society, 1500-1800* (London, 1982), especially chapter 10; K. Wrightson, *English Society* (New Brunswick, N.J., 1982), chapter 7; David Cressy, *Literacy and the Social Order* (Cambridge, 1980), pp. 128-29.

51. For a perceptive appreciation of historian Lucy Hutchinson, see Royce MacGillivray, *Restoration Historians and the English Civil War* (The Hague, 1974).

52. Hutchinson, *Life*, pp. xix-xx, xxvii; see also Hill, *Collected Essays* (Amherst, Mass., 1985), p. 299.

53. Mrs. Hutchinson's *On Theology* was published by the Rev. Julius Hutchinson in 1817 (*Life*, p. xxvii).

PART 2

*Tales of Revolutionary
Adventuring*

2

The Useful Ladies, "Gentlewomen and Tradesmens Wives"

In the 1630s and 1640s as the "free-born" males of English civil society confronted the Stuart monarchy the political rights of women was a non-issue. For English revolutionaries female political status was manifest in the twin volumes, the Old Testament and the cherished bulk of Common Law, with which they were pushing so confidently into their new order. A pamphlet of 1632 put it complacently: "Women have no voyse in Parliament, They make no Lawes, they consent to none, they abrogate none. All of them are understood either married or to bee married and their desires are subject to their husband. . . . The common Law here shaketh hand with Divinitie. . . ."[1]

However, the pamphleteer was a realistic man, and somewhat sympathetic to women as people, even deprived people: he knew "no remedy," he said, but "some" women "could shift it well enough."[2] Best not to define it, he seemed to be saying, but though walled out of the political constitution by the ordinance of God and the ancient legal monopoly of the patriarchs some women would find a way to make their wills felt.

Certainly, in the first great bourgeois revolution there is no evidence of intense debates in upper-middle-class salons of *Les Droits de la Femme*, no reasoned pleas from female writers for civil rights and the "transformation of women's place in the family and in the economy."[3] There are merely a few glimpses of women near the parliamentary eye of the revolutionary storm, shifting it and explaining themselves well enough.

Lucy Hutchinson, that voice for godliness and patriarchy, wrote a predictably negative, sermonizing text upon women in politics. Those "hands that are made only for distaffes," she said, bring "sad desolations" when they "entermeddle with the affaires of State"; the "felicity" of the reign of Queen Elizabeth was no exception since the constant policy of that princess was "submission to her masculine and wise Councellors."[4] The particular object behind Mrs. Hutchinson's reflection was Charles I's Catholic queen, Henrietta Maria, who with her flaunted court masses, French priests, and papist cavaliers had cast a black spell over the king, so thought the Puritan historian. But it was a general principle: in the nature of the marriage relationship wives became privy to the concerns of their husbands, and shared to some degree even details of the workings of state; but such wives must show themselves, and crucially know themselves, the unobtrusive and subordinate partners. Rather than Henrietta Maria, a hopeless case, women of her own class and position got Mrs. Hutchinson's sharpest barbs for transgression of this law. There was "My Lady Fairfax," Anne Fairfax, wife of the supreme commander of the parliamentary armies. Because of her personal tendencies toward Presbyterianism Lady Fairfax had "such a bitter aversion" to army Independent preachers, whom her husband preferred, that she got them dismissed. The result was, Mrs. Hutchinson believed, the pathetic decline of General Fairfax: this "great man, so pertinacious in obeying his wife . . . died to all his former glory, and became the monument of his own name, which every day wore out."[5] And poor Elizabeth Cromwell, in public life a favorite target of royalist wags because of her lack of wit and style, her dowdy country ways, and her bourgeois taste in furnishings and food, got the Hutchinson barb for perceived overweening ambition in her husband's high position: while the Lord Protector Cromwell had "much naturall greatnesse in him, and well became the place he usurp'd," his "wife and children were setting up for principallity, which suited no better with any of them than scarlett on the Ape."[6]

Mrs. Hutchinson had an insider's view of these things. Given the general silence of the sources on marital intimacy it is difficult to know the ways in which wives pressured and influenced politically engaged husbands. (Certainly Elizabeth Cromwell, almost a caricature of intellectual modesty and domesticity, did not.)[7] What is clear is that women of her class acted as Mrs. Hutchinson did, as strong women had acted in the sixteenth or fifteenth centuries, as substitutes for absent or preoccupied husbands, managing estates and business, of course, and coping in moments of extraordinary crises with ingenuity, intelligence, and courage. Men took these stand-in services for granted: ". . . women were never so useful as now," wrote Dr. William Denton to his nephew in 1646; "their sexe intitles them to many priviledges, and we find the comfort of them more now than ever."[8] The women complied cheerfully and sometimes heroically, equally as a matter of course.

Dr. Denton's words related, for one often-told example, to the services of his nephew's wife, Lady Mary Verney. The nephew, Sir Ralph Verney, was in France in self-exile from the Covenanters—the Presbyterian majority—in the House of Commons, and as an unexplained absentee from the House bleakly facing the order of sequestration of his estates. From London Dr. Denton sent him the advice: "instruct your wife, and leave her to act it with the committees," since her sex entitled her to "many priviledges." Thus Lady Mary, pregnant with her fourth child, crossed the Channel in late 1646 to give a year and a half to tedious, frustrating political lobbying (fortunately for the Verneys the parliamentary Presbyterian-conservatives fled as the Independent army marched into London in the summer of 1647), doing the "difficult political and financial business," the "man's work." She managed angry creditors and impecunious and insulting relatives; she brought a measure of order to the family estate sadly decaying with neglect and the predations of quartered soldiers; she gave birth to a third son, this marked with typical perils and drain of her physical strength. Duty presented, duty performed, lovingly and without complaint: it was an epitaph of sorts; never a robust woman, Lady Mary died in 1650, at thirty-four, of a "disease of the lungs."[9]

So normal was such activity for wives of propertied gentlemen that it was given a casual passing line: "When the Parliament sate againe the Collonell sent up his wife to sollicite his businesse in the house. . . ."[10] More unusual, though not noticeably more rewarded, was military service. In 1643 Lady Brilliana Harley, devout Calvinist surrounded by hostile royalist neighbors in Herefordshire, was responsible for the defense of the family castle, ordered to remain there while her husband worked as one of the busiest members of the House of Commons. She and the estate were irresistible game for her enemies: tenants withheld rents; the park of deer and the livestock were plundered, church and parsonage destroyed, streams poisoned. "Now, my deare Ned," wrote the Lady Brilliana in a letter smuggled out to her son, "the gentlemen of this country have affected theair desires in bringing an army against me. What spoyls has bine doun, this barer will tell you. . . . The Lord in mercy presavre me, that I fall not unto theair hands. . . ." For six weeks Lady Brilliana withstood royalist seige, until the troops were called off, needed to bolster the king's forces in Gloucester. But in a final letter she wrote: "I am now againe threatened; there are some souldiers come . . . and 3 troopes of hors." The last words of her letter were a personal note: "I have taken a very greate coold," she reported, and "it is an ill time to be sike in." Lady Harley was another casualty of the civil wars; within a week she was dead of that very great cold.[11] Lucy Hutchinson should have considered her for sainthood.

During the hammering crises of a decade of war and revolution men thought about the serviceability of their women, and set them to a variety of essential tasks. Some of them worried about the consequences. With unsupervised responsibility might not the female shift it so well as to reverse her marital role? Or, if women together were prompted to act in affairs of state, so unprecedented were the times, would they not in their intrinsic simplicity and ignorance be an erratic element, vulnerable before the wily of the Other Side?

Women came together for the first time in London as a pressure group upon government in the frenzied winter of 1642. They were "Gentlewomen, and Tradesmens-wives" carrying a petition to the House of Commons, their leader a Mrs. Anne Stagg, "Gentlewoman and Brewers Wife" of "rank and quality." They came, usefully, to perform a service for and among friends, bit players in the brilliantly organized scenario of (rich and important) Londoners' support of the Commons's confrontation with Charles I. Their presence did not arouse male suspicion or hostility there in the parliamentary yard. When the Commons had read the petition master-director John Pym—"King Pym"—appeared at the door of the House to acknowledge them. "Good Women," he said, "your petition . . . is very thankfully accepted of, and is come in a seasonable time: You shall (God willing) receive from us all the satisfaction which we can possibly give to your just and lawfull desires. . . ."[12]

To sketch in the background: the time was indeed seasonable. The Long Parliament had been sitting for over a year, in solidifying confidence and resolve to dominate royal policies. Parliamentary radicals had impeached the Earl of Strafford and Archbishop Laud, ministerial symbols of Stuart 'tyranny' and interference with the consciences, liberties, and properties of freeborn Englishmen. In May 1641 the king had had to sacrifice Strafford to London rioters convinced that the earl had plotted to import a "Popish army levied in Ireland" to destroy the English "Puritan faction."[13] Strange rioters: most of them were "Citizens of very good account," worth £30,000 to £40,000, who threatened to "send their servants" into the streets if they did not have the "justice" of the earl's head.[14] In November Irish Catholics had rebelled in Ireland and slaughtered their overlords in scenes of reported barbarity, "horrid tortures" like those visited upon the Protestants in central Europe.[15] Was this not, thought the "Puritan faction," proof of a conspiracy of a suspect king, his French-Catholic queen, and an associated English party headed by lords and bishops to use Irish and perhaps French troops against Protestant England?

December 1641: the London Puritans agitated for the impeachment of the bishops—Arminians, papists—in the House of Lords, and against the king's appointee as lieutenant of the Tower of London (good analogy here with the French revolutionary events: like the Bastille, the Tower loomed darkly over London as locus of force and ancient oppression). In the king's court there was tense talk of the "maddest" Christmas ever known, of "daily fears of uproars and disorders," of "insurrection" and of "no other discourse but of open arms."[16]

The climax was yet mounting. In January 1642 the struggle of wills between king and Commons focused on the purge of the lords-bishops and the control of the army in Ireland. Charles was driven to the extravagant gesture of an armed invasion of the House—"where never king was (as they say) but once . . . King Henry VIII"[17]—to arrest Pym and the other leaders of the Opposition. It was a farcical assault, for the famous "Five" had fled into London, received as heroes by the furious population. But what, in his humiliation and frustration, would Charles do? The next night Londoners were hysterical, a hostile reporter claimed, with "strange fears and imaginations" that "the King and Cavaleers with fifteene hundred horse were coming to surprize the City."[18] A resident, one Nehemiah Wallington, living in East-cheap, told it for the Londoners: "in the dead of the night, there was a great bouncing at every man's door to be up in their arms presently . . . for we heard (as we lay in our beds) a great cry in the streets that there were horse and foot coming against the city."[19] As the city gates were shut, defensive chains drawn across the streets, and "no lesse than 50000 or 60000 men ready provided to incounter they knew not what," the "women and children did then arise, and fear and trembling entered in all. . . ."[20]

Women improvised the art of political protest beside the armed "Citizens and Prentices," the "women and girls" if not the "ladies," in the contemporaries' distinction, conspicuous in the huge crowds milling about the Houses of Parliament and the palace of Whitehall in May and again in December and January. A courtier observed that "porters and women in this town are grown so impudent that they have attempted the persons of the Lord Keeper, the Duke of Lennox, and divers others of the nobility . . . as they came from the Parliament."[21] The ladies, "gentlewomen," participated by deputizing their menials: the throngs of demonstrators were swelled, said the king's friends, by "a rabble of Porters, and apprentices dayly sent by their Masters, but chiefly by their Mistresses, with clubs and Swords, to cry for Reformation at the Parliament doores."[22] Or by this suggestion they used more intimate tactics: the women "as M. *Peters* did instruct them in the Pulpit, have hugged their Husbands into this Rebellion."[23] But during that trembling night of 6 January 1642 there was no breakdown by rank; it was simply "women" who were outside with "hot water . . . to throw on the Cavaleeres," and with "joynt-stooles, foormes and empty tubbes" to strew in the streets "to intercept the Horse."[24]

Throughout this orchestrated turbulence, in which the Commons radicals had maneuvered the king into violation of the "privileges of Parliament," creating thereby a "constitutional crisis,"[25] the 'revival' of the use of the petition was a major stroke of political genius. The Stuart court was helpless before the flood of public opinion, apprehensive, angry, resolute, pouring into the House of Commons: the "rude multitude," snapped a frustrated royalist, "says more in a petition than armed men in battle."[26] The "Root and Branch" petition demanding the abolition in entirety of the episcopal structure of the Church of England was subscribed with "the names of above 20000, by Aldermen, Aldermens Deputies, Merchants, Common Councell men, and many others of great rank and fashion"; out of them four hundred were selected to deliver the petition, "all riding out of the Citie of London in 50 Coaches, or thereabout, to the Parliament House."[27] Petitions came from counties and towns around London, Norfolk, Northampton, Staffordshire, Worcestershire, Berkshire, Wilts, Hampshire, Southampton, Norwich, Lynn, Salop, Sarum, Lemster. The Eastcheap bourgeois, Nehemiah Wallington, by occupation a turner and by inclination an historian, noted or kept copies of them all. Proud of his private documentation of the way that the people "stirred up by God" had gone "up to Westminster" with demands for reform of "Church and Commonwealth," Wallington listed copies of forty-odd petitions including the "1000 poor peoples petition," the "15000 poor porters"—and the City women's; his collection preserved the pleas, he said, of people of "all sorts, high and low, rich and poor, of both sexes."[28]

Thus the brewer's wife Mrs. Anne Stagg and her friends of like quality and rank came up to Westminster by invitation, as it were, and doubtless with the approval of their Parliament-supporting husbands. Were they merely being useful, pawns in the political struggle undertaken by their men? The answer is not so easy. The women's public appearance was an event; however helpful, correct, and well-timed it was jarring, disturbing to male observers. Nehemiah Wallington's mention of them was not unsympathetic but his filing of their petition with those of porters and poor people was clear comment of the incongruity of powerless females in the political arena. In his account of the January-February crises the parliamentarian-historian Bulstrode Whitelock separated the women from "people": "Divers petitions, accompanied with great numbers of people," he wrote, "and one from the City dames, were presented to the parliament, against the votes of popish lords and of bishops. . . ."[29] Clarendon, the arch-royalist, identified the women's action as a "precedent": "a rabble of that sex," he called them, "appearing in the beginning of these distractions with a petition to the House of Commons, to foment the divisions, with acceptance and approbation."[30] And inevitably royalist wags rushed into print with *pro forma* ribaldry. A parody-petition published and dated December 1641 was the hasty work of some heavy-handed satirist: "The Petition of the Weamen of Middlesex; Which they intended to have presented to the High Court of Parliament, but shewing of it to some of their friends they diswaded them from it, untill it should please God to endue them with more wit, and lesse Non-sence. Subscribed with the Names of above 12000." (The text of the parody had women demanding the abolition of bishops because the starching of surplices was hard on laundresses' hands, and the elimination of church choirs of "well tuned boys, who are sufficient to put wee women which are the weaker vessels in mind of a Bawdi-house.")[31] In short, the women petitioners—extensions of their solid citizen-husbands—raised eyebrows at best, and at worst occasioned crude ridicule which lowered the tone, made a farce of a truly unprecedented and deadly serious political confrontation. Surely the men would have preferred their wives to stay at home.

The women themselves timidly but firmly explained their purposes. Like the male petitioners they had been stirred up by God to *act*, as "a duty commanded and required," for the reform of church and commonwealth. The divine message they had gotten was that God was "angry with us," that possibly there was a "curse upon the whole Kingdom" because of its festering evils: the "Popish Lords & superstitious Bishops" yet sitting in the "House of Peers"; the "Arch-enemy of our prosperity and Reformation" (that is, Archbishop Laud, who was imprisoned in the Tower) yet "not receiving his deserved punishment"; that "great Idolatrous Service of the Masse" yet "tollerated in the Queens Court." Women though they were, could they as Christians sit passive and unhearing in their homes before God's prodding wrath?

And because they were women they were afraid, in their "fraile condition" fearful of the "Domesticall dangers" of bloody religious wars. They had read the dispatches from Germany and now the news from Ireland made them "tremble": the accounts of papists' "savage usage and unheard of rapes, exercised upon our Sex," husbands and children "murthered and mangled and cut in pieces. . . . Children dashed against the stones, and the Mothers milk mingled with the Infants blood. . . ." But with England too threatened with such horrors, what should they do except join with all true Christians to help contain the "blood-thirty faction" of native papists?

In its preface and conclusion, however, the women unmistakably established the petition as their own, a project separate from sponsors or manipulators. "It may be thought strange," they said, "and unbeseeming our sex to shew our selves by way of Petition to this Honourable Assembly." But there were good reasons "why their sex ought thus to Petition, as well as the Men." The explanation followed:

> First, because Christ hath purchased us at as deare a rate as he hath done Men, and therefore requireth the like obedience for the same mercy as of men. Secondly, because in the free enjoying of Christ in his own Laws, and a flourishing estate of the Church and Common-wealth, consisteth the happiness of Women as well as Men.
>
> Thirdly because Women are sharers in the common Calamities that accompany both Church and Common-wealth, when oppression is exercised over the Church or Kingdome wherein they live; and an unlimited power have been given to Prelats to exercise authority over the Consciences of Women, as well as Men, witnesse Newgate, Smithfield, and other places of persecution, wherein Women as well as Men have felt the smart of their fury.
>
> . . . On which ground we are imboldened to present our humble Petition unto this Honourable Assembly, not weighing the reproaches which may and are by many cast upon us, who (not well weighing the premises) scoffe and deride our good intent. We doe it not out of any selfe conceit, or pride of heart, as seeking to equall ourselves with Men, either in Authority or wisdome: But according to our places to discharge that duty we owe to God, and the cause of the Church, as farre as lyeth in us, following herein the example of the Men, which have gone in this duty before us.[32]

Such a well-thought-out and carefully couched petition: the assertion of spiritual equality with men, and a like obligation to do God's work, was tempered with modesty and female submissiveness; exactly the proper balance. John Pym responded to the women both as valued constituents and as female dependents. He accepted their petition courteously, "thankfully," and promised "satisfaction" for their "just and lawfull desires." And then he dismissed them, instructing them to retire, to turn their sentiments into "Prayers at home for us"; the gentlewomen and tradesmen's wives need not linger in public.[33] These were 'good' women indeed, self-disciplined in their supportive and comforting usefulness, so good that they could write their own speeches.

From 1642 the prospect of women in politics offered welcome material for hack writers trying to turn a shilling or two: small satirical pieces appeared and apparently sold to somebody's profit through the civil wars, and into the 1650s. Fictional petitions and remonstrances had women appealing to Parliament for the "restitution and revocation" of husbands and all "deare and delicious friends" whom they wanted to enjoy at "Tavernes and other places," or proposing that "free-borne Women of England" have unrestricted choice of sexual partners in order to repopulate the nation; the frontispiece on another pamphlet had a wife ordering her husband out the door, his cuckold's horns higher than his hat, with the words, "Go to the wars."[34] Similar droll bits imagined women's parliaments, with "Rattel-head Ladies" assembling to choose their speakers, debate, and pass "Ladies Lawes." Among the latter:

First, that instead of allowing men two wives, women, especially the stronger and greater vessels, should have two or three husbands.

That women might vex, perplex, and any way torment their husbands.

That women may twang it as well as their husbands.

That women may feast, banquet and gossip, when & where they please.

Item, It is concluded and fully agreed upon, that all women shall have their husbands Tenants at will; and that: they shall doe them Knights service, and have their homage paid before every Sun rising, or at every weekes end, or at utmost betweene the quarters, and a day longer to be defer'd unlesse it be in the Dogs dayes.

Item, That man which promises a pretty Maid a good turn, and doth not perform it in 3. months, shall lose his what do you call them.[35]

Mrs. Anne Stagg and her friends set up this sort of leering burlesque (as they knew they would), but it fed upon the later activities of women less socially sedate and more politically assertive than that first delegation of London bourgeoises. Possibly there was a grand repast in the repercussions of the appearance the next year of another women's group, actually the only other to petition the House of Commons until the Levellers.[36] The feminine journey 'up to Westminster' in August 1643 was both an occasion and a *cause*; perhaps its implications were so unsettling that pamphleteers could only handle them with coarse comedy.

This second contingent of women brought a petition which urged, almost demanded, that Parliament renounce the war with the king. The social status and purpose of the women were disputed by onlookers: some said they were "a great multitude of the wives of substantial citizens" at the Commons with a "petition for peace"; others that they were "two or three hundred Oyster wives, and other dirty and tattered sluts," who "tooke upon them the impudency to come to the Honourable House of Commons [to cry] for Peace and Propositions."[37] Amidst "a fearfull Tumult and uprore" they shoved into the Parliament yard, and reviling the "Trayters" therein "most abominably" threatened to "teare Master Pym in pieces, and to pull the House of Commons downe about their ears."[38] Two troops of horse of the parliamentary army were needed to contain them, and that after bloodshed, one death for sure and reportedly others.

Behind this violent feminine enterprise was the trauma of almost exactly a year of civil war. It was in August 1642 that King Charles had set up his standard at Nottingham and called to the gentry and peers of England to assist him in punishing the parliamentary 'traitors.' From the beginning moderates on both sides tried to find means for negotiated settlement. Stalemate, however, was the result, or more to the point, a war of words: fundamentally the issues were nonnegotiable. Charles insisted upon his royal prerogative while relying on his resourceful queen, Henrietta Maria, to recruit continental (or even Irish Catholic) troops for his cause. Parliamentary radicals demanded that the king return to his 'constitutional' role to sit quietly (king-in-Parliament) as the Commons reformed church and commonwealth. Nevertheless, a 'peace party' grew even in the Puritan nerve center of London, "a not insignificant minority, having amongst them many of the wealthy merchants."[39]

The real war, meanwhile, had stumbled on with few encouraging moments for the parliamentarians. The royalists' base was in the north and west of the kingdom, from which the king's nephews, the "perfect knight" Prince Rupert and Prince Maurice with his "robber horsemen," commanded plundering attacks; by late 1642 the king's forces were aimed for London, riding "without resistance" toward Middlesex, Surrey, Sussex, and Kent.[40] It was not quite without resistance, nor counterplundering, mounted by civilians terrified of what royalist troops did and would do to Puritan estates and stronghold towns. In the countryside men and women mobilized, driven by stories of cavaliers indulging in "the like cruelty that hath been used . . . in that miserable and bleeding Kingdom of Ireland."[41] In the town of Wells in Somerset, for example, "40000 fighting men and women" gathered, with "Pitch-forkes, Dungpeeks, and such like weapons, not knowing (poor soules) whom to fight against, but afraid they were of the Papists."[42] A royalist group entered the town of South Molton in Devonshire to find this unsettling melee: ". . . both men, women, and children, about the Cross in the Market place . . . in number at least 1000, some with Musquets loaden, some with Halberts and blacke Bills, some with Clubs, some with Pikes . . . the women had filled all the steps of the crosse with great stones & got up & sate on them, swearing if they did come there they would braine them. . . . a woman which is a Butchers wife, came running with her lapfull of Rams hornes for to throw at them, some of the Gentlemen were comming towards the Crosse. . . . presently the people gave a shoute, and did cry, they be come, at which they were all ready to stand against them. . . ." Prudently, the royalist "Gentlemen" retreated, "betooke themselves every one to house, and after that did not one of them nor their servants, durst show themselves in the street."[43]

The royalist armies pressed on even as Charles was pretending to negotiate with Parliament, by November 1642 coming as close to London as Brentford, which was taken and sacked. Prince Rupert's soldiers took "from the Inhabitants, their Money, Linnen, Woolen, Bedding, wearing Apparell, Horses, Cows, Swine, Hens, &. and all manner of Victualls," and "Pewter, Brasse, Iron pots, and Kettles, and all manner of Grocery, Chandlery, and Apothecary ware. . . ." They burned fishermen's boats, "spoiled" fruit trees, and ruined crops, cut up the "ticks" of featherbeds they could not carry away, and so randomly robbed that they snatched from an "ancient Gentlewoman" the "Mantle from her back." They cocked "pistols at womens breasts" and terrorized the townspeople with threats to "cut off their Noses, and pull out their eyes," calling them "Parliament doggs, Round-headed rogues. . . ."[44] There was not, said a witness, a town "so ruined and defaced" in Germany.[45]

In London the parliamentary population rallied magnificently against the advance of the royalist educators: people of all sorts worked to "secure and defend the City and the Suburbs," women laboring "as heartily as the men";[46] and at Turnham Green Charles's armies were stopped by the "trained bands." But with the parliamentary capital the prize which would seal the king's victory, the spectacle of brigades of citizen-defenders became common sight in the following months: ". . . great numbers of men, women and young people, many of them being house-keepers of very good rank and quality, went out of the city and Suburbs of London, with baskets, spades, and such like instruments, for digging of trenches, and casting up brest-works from one fort to another round the city, and suburbs thereof."[47] City defense had been made into a vast collective celebration: "all the trades . . . whole inhabitants . . . ladies, women, and girls . . . interlarded" set to with exalted determination; with "roaring drummes, flying colours, and girded swords" the Londoners of both sexes, "the indefatigable multitude and strength of the city," erected and dug a "circuit" of fortification around "above five hundred thousand dwelling houses" of "three millions of soules."[48]

Thus the London women's petition and riotous demonstration *against* Parliament in August 1643 was startling and embarrassing to Commons leaders. "I shall relate the whole matter as neere as I can," wrote the editor of the supportive *Kingdomes Weekly Intelligencer*, "concerning the womens coming to Westminster to the Parliament House, on Wednesday-last, to Petition for Peace." It was a discomfitting accident "that they were some wounded and some slaine," especially with the "Malignants" sending reports around the country—"to incence the people against the Parliament"—that the petitioners had only been asking for peace.[49]

The women had appeared in the midst of a strained debate of "propositions" for negotiation with the king which had originated in the House of Lords and been sent to the Commons. Radicals in the second House were appalled: the propositions from their reading would have yielded to the king all the points of the conflict, handed London to him, and excused the "Popishly affected" around him from their assault upon "our Religion, Lawes and Liberties." The strategy of the Lords was to organize the "Malignants" so as to convince people that the Commons resisted peace, "a thing," protested the *Weekly Intelligencer*, "then which nothing is more likely in the world."

But were the women the manipulated, or the initiators? According to the *Weekly Intelligencer*, "those women that were Ring-leaders of the crew" persuaded "such women in and about the City of London and Suburbs, as were desirous of Peace, which was to the women (nay to all Christians ought to be) a pleasing thing, and thereupon some out of an earnest desire of Peace, others out of designe, came . . . to Westminster, with white silke Ribbands in their hats, and cryed for Peace."

The first day the women came with their petition, as all citizens were entitled to do, and there was in it "little exception to be taken," except an undertone of disrespectful sarcasm.[50] But in any case all was proceeding as usual: the Commons accepted and read the "Humble Petition of many Civilly-Disposed women" and delegated a member to talk with the petitioners, "to returne them an answer, satisfactory enough," said the *Weekly Intelligencer*, "if they had beene reasonable Creatures. . . ."

But then the women became noisy and ugly. They had increased in number by "five or six thousand at least, besides the men Malignants that were amongst them, who clapt them on their backes and bid them not to be afraid, but to go on (not withstanding their Petition) to the House of Commons doore, and cry for Peace." The women pushed up the stairs to the door of the House, shoving and knocking down the "part of the Trained Band, that usually stood Centinell there"; they blocked the entry and "would suffer none to come in or out of the Parliament house for two hours together." More soldiers arrived; they fired only powder at the women at first, but when they got brickbats and stones in return they "were forced to shoot bullets in their own defence" (in this they managed to hit only an innocent observer). The provocation was intolerable, said the *Weekly Intelligencer*: "except some few women" the crowd was of the "meanest sort," made up of "Whores, Bawdes, Oyster-women, Kitchen-stuffe women, Beggar women, and the very scum of the Suburbs, besides abundance of Irish women." The proof of their breeding was that they were not "any whit scared or ashamed of their incivilities, but cryed out so much the more, even at the doore of the house of Commons, Give us Pym in the first place. . . ." It was a civilian seige: "all this while the Parliament was in a manner Prisoners, the guard could not in two houres make way to the House, to bring them downe, being loath to offer violence to women. . . ."[51]

He would "let the world judge," said the *Intelligencer* reporter, "if there were any possibility (all faire meanes taking no effect) to appease these Tumults without mischiefe." Ten troopers advanced on the crowd, were surrounded and assaulted, "violent hands upon them." The soldiers used their swords "flat wayes" at first, then in desperation with the pressing women they "cut them on the face and hands, and one woman lost her nose, whom they say is since dead. . . ." The sight of blood finally scattered the rioters "into the Church-yards, Pallace and other places"; a troop of horse rode in with "Kanes" flailing, "cudgelled" and dispersed them. There was a last, certain fatality: accidently and "unhappily," a "maid servant" passing through Westminster churchyard was shot: "unfortunate," said the *Intelligencer*, but a "warning to people to keep out of unlawful Assemblies."[52]

Some of the women rioters had answered the queries of "divers people" about "who put them on to this businesse." They said, according to the *Intelligencer*, that "they were at such a Lords House, and he bid them go to the house of Commons, for they were against Peace." Asked where they had gotten "so many hundred yards of silke Ribbin" for their hats, they mentioned several "ladies" homes in Westminster, Southwark, and the suburbs. The *Intelligencer* concluded that the demonstration had been the "Master piece" of "Malignants here" who carried out the "designes laid at Oxford [where the King had his headquarters and capital] to breed a division and distraction in this City"; it had been a plot, "by this beginning (by women) to get an opportunity to rise in Armes, and to sacrifice the Parliament," so that the Cavaliers may the more easily enter the City."[53]

Naturally, opposition partisans did not answer the parliamentarians' defensive argument that the women's riot had been masterminded by royalists (lords *and* ladies). Excellent political points were to be made in reiterating the "cruel and barbarous" treatment of females by the "enemies to all kind of peace" in the Commons and their army. The king's man, Clarendon, stamped the episode with a semiofficial royalist account. He granted the women's initiative in the peace petition (and from his side they were not of the "meanest sort" of Londoners—it was he who claimed they were the wives of "substantial citizens"), in fact observed that they had "expressed greater courage than the men" in acting against the war. But immediately following that praise came his narrative of the army troopers behaving themselves "with such inhumanity" that they "charged among the silly women as an enemy worthy of their courage"; furthermore, the upshot of the whole project was a signal defeat, the exposure of the peace party in Parliament, and the flight of its members to Oxford, to the "protection of the King."[54] Courageous or silly, the women's interference had discomfited the royalists as much as it had enraged and embarrassed the parliamentarians.

But, in sum, the female interlopers were only a sideshow in the revolutionary crisis in London. The useful gentlewomen and tradesmen's wives came but once to the halls of political decision. Could the manipulated "viragoes" of the summer of 1643 have failed to prejudice their initiative, even for themselves? The next time women came to Westminster in numbers they were Leveller wives, by definition the 'meaner sort' of females. And then the pamphleteers would have a field day, hitting all the old themes of rebellious, lustful Amazons, intent in "beating up men."[55]

NOTES

1. *The Lawes Resolution of Womens Rights* (London, 1632), p. 6.

2. Ibid.

3. Paule-Marie Duhet, *Les Femmes et la Révolution, 1789-1794* (Paris, 1971), p. 57 and passim on Olympe de Gouges and Condorcet; *Women in Revolutionary Paris, 1789-1795*, ed. Darline Gay Levy, Marriet Branson Applewhite, and Mary Durham Johnson (Urbana, Ill., 1979), p. 4.

4. Hutchinson, *Life of John Hutchinson*, p. 48.

5. Ibid., pp. 168, 195.

6. Ibid., pp. 208-9.

7. Antonia Fraser, *Cromwell: The Lord Protector* (New York, 1973), pp. 27-28.

8. Frances Parthenope Verney, *Memoirs of the Verney Family during the Civil War* (London, 1970), 4 vols, 2: 240.

9. Ibid., 2: 413; for recent work on the Verneys, see Miriam Slater, *Family Life in the Seventeenth Century: The Verneys of Claydon House* (London, 1984).

10. Hutchinson, *Life*, p. 236.

11. *Letters of The Lady Brilliana Harley* (New York, 1968), Camden Series, 1, 58: 208-9.

12. *A True Copie of the Petition of the Gentlewomen and Tradesmens-Wives, in and about the City of London* (London, 1641/42).

13. *State Papers Domestic* (hereafter SPD), 17: 568; 18. 241.

14. Ibid., 17: 569.

15. Bulstrode Whitelock, *Memorials of the English Affairs* (Oxford, 1853), 4 vols., 1: 150.

16. *SPD*, 18: 217, 216, 240, 243.

17. Ibid., 18: 245.

18. *A Letter from Mercurius Civicus to Mercurius Rusticus*, 25 August 1643, E.65(32). The abundance in the notes ahead of the familiar British Library reference and shelf-mark number "E" of the Thomason Tracts will give a quantitative sense, at least, of my appreciation of the riches of that collection.

19. Nehemiah Wallington, *Historical Notices* (London, 1869), 2 vols., 1: 289.

20. *Mercurius Civicus to Mercurius Rusticus*, 25 August 1643; Wallington, *Notices*, 1: 289.

21. *SPD*, 18: 274.

22. *Persecutio Undecima* (London, 1648), p. 64.

23. *Mercurius Civicus*, 25 August 1643. The Puritan preacher Hugh Peter probably did so instruct his congregations. See R. P. Stearns, *The Strenuous Puritan* (Urbana, Ill., 1954).

24. *Mercurius Civicus*, 25 August 1643.

25. *SPD*, 18: 274; Valerie Pearl, *London and the Outbreak of the Puritan Revolution* (London, 1961), p. 229; for the "two competing myths" which forced the crisis, see Anthony Fletcher, *Outbreak of the English Civil War* (New York, 1981), p. 189.

26. *SPD*, 18: 274.

27. Wallington, *Notices*, 1: 24-28.

28. Ibid., 2: 14.

29. Whitelock, *Memorials*, 1: 158.

30. Clarendon, *The History of the Rebellion* (Oxford, 1958, 1969), 6 vols., 3: 139.

31. *The Petition of the Weomen of Middlesex*, E.180(17).

32. *A True Copie of the Petition of the Gentlewomen and Tradesmens-Wives*, 4 February 1641-42.

33. Ibid.

34. *The Petition of Wives and Matrons for the Cessation of these Civil Wars*, E.88(13); *A Remonstrance of the Shee-Citizens of London*, E.404(2); *The Resolution of the Women of London to the Parliament*, E.114(4).

35. *A Parliament of Ladies* (1647), E.384(9).

36. See Chapter 3.

37. Clarendon, *History of the Rebellion*, 3: 139; *Certain Informations* (7-14 August 1643), E.65(8).

38. Ibid.

39. Samuel Gardiner, *History of the Great Civil War* (London, 1886), 3 vols., 1: 62, 44, 61, 169, 172; Pearl, *London and the Puritan Revolution*, "Conclusion."

40. Gardiner, *History of the Great Civil War*, 1: 196, 60.

41. *A True Relation of his Majesties coming to the Town of Shrewsbury* (London, 29 Sept. 1642), E.119(3).

42. *A True and exact Relation of all the Proceedings . . . in his Majesties Coming to Somerset* (London, 19 Aug. 1642), E.112(33).

43. *Declaration, A True Relation of the Great Battle between Prince Robert and the Parliament forces at Worcester*, "A Copy of Letter sent to a worthy Gentlemen in London" (Sept. 1642), E.119(11); also R. W. Cotton, *Barnstaple and the Northern Part of Devonshire during the Great Civil War, 1642-1646* (London, 1889), pp. 66-69.

44. *A True and Perfect Relation of the Barbarous and Cruell Passages of the Kings Army at old Braineford, neer London* (Nov. 1642).

45. *Diary of John Rous* (New York, 1968), Camden Series 1, 66: 129.

46. *Englands Memorable Accidents*, 24-31 Oct. 1642, E.240; Gardiner, *History*, 1: 60.

47. *A Perfect Diurnal of the Passages of Parliament*, 1-8 May 1643, E.201(7).

48. William Lithgow, *The Present Surveigh of London and Englands State* (London, 1810), *Somers Tracts*, 4: 537-38, 541.

49. *Kingdomes Weekly Intelligencer*, 8-15 Aug. 1643, E.65(11).

50. See John Rushworth, *Historical Collections* (London, 1721), 8 vols., 5: 357-58; *The Humble petition of many Civilly-Disposed Women, Inhabiting in the Cities of London, Westminster, the Suburbs and Parts adjacent*, 7-9 Aug. 1643.

51. *Kingdomes Weekly Intelligencer*, 8-15 Aug. 1643, E.65(11).

52. Ibid.

53. Ibid.; also Rushworth, *Historical Collections*, 5: 357-58.

54. Clarendon, *History*, 3: 139.

55. Simon Shepherd, *Amazons and Warrior Women: Varieties of Feminism in Seventeenth Century Drama* (New York, 1981), chapter 14, especially, has a nice discussion of these themes.

3

"Seagreen" *Révolutionnaires*

"There were, we may oversimplify," wrote Christopher Hill, "two revolutions in mid-seventeenth-century England." The primary one "established the sacred rights of property . . . gave political power to the propertied . . . and removed all impediments to the triumph of the ideology of the men of property—the protestant ethic." Then there was the other revolution, which "never happened, though from time to time it threatened." This unsuccessful revolution "might have established communal property, a far wider democracy in political and legal institutions, might have disestablished the state church and rejected the protestant ethic."[1]

It should be plain in the foregoing chapter that women played so marginal a part in the primary, successful English Revolution that one must labor to wring out of it the evidence of their participation. In the other revolution there is not exactly a direct contrast: it is not that one sees here an independent 'women's history.' Rather, in the popular revolt, out of "the lower fifty per cent of the population" upon whom Hill focuses in *The World Turned Upside Down*, one is constantly aware of the omnipresence of women, and of the centrality of their cooperation and contributions.

Women were particularly visible within the popular movement which might have established a wider political democracy, among those people "commonly though unjustly styled Levellers" whose challenge between 1645 and 1649 racked the new England being shaped by the capitalist landowners and great merchants, Presbyterian parliamentarians, and army "Grandees." The women we see were the mothers, wives, sisters, daughters of the urban "middling" sort of men, the petite bourgeoisie of trades and crafts. No group consciousness or self-interest motivated them; not once did they object that the franchise demanded by Leveller men excluded them as 'dependents,' denied them the vote along with wage-earners and servants. They were simply there as equally concerned and committed as their men, and enormously useful in organizing, petitioning, and demonstrating.

Keith Thomas observed long enough ago to have had someone take up the challenge that the "place of women in the Leveller movement" was "well worth investigation."[2] Surely it is a tempting subject: Leveller women were of the sort who impressed Alice Clark with their confidence and independence, responsible as expected in family enterprise, from supervising apprentices to tending shop counter.

It is also a frustrating subject, regularly slipping away into blind passages. A small example: H. N. Brailsford, the Leveller historian, was sure that male Levellers did not compose the women's large petition presented to the House of Commons in May 1649; the "most likely author," he said, "was, surely, Mrs. Chidley."[3] "Likely," "surely"? By 1649 Katherine Chidley had been for almost thirty years a Brownist preacher and writer. More recent research recognizes her style in that petition, and especially in one of the 1653 petitions in behalf of John Lilburne. But then the reporter in 1653 identified as the leader of the women's delegation the "wife to one Chidley, a prime Leveller," that is to say, the wife of Katherine Chidley's excellent son, Samuel.[3]

Though, or because, the clearest message in the legacy of Leveller sources is the futility of disentangling the female contribution, let us begin with a resumé of the male-constructed movement, with chief focus on its founder, its self-declared "touchstone," John Lilburne. The sparse facts of the women's activities will follow. And then we will cut back to the *Lilburnes*, to the individual story from which we may form some hypotheses—if not, large-scale, of "the place of women" in the movement—of at least the place of one wife in the political career of one husband.

"Free-born" John Lilburne was from Durham, from a family of the northern minor gentry. A younger son, he was apprenticed to a London cloth merchant, though he never engaged in the trade. He was a brewer at the start of the 1640s, and briefly tried to set up as a soap dealer at the end of the decade. Earning a living was for him an irritating necessity, a dreary distraction from the nation-building work that obsessed him; besides, when he tried to "set up a Shop in the City" he was thwarted by the power of the "Corporations and Monopolies" and the "court of Aldermen" so "oppressive in their Government"[4]—reminded always, in short, of the primary task of democratic control of the great and the rich.

Lilburne was the touchstone of the Leveller movement because, as he explained incessantly, every portion of its program emerged from his living experience. When scarcely more than an apprentice-youth, pulsing with Puritan zeal, he had gotten involved in the printing and publishing of unlicensed books asserting in essence that "all Authority [was] corrupted and perverted from the true end, (the preservation and freedome of the people)." For this (it was the late 1630s) he was brought before Archbishop Laud's Star Chamber, interrogated unjustly and illegally, as he pronounced it, and sentenced to savage punishment and imprisonment.[5] Quick martyrdom: his was one of the first cases taken up by the Long Parliament when it met in 1640; he was freed upon the parliamentary judgment that the Star Chamber proceedings had been "bloody, wicked, cruel, barbarous, & tyranni-call." Lilburne made it the symbol of a new age, a new England governed by an elected body of representatives of the people, a nation in which it would be "unnatural, irrational, sinful, wicked, unjust, devilish, and tyrannical . . . for any man whatsoever, spiritual, or temporal, clergyman or layman, to appropriate and assume unto himself a power, authority and jurisdiction, to rule, govern or reign over any sort of men in the world without their free consent. . . ."[6]

Naturally Lilburne joined the parliamentary army to fight the "norman yoke" of royalist tyranny, "ventured his life freely" in "faithfulnesse and valour" for "his Countrey." But even as he learned to be a soldier he discovered the deceitfulness of the new governors of England. He resigned his commission as a lieutenant colonel in disgust with the "corrupt managing" of the war, and with the strong suspicion that his senior officers and parliamentary leaders alike were acting not "for justice sake, but rather to advance a party whereby to compasse their own ends, and not the publike good."[7]

His mistrust was confirmed when he resumed civilian status in London. He who was not "a changer with the times" spoke out in his first pamphlets for freedom and the "publike good," and was instantly in trouble with Parliament. Under the Presbyterian reaction of 1645 he was arrested, tried, and convicted by the House of Lords for writing works judged libelous and seditious; his appeals from prison to the House of Commons were either unanswered or rejected. Lilburne had no doubt now: the Lords were hopelessly royalist, traitors to the new England; the Commons because of "long continuance" had "changed their interest from that of the peoples," and were "hand in hand" with the Lords; and the "great ones of the Army, what ever they pretended," were "of nearer relation, and more strongly contracted to the Lords and great ones of the Nation."[8]

In jailing Lilburne the Lords and the Presbyterian power mongers of 1645-46 had the proverbial tiger by the tail. No matter how close the prison surveillance he could not be silenced. In smuggled-out and surreptitiously printed pamphlets he decried his unjust sentence, imposed, he charged, because the betrayal of the promises of 1640 by the "great ones" had been "discerned by him sooner than other men"; he vowed he would spare "neither paines, cost nor hazard, forthwith" to share his "forwardnesse" with the "true part of England."[9]

By the spring of 1647 a party was forming around Lilburne; one new friend, a printer and brilliant pamphleteer named Richard Overton, was in prison with him. And a party program was emerging in pamphlets, position papers, petitions to the Commons. (The malicious nickname of "Levellers" was not applied yet: the leaders would be tagged with it at the remarkable Putney debates in October by Oliver Cromwell and the other army grandees; it was used for shock effect—the seventeenth-century equivalent of the label "communist.")

The program built upon the theoretical foundation of the "Norman yoke," largely mythical but powerful because familiar: it had been the common coin of discourse among parliamentary theoreticians. Thus the eleventh-century Norman conquest had ruthlessly trampled the rights of "free-born" Englishmen; Norman kings had usurped the sovereignty of the people's councils; Norman lords, their heirs still sitting in the House of Lords, had established themselves as rulers of the people's lands and villages; the Norman church, censor of conscience and extractor of wealth, had spread its tentacles, punitive and plundering; Norman law had "erected a trade of judges and law and lawyers, to sell justice and injustice."[10]

Now, the Levellers maintained, the long Norman night was ending, its tyranny first assaulted in the glorious events of 1640. The next great advance must be that the Parliament elected in that year dissolve themselves, return their authority to its rightful place, to the whole body of the people of England. Exercising their sovereignty through manhood suffrage, again excluding those dependent upon another's will, wage-earners, servants, and women, the people would elect and grant limited representational capacity to annual parliaments. The pamphleteers repeatedly denied that the new commonwealth would attack property, bring the 'levelling' of estates. As they explained it, their projected democratic franchise would ensure *political* equality, legal justice, and the protection of every man in his enjoyment of what was his by his labor and inheritance.

They insisted further upon a list of immediate reforms, to be made through "An Agreement of the People." Freedom of conscience was an absolute, the toleration of public exercise of opinion for all separatists and Independents as well as for Anglicans. The total abolition of tithes, "enforced maintenance" of the Anglican clergy was to be decreed. The great trading companies were to be outlawed, especially (Lilburne's resented target) the Merchant Adventurers: "the oppressive monopoly of Merchant Adventurers," said the Levellers, "do still remain, to the great abridgement of the liberty of the people, and to the extreme prejudice of all such industrious people as do depend on clothing or woolen manufacture . . . and to the great discouragement and disadvantage of all sorts of tradesmen, seafaring men, and hindrance of shipping and navigation." Imprisonment for debt, that scourge of the petit bourgeois, was to be eliminated. The law, root and branch, would be reformed, with courts made honest and to all accessible. The new commonwealth was to undertake relief, in the worsening economic conditions of the civil war, assume responsibility for the "many thousand poor Tradesmen . . . ready to famish through decay of Trade," for the "Oppressed," the poor, the widows and orphaned children.[11]

Surely the "hand in hand" alliance of the "great" in England was manifest now. Frantically backpedaling from the principles of 1640 Commons Presbyterians were negotiating to restore the king, and planning to disband the New Model Army (with minimal pay to its soldiers): settlement of the erstwhile conflicts among the rulers; restoration of peace and privilege, law and order. Shaken by evidence of popular support for the Leveller program, the Commons spread a reign of terror in London, not only refusing petitions signed by thousands of names but ordering them burned by the public hangman, sending out soldiers to hunt down Leveller neighborhood presses, to raid taverns known as Leveller meeting places, and to burst at early dawn into Leveller homes for search and arrest. John Lilburne they had but had not; still in the Tower, smuggling out ever more furious pamphlets and directing the popular organizational activity, he pronounced Parliament "a conspiracy and confederacy of lawlesse, unlimited, and unbounded men," whose "distruction" he had "no scruple of conscience" to "help forward."[12]

Amazing "Honest John": he forewarned the Great of popular rebellion, not that he regarded it as rebellion, since the parliamentarians were the "reall Rebells and Traitors." "I am now in good sober resolved earnest," he wrote, "determined to appeale to the whole Kingdome and the Army against them." This young man, barely in his thirties, penning that threat in a prison cell, at the mercy of his jailers, could do precisely what he said. Lilburne made his appeal to the "free people of England" including the plain, russet-coated citizen-soldiers of the New Model Army, Independent in politics as in religion, in May 1647; by June, New Model Army troopers were Leveller.[13]

With Lilburne raging in the Tower, the "revolt within the Revolution" exploded in the summer of 1647. The Great Ones split over the prospect of a restored king demanding his full prerogatives and toying with plans for renewed civil war. Army grandees had to ask themselves, "What have we fought for?" and to decide prudently that it was better to be within rather than on the outside of the popular uproar. Commander in Chief Sir Thomas Fairfax rode before army regiments to wild acclaim; Oliver Cromwell rejoined to the same celebration, and his son-in-law Henry Ireton probably composed the famous phrases of the "Solemne Engagement" addressed to Parliament from the summer rendezvous of the Army: "Considering that we were not a meere mercenary army, hired to serve any arbitrary power of a state, but called forth and conjured by the several declarations of Parliament to the defence of our own and the people's just rights and liberties . . . we shall, before disbanding, proceed in our own and the kingdom's satisfaction and future security. . . ."[14] An army lieutenant with a troop of five hundred horses seized the king, for 'safe-keeping' from Presbyterian/royalist restoration. In August, with its generals at the head, the army marched to occupy London, to 'oversee' parliamentary proceedings. In October, in formal debates with (appalled) generals at army headquarters at Putney junior officers and enlisted men endorsed the Leveller constitutional proposals, An Agreement of the People.

John Lilburne was granted "limited" liberty in November, and was reimprisoned in the Tower in January 1648. This ominous signal occurred in a bewildering swirl of events. *An Agreement of the People* was published for mass circulation. The king escaped to the Isle of Wight amidst rumors that he had Scots, French, and Irish troops readying for a second civil war. Several regiments of Leveller soldiers in the New Model Army mutinied, demanding the immediate acceptance of *An Agreement of the People*; Cromwell faced them down, and was formally thanked by the House of Commons for suppression of "sedition." The parliamentarians used the same word about civilian activities. In London, by the lament of an M.P., "the old friends, joint-actors, and constant assistants of the parliament with their lives and fortunes, become full of sedition and averseness towards them, question their integrity, reproach them, and seek to cast them off." People were massing, "under a colour of a petition"; it was "a design by many thousands," with the likelihood of sustained "tumults" in the City, and a "great meeting" in Kent of "the many thousands of freeborn people," all of them "speaking disgracefully of Parliament."[15]

John Lilburne was outmaneuvered in 1648, though it does not seem that he and the Levellers could have done other than they did. The lords and gentlemen of England, and most effectively their cousins of the army command, did not intend polling the nation's freeborn males toward an Agreement of the People. Henry Ireton said at Putney that he would keep the franchise with those having "a permanent fixed interest" because he had "an eye to property." But with the reopening of civil war Lilburne himself set aside the constitutional challenge and pledged his cooperation with the army grandees against the king who was again in arms and bolstered by northern allies; "not loving a Scotch Interest," he related, he "applyed" his hand to help Cromwell "up again."[16] No Leveller revolt within or without the military campaign undermined the effort which ended with the August 1648 defeat of the king and the Scots army at Preston. And after that it was too late.

Lilburne was consigned to a lasting martyrdom, and the Leveller movement to a futile revolutionary posture, after Preston. Their blueprint for the new England was so clear to them, compelling real; and it was so irrelevant, though practically dangerous, politically tricky, to those in power. On 11 September 1648 the "most excellent," the mightiest, of Leveller petitions was presented to the House of Commons as definitive restatement of *An Agreement of the People*, a proposed constitution for a pristine (near) democratic nation. It was ignored: the men of big property were in boiling debate about the execution of a king, and improvising a government with an executive "Council of State." Lilburne sat out the trial and condemnation of Charles Stuart. His position was that that exemplary action should have waited upon the election of a representative body through the mechanisms outlined in the Leveller program: and a king who accepted *An Agreement of the People* would not have had to be killed. He was quiet for a month after the royal execution, and then came roaring back with two pamphlet-petitions: *Englands New-Chaines Discovered*, parts one and two. The first was still within the bounds of toleration to the big bourgeois rulers of the Commonwealth though surely pressing against the outer limits. The king is dead, said Lilburne, but where is the new constitution, the country-wide planning and agreement for a new "Representative"? What is this thing, the "Council of State," manned by those high officers who had shown so "much bitternesse against the most Conscientious part of the [Leveller] souldiery"? Could this self-appointed executive body be the "guardians" of the liberties of freeborn Englishmen, even as it decreed anew the "stopping of our mouths from printing"?[17] But the last words give it away: Cromwell's Council of State was closing in on the Levellers and their chief.

With the publication of *The Second Part of Englands New-Chaines* the fist of the Cromwellian government descended upon Lilburne and his associates, Richard Overton and the merchants-Levellers Thomas Prince and William Walwyn. It was March 1649 and the threat real enough, as London and other cities trembled with popular agitation, as army soldiery and junior officers poised for mutiny against their generals. Lilburne and the others had written an irrefutable history of the strategems by which the 'middling sort' of people had been "mock'd and Cheated," of the methods used by "a few lofty and imperious" men to make themselves "absolute masters over the Commonwealth." Upon orders of the Council of State the four Levellers were arrested, roughly: "about a hundred or two hundred armed men, Horse and Foot" came at "foure or five a clock in the morning." They were charged with the high treason of seditious writing. After individual interrogation the four were together in an anteroom where they plainly heard Cromwell addressing his colleagues, in words which made, Lilburne wrote, "the blood run up and down my veines . . . (being scarse able to contain myself) that so I might have gone five, or six stories higher than I did before. . . ." Cromwell said, "very loud, thumping his fist upon the Council Table, til it rang, . . . I tel you Sir, you have no other way to deale with these men, but to break them in pieces. . . . if you do not breake them, they will break you; yea, and bring all the guilt of the blood and treasure shed and spent in this Kingdom upon your heads and shoulders . . . as the most contemptiblest generation, of silly, low spirited men in the earth, to be broken and routed by such a despicable contemptible generation of men as they are; and therefore Sir I tel you againe, you are necessitated to break them."[18]

The Leveller movement was broken in 1649. Lilburne had one of the high triumphs of his turbulent political career in October, when a jury of his peers in London acquitted him totally of the charges brought against him by the Council of State (and freed as well his three friends). But the Leveller mutineers in the army had been crushed; Lieutenant General Cromwell personally was in command of the arrest and summary punishment. To official stoniness the civilian Levellers had held their mass protest demonstrations and funeral marches for their imprisoned and dead comrades, carried "humble" petitions signed by thousands expressing outrage and defiance. The passion of it was ebbing, however, the committed drifting away, some, to be sure, to the different kind of enthusiasm of the millenarianism of the Ranters and Seekers or to the rigorous radical secularism of Gerrard Winstanley's "True Levellers," most to resignation and apolitical acceptance of the rule of the Saints of the Cromwellian Protectorate.

A few with John Lilburne nursed the 'fire in the belly' and awaited a fresh resurgence of the sovereign people, punctuating with scathing documentation Cromwell's frustration in rooting a foundation for a government of the progressive upper bourgeoisie. Or, Lilburne maintained the passion and defiance for another half dozen years, through angry exile in the Low Countries, imprisonment upon forbidden return, yet another trial and acquittal, and finally, Cromwell openly punitive now, the sentence of permanent exile on the island of Jersey. In the last year of his life he declared himself a Quaker, and in intellectual and emotional peace. He died in 1657, aged forty-two years.

Not the least intriguing fact about John Lilburne and other Leveller leaders is that they talked openly and artlessly of the assistance of their wives, a not inconsequential point. Protestant preachers and social mannerists alike labored over the portrait of the unblinkingly supportive wife, but in the real-life scene she was to be invisible, unacknowledged: 'virtue is its own reward.' On upper-class levels only male activities in the public sphere were properly recorded. Oliver Cromwell was surrounded all his life with women, adored by mother, sisters, and daughters, and faithfully served by a loving homebody of a wife. That he would have done the unmanly thing, however, of seriously discussing his encircling females before parliamentary committee or Council of State is unimaginable. But John Lilburne, in the speeches, petitions, and pamphlets which amounted to a kind of serial autobiography, constantly referred to his wife with almost total lack of male inhibition. It was a rare and maybe tongue-in-cheek occasion when he spoke of going below his "accustomed principles of Resolution" in publicly avowing the "indearednesse of affection" which was "betwixt" him and his Elizabeth.[19]

William Walwyn, successful merchant and enlightened, self-educated man, discoursed regularly, he said, "before my wife," upon his favorite writers, Lucian and Montaigne. Mrs. Walwyn had done her woman's bit: married for twenty-two years she had produced "almost [!] twenty children"; she had so much "more wit than ordinary" that her husband quoted at length her sensibly acerbic comments on the class rulers of the Long Parliament.[20]

Mary Overton was the sharing wife of perhaps the most intellectually audacious of Leveller men. Husband Richard was author of pamphlets not only seditious but blasphemous to the English establishment. Besides sending "Arrows" against "all Tyrants" he punctured "the ridiculous invention of the Soule," the "absurd" notion that "the Soule liveth, when the Body dyeth," and the "fancies" of the reality of Heaven and Hell. "Naturall Reason" proved to him that there was no division between body and the soul, which he called human conscience; there was no instant entry upon death "into glory and salvation," rather "all are dust and to dust must return."[21]

Both Overtons were arrested in 1646 by order of the House of Lords, Richard first, for writing in his infuriatingly witty style a blast against the Lords' imprisonment of Lilburne, Mary for possessing, concealing, and protecting his papers. Each chose to resist arrest, passively, because they said the officers had no legal warrant. Overton's description of the scenes is too good to abridge. He would not "be so base," he wrote,

> to my Country, and to my self in particular, as to yeeld these Arbytrary Lords, so much Villain service, as to become their Lordships *Prerogative Porter*, to carry my self to the stinking, lowsie, barbarous Goal of Newgate. . . . I was not minded to be their DRUDG, or to make use of my feet to carry the rest of my body to the Goale, therefore I let them hang as if they had been none of my own, or like a couple of farthin Candles dangling at my knees, and after they had dragged me in that admireable posture a while, the one took me very reverently by the head, and the other as reverently by the feete, as if he had intended to have done Homage to His Holinesses great toe, and so they carried me: but truly Sir, I laughed at the conceit in my sleeve. But . . . they were a little wearie, they let my bodie fall upon the stones . . . and just as if I had been a dead Dog, they drag'd and trayl'd my body upon the stones, and without all reverence to my cloth, drew me through the dirt and mire, and plucked me by the hair of the head. . . . And in this like unheard of barbarous manner they brought me into the lower roome in *Newgate*; called the Lodge, and there they threw me down upon the Bords. . . .[22]

As her husband told it Mary Overton got quicker brutal treatment. She was "with child and had a young sucking Infant in her Armes," but "like a true bred Englishwoman" she resisted arrest "to the utmost testimony of her weake power." She "told the Marshall that she would not obey it, neither would she stir after it, so much as to set one legg before another in attendance thereto." She further told him that *"if he brought any Order or Warrant from the House of Commons, she would freely and willingly yeeld all humble obedience and subjection thereto*, which was as absolute an evidence of her acknowledgement and submission unto *Englands* legitimate lawfull authority as the other was of defiance and contempt to all arbitrary usurpation whatsoever." The arresting officer was enraged by her spirit: "no sooner had this *Turky-cock Marshall* heard of her uprightnesse to the Commons of England, but up he brisled his feathers and looked as bigg and as bugg as a Lord, and in the height and scorne of derision (just as if he had been Speaker to the House of Peers pro tempore) out he belched his fury and told her, that *if she would not go, then she should be carried in a Porters Basket, or else draged at a Carts Arse."* There were no porters to be found (in sympathy, solidarity?) so Mary Overton too was propelled to jail. The Marshall tried "to pluck the tender Babe out of her Armes," while she fought to keep it "despite of his Manhood." The soldiers "laid violent hands upon her, and drag'd her down the staires, and in that infamous barbarous manner, drew her headlong upon the stones in all the dirt and the mire of the streets with the poore Infant still crying and mourning in her Armes . . . calling her *Strumpet and wild Whore,* thereby to possesse the people, that she was no woman of honest & godly Conversation, whom they so barbarously abused, but a vile strumpet or whore, and were dragging to *Bridewell* that common shore & sinke of Bauds & Whores, etc." Thus was she "shamefully used," to "blast her reputation for ever," to ensure that "she should not passe the streetes upon her necessary occasions any more without contumely and derision, scoffing, hissing, and poynting at her, with such or the like sayings, as, see, *there goes a Strumpet that was dragged through the streets to Bridewell. . . .*" Thus "is the honour," Overton concluded, "that their Lordships are pleased to conferre on the free Commoners wives who stand for their Freedoms and Liberties," the manner in which the Lords "reproach, revile, and dishonour modest, chaste, and civil women."[23]

In various of Leveller petitions, actually restatements of *An Agreement of the People*, male authors routinely spoke of the grievances of men and women. The editor and contributors of the Leveller newspaper, *The Moderate*, reported women's activities in the climactic spring of 1649 in a way both respectful and matter-of-fact: noting the contingents of thousands of females wearing the "seagreen" ribbons of the Leveller emblem at great demonstrations and marches; reprinting in full their petitions to the House of Commons.[24] Many of these women must have been by then movement veterans, seasoned as special messengers between 'safe' houses and taverns, distributors of leaflets and hawkers of pamphlets, community and neighborhood organizers. A story of Lilburne's from the time of his prison sentence in 1646 is relevant in tone and content: from the Tower he "paid" the Lords, he wrote, "prety well my self" by writing "two large books," and "by a large Petition of my Wives, and accompanied at the delivery of it with divers of her feminine friends"; the women's petitioning was so successful, he added, that they got his "business" and he himself heard before the House of Commons.[25]

In sum, through this first 'modern' moment of democratic politics female efforts were naturally integrated with those of the men: the latter did not need to advise one another of the use-value of their womenfolk. Though the inequality was just as obvious, the subordinate partner behaved and was treated with dignity. In one of his fast narratives Lilburne had himself sitting down to ghostwrite a statement for his wife, Elizabeth, to submit in her interrogation before the House of Commons.[26] Richard's hand is obvious in Mary Overton's petition of complaint to the Commons about her incarceration in Bridewell in 1646: the same phrases occur in his petition and hers in relating the brutality of their arrests, and in their indictment of the Commons for failing to restrain the arbitrary power of the Lords. But Elizabeth Lilburne pointedly read, assented to, and signed the statement written by John. And on the published title page of the *Humble Appeale and Petition* of 24 March 1646 is the bold legend, "Per me, Mary Overton." For that matter it would be a strange sort of historical imagination that thought Mary Overton incapable of this pithy passage from Bridewell to the House of Commons: ". . . when we have appealed to this House both for judgement and redresse, all approaches to justice have beene interrupted and hitherto delayed, our Petitions and Complaints slightly rejected or disregarded, our friends wearied, vexed and molested with long & fruitles attendance, while we, our husbands, bretheren, friends and servants, contrary to all Law (severally, and in a forced and unjust separation from our husbands) are kept and mewed up in your severall starving, stinking, murtherin prison-houses, and if at any time we get access, or a Petition read, which is seldome obtained, we are referred over to one Committee or another, who never will bring their reports unto the House, to the obstructing and perverting the whole course of Justice. . . ."[27]

Finally, the best episode reveals the seasoned veterans of Leveller women acting alone and speaking their own words in the terrible weeks of April and May 1649. With the Leveller leaders in the prisons now of the republican Commonwealth and the Leveller soldiery moving ineluctably to the mutiny-disaster at Burford, the women were organizing their part of mass demonstrations in London. A petition of "divers well-affected WOMEN" of the City and suburbs was circulated before delivery to the Commons, and bore this instruction at its end: "All those Women that are Approvers thereof, are desired to subscribe it, and to deliver in their Subscriptions to the women which will be appointed in every Ward and Division to receive the same, and to meet at Westminster Hall upon Munday, the 28 of this instant April 1649, betwixt 8 and 9 of clock in the fore noon."[28]

On Monday, 28 April, "many hundreds of women," by the account of the newssheet *Mercurius Militaris*, "waited upon the house with a Petition of about 10000 hands to it," demanding the release of the Leveller chiefs and the immediate consideration of the *Agreement of the People*. The delegation was blocked by army troopers, the soldiers "most uncivill and inhumane towards them," holding "Pistols ready cock'd at some of their breasts. . . ." About twenty of the women were admitted into the lobby of the House where an angry M.P. told them "it was not for women to Petition, they might stay at home to wash their dishes." Furious, the "Gentlewoman" at the delegation front answered, "we have scarce any dishes left us to wash, and those we have we are not sure to keep them." Joining the scene another member of the House repeated that it was "strange" that females petitioned; the woman shot back, "Sir, that which is strange is not therefore unlawfull, it was strange that you cut off the Kings Head, yet I suppose you will justifie it."[29]

In another newspaper report the women got a more formal rejection in this contemptuous reply sent through the sergeant-at-arms: "You that are the women Petitioners: Mr. Speaker (by direction of the House) hath commanded me to tell you, That the matter you petition about, is of an higher concernment then you understand, that the House gave an answer to your Husbands; and therefore that you are desired to goe home, and look after your own businesse, and meddle with your industry."[30]

On 5 May the women returned to Westminster to answer the insult: "whole *Troopes of Amazons*," gloated the royalist press, came to "spit defiance in the teeth of Authority."[31] In that week a popular young Leveller soldier had been summarily shot as a mutineer, and others humiliated, cashiered, imprisoned. The women's mood was beyond the formalities of political intercourse:

> . . . since we are assured of our creation in the image of God, and of an interest in Christ equal unto men, as also of a proportionable share

in the freedoms of this commonwealth, we cannot but wonder and grieve that we should appear so despicable in your eyes as to be thought unworthy to petition or represent our grievances to this honourable House. Have we not an equal interest with the men of this nation in those liberties and securities contained in the *Petition of Right*, and other the good laws of the land? . . . And can you imagine us to be so sottish or stupid as not to perceive, or not to be sensible when dayly those strong defences of our peace and welfare are broken down and trod underfoot by force and arbitrary power?

Would you have us keep at home in our houses when men of such faithfulnesse and integrity as the *four prisoners* our friends [are] in the Tower, are fecht out of their beds, and forced from their Houses by Souldiers, . . . [when] such valiant religious men as Mr. Robert Lockyer be lya-ble to Law Martial, and be judged by his Adversaries, and most unhumanly shot to death? . . . And are we Christians, and shall we sit still and keep at home, while such men as have born continual testimony against the unjustice of all times, and unrighteousnesse of men, be pickt out and be delivered up to the slaughter, and yet must we shew no sence of their sufferings, no tendernesse of affection, no bowels of compassion, nor bear any testimony against so abominable cruelty and injustice?

. . . No, far be it from us: Let it be accounted folly, presumption, madness, or whatsoever in us, whilst we have life and breath, we will never leave them, nor forsake them, nor ever cease to importune you. . . . Nor will we ever rest until we have prevailed, that We, our Husbands, Children, Friends, and Servants, may not be liable to be thus abused, violated, and butchered at mens Wills and Pleasures. But if nothing will satisfie but the bloud of those just men, those constant undaunted Asserters of the Peoples Freedoms will satisfie your thirst, drink also, and be glutted with our bloud, and let us all fall together: Take the bloud of one more, and take all: Slay one, slay all.

Just once in this hard petition did the Leveller women use the ritual female phrases: they entreated the Commons not to "slight" the points of their "last petition" because they had been made by "the weak hand of Women"; it was the "usual" way of God, they said, "by weak means to work mighty effects." But in peroration they declared themselves "no whit satisfied" with the Commons' answer to their husbands and themselves. "Nor shall we be satisfied," they concluded, "however you deal with our Friends, except you free them from under their present extrajudicial imprisonment . . . and give them respect from you, answerable to their good and faithful Service to the Commonwealth." And until the Commons granted their demands and intended "good to this miserable Nation" their houses were "worse then Prisons," and their "Lives worse then death. . . ."[32]

NOTES

1. Christopher Hill, *The World Turned Upside Down* (London, 1972), p. 12.

2. Keith Thomas, "Women and the Civil War Sects," *Past & Present* 13 (April, 1958): 62 n.97. A solid response is in Dorothy F. Ludlow, " 'Arise and Be Doing': English 'Preaching' Women, 1640-1660" (Ph.D. diss., Indiana University, 1978), pp. 242-59.

3. H. N. Brailsford, *The Levellers and the English Revolution* (Stanford, 1961), p. 318 n.8; Ludlow, "Arise and Be Doing," pp. 119-26.

4. John Lilburne, *The Legal Fundamental Liberties of the People of England Vindicated*, 8 June 1649, E.560(14), p. 60.

5. J. Lilburne, *Englands Weeping Spectacle, or the Sad Condition of Lieutenant Colonel John Lilburne*, 29 January 1648, E.450(7), p. 2.

6. Lilburne, *The Free-mans Freedom Vindicated*, 16 June 1646, E.341(12).

7. Lilburne, *Englands Weeping Spectacle*, pp. 4, 6.

8. Ibid., p. 9.

9. Ibid., 9, 12.

10. *Remonstrance to Commons of the Many Thousands of Citizens and other Free-born people*, 7 July 1646, E.343(11), p. 15.

11. *To the right Honourable and Supreme Authority of the Nation, the Commons in Parliament Assembled, The humble Petition of many thousands. . .*, 19 September 1648, E.464(19), p. 3.

12. Lilburne, *Rash Oaths unwarrantable*, 23 June 1647, E.393(39), p. 8.

13. Ibid., p. 56.

14. *A Declaration, or Representation from his Excellency, Sir Tho. Fairfax, and the Army under his Command*, 14 June 1647, E.392(27), p. 4.

15. Bulstrode Whitelock, *Memorials of English Affairs*, 2: 242, 264.

16. Lilburne, *Legal Liberties*, p. 28.

17. *Englands New Chains Discovered*, by Lieut. Col. John Lilburne and divers other Citizens of London and the Borough of Southwark, 26 February 1649, E.545(27).

18. *The Picture of the Councel of State*, by Lieut. Col. John Lilburne, Mr. Thomas Prince, and Mr. Richard Overton, 11 April 1649, E.550(14), pp. 14-15.

19. Lilburne, *Anatomy of the Lords Tyranny*, 1 November 1646, E.362(6), p. 16.

20. William Walwyn, *The Fountain of Slaunder Discovered*, 30 May 1649, E.557(4), p. 2; *Walwyns Just Defence*, in *The Leveller Tracts, 1647-1653*, ed. William Haller and Godfrey Davies (New York, 1944), p. 373.

21. Richard Overton, *Mans Mortalitie* (Amsterdam, 1643-44), pp. 11, 15, 6-7.

22. R. Overton, *The Commoners Complaint*, February 1646-47, E.375(7), pp. 13-14.

23. Ibid., pp. 17-20.

24. *The Moderate*, 24 April-1 May 1649.

25. Lilburne, *Legal Liberties*, p. 26.

26. See below, pp. 76.

27. *Humble Appeal and Petition*, E.318(10).

28. *The Humble Petition of divers Well-Affected Women*, 24 April 1649, E.551(14), p. 8.

29. *Mercurius Militaris, or the Peoples Scout*, 17 April to 24 April 1649, E.551(13).

30. *The Kingdomes Weekly Intelligencer*, 24 April-1 May 1649, E.552(21).

31. *Mercurius Militaris*, 22-29 May, E.556(22).

32. *The Humble Petition of divers Well-affected Women*, 5 May 1649, 669f.14(27). See A. S. P. Woodhouse, *Puritanism and Liberty* (Berkeley, 1951), p. 367n, for the observation that it is "improbable that this petition was actually composed by the women," though its "principles" are "none the less interesting." As we have seen, Brailsford and Dorothy Ludlow thought Katherine Chidley wrote it (above, pp. 54).

4

Leveller Husband/Leveller Wife

Despite their relative visibility, we know next to nothing about Leveller women. Straight-talking Mary Overton told Parliament in her petition from Bridewell that their soldiers had taken away "her goods, which were her then present livelihood for her imprisoned husband, her selfe, and three small children."[1] She suckled one baby, carried another, and possessed trunks filled with perhaps profitable merchandise: end of information. Who was the woman who spoke for the delegation of petitioners in the Commons lobby and silenced the M.P. with her thrust on the extralegal execution of the king? There is another story of her stopping Oliver Cromwell on that April day of 1649 (in a 1973 Cromwell biography the woman is called a "harpy").[2] She took hold of Cromwell's cloak and told him "there were many hundreds of them" who had waited "from morning" to deliver the petition, but the Commons "would not hear it." Time "hath been," she said, "when you would readily have given us the reading of Petitions, but that was when we had money, plate, rings and bodkins to give you. . . . you think we have none now, but we have a little left, but not for you, and blood too, which we shall spend against you." Nonplussed, Cromwell asked, "What would you have?" She answered, "Those rights and freedoms of the Nation, that you promised us, and in particular the deliverance of our friends which you have imprisoned contrary to the forme and Method of Law, and Sir their Liberty we will have, or we will loose our lives." Cromwell was impatient: "Well, well, there is Law for them," he said. The woman held on to make him hear her point: "Sir, if you take away their lives, or the lives of any contrary to Law, nothing shall satisfie us but the lives of them that doe it, and Sir we will have your life too if you take away theirs. . . ."[3]

Of only one woman is there more than a tantalizing glimpse. In that serial autobiography of the Leveller founder Elizabeth Lilburne runs along in her husband's footnotes, frequently making it up to the

light of the pages proper. Everything we have about Elizabeth Lilburne comes from John's narrative of his own life, which is to say
that we see her always in tandem with him, the portrait controlled
by his compulsion to talk of himself: unless the petitions for state
support of the Widow Lilburne count, there is not a shred of evidence
of an autonomous Elizabeth. But that, almost needless to add, is the
point of her story.

The most, arguably the only, extraordinary thing about Elizabeth
Lilburne is her marriage to John. (It is also the most puzzling, though
the obvious may be assumed from Lilburne. He chose her; how could
she have refused?) Coupled with one of the supremely original personalities of this amazing age she was a prototypical 'normal' wife,
the 'little woman' really wanting nothing more than a husband, children, and a nice property, with a few good friends for company,
gossip, and assistance in her lyings-in. She was not dull-witted: she
had intelligence and initiative. She must have been socially charming.
Oliver Cromwell, fond of interesting women, ever found her so. With
Lilburne she was not only "unweariedly" devoted, but understanding,
warm, and responsive. He loved her inordinately (until almost his
end), told anyone and everyone that she was his "chiefest earthly
delight" whose "company" he desired more than that of any worldly
being. But through all the turbulence of her fifteen years of marriage,
with John pulling her up to soaring peaks of political crusade, Elizabeth Lilburne remained essentially unchanged. She was a very consistent bourgeois woman.

Probably born and raised a Londoner, Elizabeth was the daughter
of a City merchant, Henry Dewell, and a "gentlewoman," as Lilburne
noted (he was fierce about rank, insisting that he be recognized as a
gentleman and son of a gentleman). By the conditions of her first
acquaintance with Lilburne it might be that she was an intense youthful Puritan. Or she may have been a late-adolescent prone to hero-
worship. Or again, perhaps it was simply that, as his biographer says,
Lilburne was "always attractive to women,"[4] even as he was being
beaten in London streets. Whatever her reasons Elizabeth Dewell
visited him in 1638 in Fleet Prison were he lay in chains after the
terrible sentence imposed upon him by Archbishop Laud's Star Chamber Court—fathers punishing the obdurate son who would not kneel
to their authority. The twenty-three-year-old Lilburne was the martyred hero for all London Puritans as he was whipped at the cart's
tail from Fleet Street to Westminster—five hundred blows, according
to spectators—and as he stood two hours immediately thereafter in
the pillory, shouting his indictment of the bishops, incredibly even

pulling 'subversive' pamphlets from his pockets and throwing them to a spellbound crowd. Returned to his cell, with minimal medical attention, his tortured body in irons, half-starved and hallucinating in spiritual certainty of God's "work for him to do" in the "preservation and freedom of the people," he was visited by several women. One of them was Elizabeth, the gentlewoman who would become his wife, here "honouring and comforting him . . . when he was more like *Job* upon his dunghill by his sufferings then a man at that time for her society. . . ."[5]

They were married sometime during the 1641-42 furor of the parliamentary challenge of Charles I. Lilburne was in his mid-twenties; Elizabeth Dewell's age was not recorded. Nor have the details of a marriage contract survived, though circumstantially the prospects of the pair were typically those of their small gentry and merchant middle class. Elizabeth must have brought a respectable portion, and John, whose father was a landed gentleman and of a family of successful merchants in and around Newcastle in north England, was establishing himself as part owner, with an uncle, of a London brewery. To anticipate: unlike many Leveller women, "divers" of the feminine friends with whom she would go petitioning, Elizabeth was never a working wife, had apparently no contact with the brewing and soap-boiling trades in which John half-heartedly dabbled. Unless she was engaged in his political aggressions, the ways in which she spent her days were irrelevant to Lilburne's narratives. From other sources[6] we know that she had nine pregnancies, with three surviving children.

With her marriage vows, matron Elizabeth Lilburne entered her future with sufficient complacency. She had a honeymoon of sorts: though as "high" for Parliament as any man in England, and so conspicuously belligerent in street demonstrations and rioting in 1640 that he had been briefly arrested,[7] husband John was quiet for a few months. Years later he wrote to a just-wed friend that he knew "by experience, that divers moneths after marriage are mostly commonly a time of dotage . . . even in the solidest persons," a time for "negligence and remissnesse," for "delight and joy."[8] Never a man to do things by halves, Lilburne was surely as passionate in love as in politics. Through the coming years, so many of them spent in prison, he complained bitterly when separated from Elizabeth. "I had rather," he told a jailor, "you would immediately beat out my braines, then deprive me of the society of my wife."[9] Reasonable, then, that the new Mrs. Lilburne might have underestimated the driving power of that youthful "conscience . . . awakened upon his Masters call."[10]

"Well," in typical Lilburne transition, "in the next place the Wars begun betwixt [Parliament] and the King." John was chafing to fight, and joined a London foot regiment as a captain. Elizabeth went with him; wives lived in rear quarters and moved with the baggage trains. The first civil war must have seemed to her only a lull, unprecedented and dangerous, but still a time of postponement before (God willing) regaining the normality of merchant privacy and accumulation, and further ahead, perhaps, the prize of an estate of Lilburne land near Durham.

As consequences of their short-lived displacement in the military the Lilburnes had a frightening episode, which included a test of Elizabeth's mettle and resourcefulness that should have provided a single favorite story for grandchildren by the fire. Lilburne was captured at Brentford in late 1642, after commanding a gallant holding action against a far superior royalist army. Taken to the king's capital at Oxford he was tried for treason by enemies who had already marked his name: he was "much known and talked of," wrote the king's minister; at his trial he "behaved himself with so great impudence in extolling the power of Parliament, that it was manifest he had an ambition to have been made a martyr for that cause."[11] He would have been shot, had Elizabeth not acted. Back she traveled to London, "to solicite the House of Commons daily and hourely . . . for his preservation"; she "took the boldnesse to present her self at the Commons Barre, there begging and importuning their care of her husbands life," and at last obtained an official letter which threatened parliamentary reprisal against noble royalist prisoners if Lilburne were executed. On her return journey to Oxford, through army lines, she matched the hero in heroism: wrote John proudly, "With which letter (big with child as she was) she undergoes a task through all the strong Courts of Guard, which none else (as things then stood) durst undertake; in performance whereof, she met with so many sad and difficult accidents, to a woman in her condition, as would force tears from the hardest heart, to heare them related, but they are too large for this place, though those that know them, cannot but remember them to her perpetuall commendation, who by wisdome, patience and diligence overcame them all, and for her reward both saved her husbands life, and after a season his liberty."[12]

Elizabeth Lilburne had well earned her normality, prosperity, and privacy. John was exchanged in 1643, "high above my quality and condition," he said modestly, and on his homecoming offered "a place of honour and profit . . . reputed worth about £1000 per annum." Here for Elizabeth was the stamped finale of the military lull and its postscript reward. She was ecstatic—for the second before Lilburne rejected it, "conscienciously scorned and slighted" it. Husband and wife seem to have surprised one another. His decision, John noted, caused his wife "extraordinary grief," and he was compelled to explain it to her: "I must rather fight (though it were) for 8 pence a day," he told her, "till I see the liberties and peace of England setled, then set me down in a rich place for mine own advantage, in the midst of so many grand distractions of my native Country as then possessed."[13] Obvious—except, beforehand, to Elizabeth. But in stinging disappointment she was learning her Puritan martyr: with his head filling with ideas culled from the Magna Carta and the *Petition of Right*, and the duty plain to rid the land of the "Norman Yoke" in order to recover the fundamental liberties of freeborn Englishmen, he was only beginning his crusade.

A thick sheaf of lessons accumulated for Elizabeth Lilburne in 1644 and 1645. John resigned as a lieutenant colonel from an army he considered riddled with royalists, Oliver Cromwell and the New Model freedom fighters excepted. In London residence he became the furious focus of resistance to the House of Lords and the Presbyterian majority riding high in the Commons. As he saw it, and surely further explained to his wife, he was specifically tapped to do battle with evildoers: in "conscience to God, and safety to my self and bretheren, I was inwardly compelled to deal with [them] that sought to destroy the generation of the righteous." However 'they' were always the initiators: the Lords, not just unrighteous but illegal, since Lilburne denied their jurisdiction over commoners, would "fall upon my bones, and Vote me to prison I know not wherefore."[14] Or, as he objectified his innocent self: "diverse unworthy officious men were set awork both upon him and all that loved him and his cause, even by printed, railing, and lying pamphlets, to abuse, vex and provoke him, unto which he answering & replying in way of justifying himself and his friends, is hastily complained on to the Parliament, his person summoned by Warrants from the Committee of Examinations, where (as before in Starchamber) he is demanded questions against himselfe, which he refusing to answer, they make no longer debate, but immediately send him to Newgate, purposely to provoke him more and more. . . ."[15]

So Elizabeth Lilburne was drawn into an embattled existence, or without choice, she was overwhelmed by it. She could only stand by John's side, at her committed best in the unremitting confrontations he forced with the powers of England. In his examinations at parliamentary bars Lilburne developed ingenious delaying tactics, used to display his growing and formidable knowledge of law, Coke's *Institutes* his cherished authority, and to make his case for civil liberties, equal justice, and "lawfull" court procedures; and all the while, during stretched-out sessions, he played to a crowing throng of fans who hung about the halls of Westminster in anticipation of just such fireworks. It was an amused royalist journalist who made a point of Mrs. Lilburne's absorbed presence: Lilburne "Baits and whips the House of Lords as if they were so many blind Beares," read the newssheet *Mercurius Elencticus*, and "hath declared their proceedings illegal, and challenged forty of the best lawyers to dispute the point with him"; but, continued the writer, "let them be assured John Lilburne hath not play'd the Truant, he hath not his lesson to learne, nor must they thinke to abate his courage, so long as *Elizabeth* stands by, and is his promptuary."[16]

With this behind her perhaps Elizabeth Lilburne was prepared for the moment when John ran out of delays, when the House of Lords, that "Spanish Inquisition," as he labeled them, ordered him to receive their judgment. "I marched in amongst them," Lilburne related, "with my hat on, & not only refused to kneel at their Bar, But also with my fingers stopt both my ears when they went about to read my pretended Charge."[17] For that outrage he was fined £4,000 to be paid to the king, given a prison sentence of seven years, and forbidden for life to hold civil or military office. And to silence him totally, as the Lords fervently wished to do, he was denied in his Tower quarters reading and writing materials *and* the company of his wife.

The preparation was so sufficiently advanced that Elizabeth Lilburne immediately became John's outside runner. For the few months he was kept in solitary sentence she communicated with him from the window of a building forty or fifty yards away. When she was permitted to be with him in the Tower (not even the goaded Lords had the stomach for responsibility of separating husband and wife) she more directly managed his widening organizational affairs. She smuggled his manuscripts to printers working in tiny streets and back alleys, and distributed the finished pamphlets to the booksellers who would spread them city and county-wide to people of the middling sort. She carried letters of appeal to the sheriff of London, and to Oliver Cromwell, whom Lilburne yet considered a stalwart in his cause. Cromwell's letter bore the introduction that it was brought "by the gravest, wisest, and fittest messenger I could think of, and though a Feminine, yet of a gallant and true masculine Spirit."[18] And she became in earnest a political lobbyist: she and "divers of her feminine friends" took that "large Petition" to the Commons whereby Lilburne got his hearing before that House (but no progress on his release: his friends in the House minority were either afraid or unwilling to challenge the Lords' jurisdiction).[19] Lilburne's words to his jailor date from this campaign: "God hath so knit in affection," he said, "the heartes and soules of me and my wife, and made us so willing to help to bear one anothers burdens, that I professe, as in the sight of God, I had rather you should immediately beat out my braines, then deprive me of the society of my wife."[20]

It was April 1647, Lilburne in the Tower, busily baiting the Lords with manuscripts for the hidden presses and the slippery street carriers. House of Commons Presbyterians decided to intervene to stop the flow of incendiary prose; though they could not snuff out its source which was Lilburne and Overton, they hoped to ferret out the presses and round up the carriers. From the House Committee "for suppressing scandalous Pamphlets" a warrant was issued for the arrest of Elizabeth Lilburne for "dispersing" her husband's books. What followed was a matchless moment in the Lilburnes' first battle with the authorities and Establishment of England. Here, verbatim at the start, is Lilburne's account:

> . . . Lewis a servant to the Sergeant at Armes, came to my lodging in the Tower, and shewed me a Warrant he had to take my wife into safe custody, for dispersing some of my last bookes, and I told him it was very hard, for an Committee of Parliament, to send forth a warrant to make my wife a Prisoner, before they had heard her speak for her selfe, or so much as summoned her to appeare fore them, and I plainly told him it was more then by law they could justifie, but how ever, I bore so much honourable respect unto the House of Commons, and all its Committees, that I would not perswade my wife to contemne their warrants, but if he pleased to take my word for her appearance, I would ingage my life for her, that she should be punctually at the houre appointed, to waite upon the Committee to know their pleasure: which ingagement he was pleased to take, but withall told me, he had brought a warrant, to the Lieutenant of the Tower, to carrie me before the Committee at two o'clock in the afternoon, but I told him, unlesse I see and read the warrant, I should not goe, but by force and compulsion, and therefore if he pleased to goe with me to the Lieutenant, and get him to let me read the warrant, I should readily obey it, which he did accordingly, but time being very short, I considered with my selfe what was most fit for me to doe, for I assured my selfe I was to goe before those, divers of which, would bend all their insensed mallice and indignation against me, and make use of all their power and wiles, to intrap and insnare me, and therefore, I lifted up my soule to my old and faithful Counceller, the Lord *Jehovah* . . . [who] gave me that present resolution that was

able to lead me, with a great deal of assured confidence to grapple with an whole host of men. . . .

His part thus simply rehearsed, Lilburne turned to Elizabeth's problem, "to doe something for my wife as the weaker vessel, that so she might not be to seek in case she were called before them, and for that end, I drew her presently up a few lines, which I read unto her, and gave her instructions, that upon the very first question they should aske her, she should give them her paper, as her absolute answer to their question: unto which she readily assented, and set her name to it."

The points of the paper written for Elizabeth, to cover her speechlessness, were based on statue law from the reign of Edward III and the *Petition of Right*, insisting that "no man be put to answer with out presentment before Justices, or matter of record, or by due process and writ originall according to the Law of the Land, and if anything . . . be done to the contrary, it shall be void in the Law, and holden for errour." Lilburne carefully made a second copy, for printing and circulation.

Husband and wife appeared together at two o'clock before the House Committee, Elizabeth in the background as John at the bar readied to follow his own script. The chairman of the committee, a Mr. Corbet, began by asking if Lilburne were the author of a "little book," which he held up, entitled *The Oppressed Mans Oppression Declared*. Lilburne said that he would answer after he had had an opportunity to "speake a few words"; first, said Mr. Corbet, "answer the question." Round and round they went with that, Lilburne creating the impasse to make his stinging points, Corbet repeating with helpless exasperation, "answer the question." This was not a court of justice, Lilburne protested, but if it is being so declared, then "by law you are bound. . . . I will not answer you till I have liberty to speak." The patience of a weary member of the Committee snapped: "Let him speak. . . ." Lilburne could chalk up the first advantage.

He then observed that if this were indeed a court of justice, rather than a "Cabinet Counsell," its proceedings must be "held openly and publiquely," so that "all the people, that have a mind to heare and see you, and beare witness, that you proceed with justice and righteousnesse, may without check or comptrole, have free accesse to behold you." This demand caused a "mighty stir by some Parliament men," which Lilburne countered, saying "blessed God, I am not now before a Spanish Inquisition, but a Committee of an English Parliament, that have sworn to maintaine and preserve the lawes of the Kingdome. . . ." Easy second round: the doors were opened, to the joy of an expectant audience. (And, according to Lilburne, "people cryed out, they would never answer to close Committees any more, being the doores ought to be open, which they never knew before.") That settled, Lilburne took notes from his pocket: "Now Sir," he said, "with your favour, I shall expresse my selfe a little further to this Committee."

Elizabeth Lilburne was silently watching this test of wills, brilliant John at the bar, the committee members an apoplectic body, shouting that they would not be compared to the Spanish Inquisition and commanding him to answer the question. Suddenly, addressing her husband, she "burst out with a loud voice": "I told thee often enough long since, that thou would serve the Parliament, and venture thy life so long for them, till they would hang thee for thy paines, and give thee *Tyburn* for thy recompence, and I told thee besides, thou shouldst in conclusion find them a company of unjust, and unrighteous judges, that more sought themselves, and their owne ends, then the publique good of the Kingdome, or any of those that faithfully adventured their lives therefore."

Lilburne must have glanced at his wife, but he paused only long enough to tell Mr. Corbet "to passe by what in the bitternesse of her heart being a woman she had said unto them." Domestic distractions he did not need in his concentrated maneuvering against the "power and wiles" of his opponents. He would conclude his written statement, he informed the Committee, and then "return" to the "answer to their question." Worn down, the members consented to their final humiliation.

Completely in charge, Lilburne made a triumph of his answer on the authorship of *The Oppressed Man Oppression Declared.* That is to say, *he* was triumphant: one imagines Elizabeth listening to his mocking and defiant reply in despair. Lilburne explained to the Committee:

> I came before you with an absolute resolution to owne and avow that booke (though I have been much by some of my friends persuaded to the contrary) always provided I could get some thing effected before I did own it, which I have already done, (that so I might set it in a way to come to a legall justification). For first I have got the doore openned, that so I might have a publique hearing as my right by law. And . . . have obtained liberty (though with much adoe) to declare before you, in the presence and hearing of all these people, the illegality of all yours, and all other Committee proceedings, inforcing the free men of England, (against the known and fundamentall lawes, of the land, and your own oathes,) to answer to selfe accusing interrogatories, and now having fully effected what I desired and thirsted after, I come now with as much

willingnesse and readinesse to answer to your question, as you are to have me answer to it, and avowedly I tell you, I invented, compiled and writ that booke, and caused it to be printed and dispersed, and every word in it I will own and avouch to the death, saving the Printers Erratas, which if you please to give me the booke, and liberty of pen and inke, I will correct and amend them under my own hand, and return you the booke again, with my name annexed, under my own hand at the conclusion of it.

That "little digression" finished, Lilburne had a last demand, though he presented it "humbly" to the Committee. He asked that the charges against his wife be dropped, for, he said, though she indeed dispersed his books, "she is my wife, and set at worke to doe what she did at the earnest desire of me her (unjustly imprisoned) husband, and truly I appeale to every one of your own consciences, whether you would not have taken it very ill at the hands of any of your wives? If you were in my case, and she should refuse at your earnest desire to doe that for you that she by my persuasion hath done for me, therefore I entreat you to set her at liberty, and set the punishment of that her action upon my score." That logic impressed all but one committee member; Elizabeth was discharged, for which, John noted, "I thanked them."[21]

And the Lilburnes were returned to the Tower, John a state, Elizabeth a private, prisoner. What was she thinking? She would serve and assist her husband in his political warfare; she understood and valued his superbly courageous combat for the true law and the rights of freeborn Englishmen. But ultimately it was not his principles but his *person* which she cherished and for which she was responsible. She had cried out in the courtroom against the awesome weight of power represented there, that would inevitably crush her husband, making his righteous principles for naught. Lucy Hutchinson played but one scene of this excruciating wifely dilemma, and (grudgingly) perceived it as a moment of weakness and failure. Elizabeth Lilburne was less high-minded, perhaps, less 'intellectual'; she suffered, irresolute, through repetitive acts of a drama which ended only when her 'womanish' vision had become the fact.

A day in January 1648: Elizabeth Lilburne had a terrifying experience. John was out of prison and of course at the center of Leveller turmoil in London. A warrant was issued again for his return to the Tower, this from both Lords and Commons, an illegal warrant, Lilburne naturally declared it, in violation of the basic law of Coke's *Institute*, of habeas corpus and the guarantees of just and speedy trials. He and "friends" went to the House of Commons, Lilburne vowing that, he told the crowd, "I would loose my life before I would be a trayter to the Liberties of England," which he would be if he "obeyed that illegal Warrant." He stood at the Commons door "preaching the law and advice out of Sir Edward Cookes Institute (then in [his] hands)" and the Parliament's "own declarations" so stridently that a specially reliable army detail had to be fetched to stop him. A Colonel Baxter with a "fresh guard" arrived. He "most imperiously," said Lilburne, "commanded me to cleare the Lobby of all my friends; and not knowing but his intention was to murder me at the House of Commons doore . . . I gave my books, staffe, and gloves to my friends, being resolved (if possible I could) to seize upon the very wind pipe of him that first laid hands upon me." The crowd was so thick, however, that Lilburne's "very armes were pinnioned," and "abundance of swords were drawn" dangerously about him. As soldiers came "at a tilt" at him he cried out "murder, murder"; they would have, he said, "undoubtedly dispatched me, *had not my wife stood betwixt me and them*"[22] (italics mine).

During the rest of 1648 Elizabeth Lilburne might have nursed the small hope that there would come an end to her fear and tension. With the Presbyterian reactionaries driven from Parliament John was free, pardoned and promised his soldier's arrears and reparations by the Commons: the Leveller chief was essential to the Cromwellians in the last military showdown with the king and his Scots supporters. But she was closest to his fretting restlessness. Lilburne said he was now going to devote himself "to provide for the future well-being" of wife and three children, which meant finding an income for the first time since 1642. He went north to look at the land offered him as reparation, to satisfy his rigorous conscience about accepting a sequestered estate (he knew the gross details of the ways in which the "great ones" were accumulating fine fortunes in grabbing royalist estates); but in any event the grant was barely enough to cover his debts of six years' standing. He was offered as well a "publick place," which he refused for two reasons. First, he said, the Parliament had no mandate from, did not represent, the whole of the people; purged of Presbyterians, "pick'd and culled" by Cromwell, the government was a farce, and should have been dissolved. Second, he would not be among those "many men in the Parliament, and elsewhere of their associates (that judge themselves the onely Saints and godly men upon earth)," who with salaries of thousands of pounds a year lived "upon the sweat of poor peoples brows," upon the backs of "thousands of Families having never a penny in the world . . . but what they earn . . . in sad and deplorable condition." State employment rejected, he had to be either a farmer or a tradesman. Farming was absurd because, he said, any profits would be eaten up by the "lazy, antichristian, time observing Priests"; and besides tithes, taxation, excise, and "that unfathomable gulf of free-quarter" from any officer who bore him "a spleen" would force him "out of house and home." Which left trade of some sort, where he would have to "hazard the losse" of goods and shop or "else go to Law for it" in unequal competition with the rich corporations and monopolizers (and both, Lilburne charged, "against the fundamental Laws and Liberties of England," as "notably proved by Cook in his exposition of the Statue of Monopolies, 3 part Inst. fol. 181, 182 &c"). He was an "old weather-beaten ship," needing "ease and rest," Lilburne complained, as he eliminated every occupation except that of professional political agitator.[23] And with the conclusion of that soliloquy Elizabeth doubtless realized that her small hope was a withered stillborn.

Early 1649: Lilburne was expending a fraction of his energy and anger to expose the monopolizers thwarting his infant enterprises as soap dealer or Holland merchant; most of him was engaged in furious note-taking on the government of the new Republic, its parliament perpetuated "for ever," its "erected Councell of State" and "councell of Warr" ruling "this declared Free Nation arbitrarily . . . that none for time to come should dare to stir. . . ."[24] Publication of *Englands New Chaines Discovered* was hurled assertion that he would not be a private citizen. By March 1649 he was back in prison with Overton, Walwyn, and Thomas Prince, this time with an implacable Oliver Cromwell, rather than wavering coalitions of parliamentarians, dictating the disposition of his case.

So in less than a year Elizabeth Lilburne was again a prison wife. Again, as John churned out raging pamphlets against the "mock" Parliament and the Cromwellian "Junto," she "unweariedly laboured to the often hazard of her life" for his "reliefe and preservation." "Unweariedly"? For once, perhaps, on the choice of one word, Lilburne's veracity might be questioned: this time, as all her appeals, her "journeys, petitions and sollicitations to the Parliament & Members thereof" were utterly "fruitles,"[25] Elizabeth must have gotten very weary. Perhaps in the battering the Leveller movement took in the spring of 1649 she understood sooner than John that challenging the Cromwellians was ominously different than baiting uncertain cliques of Presbyterians. She could not have been surprised with the Commons' rejection in May of the women petitioners. Nor was it then unexpected that male petitioners were rejected too, informed that the Commons would not accept "any Petition in Lieu. Col. Lilburnes behalf" (even as they protested that it was "the Right of the People of England to Petition, and their Duty to receive Petitions").[26] To what levels of "tyrannie" would this iron-fisted government not descend when in May, *two months* after they were arrested, it had passed a new Treason Law upon which the Leveller leaders were indicted and would be tried? In any case, in his narration of the dreadful mid-months of 1649 John in effect retracted his description of the unwearied resourcefulness of Elizabeth's activities. At my "tryall," he wrote, "my faithfull and endeared wife" was "little less then perfectly distracted" with "insupportable griefe and care for my life," which she "judged to be no other then absolutely lost."[27]

In that summer of 1649 Elizabeth Lilburne had more to bear than premonition of John's conviction for treason. For once her domestic concerns surface, break through the political autobiography in pathetic detail. In July her oldest son fell ill of smallpox; the next child, also a boy, took the "violent sicknes," then the baby, a girl still at "its mothers brests," and finally Elizabeth too. The little boys died; mother and baby survived. To his sympathizers in the Commons Lilburne wrote from the Tower a letter expressing insupportable frustration, mingling grief, bitterness, vengefulness, self-pity. He wanted "a few dayes liberty for me to go see my distressed Wife," told his friends that as the older boy sickened Elizabeth had vainly called upon and begged officials to allow him a brief parole, that the child had died in torment, crying out "TO SEE HIS FATHER OR BEE CARRIED TO PRISON TO HIM," that now in her "exceeding illnesse" Elizabeth had an "exceeding desire" for her husband's presence. Upon the quiet intercession of the Commons acquaintances Lilburne was given "liberty upon the day time" to be with his wife and family.[28]

Still ill and drained Elizabeth Lilburne did not witness John's trial on 24-25 October 1649. She could not have missed hearing the delirious street celebrations of the aftermath of his unconditional acquittal by a jury of his peers of "all Treasons, or any of them that are laid to his charge," or seeing in the London sky the leaping victory flames of myriad all-night bonfires. The trial record, 135 pages of transcript, and the newssheets' resume of the triumph of Honest John and the "people" might have cheered or distracted her positively. It was, is, wonderful reading. There was Lilburne informing the court after grueling hours of parry and thrust that in English legal tradition the jury members were the real judges of *law* as well as fact, that the so-called judges were no more than "Norman intruders," and "in truth," only "cyphers" to pronounce the jury's verdict![29] There was

John demanding and being refused time to prepare his defense against a long indictment which he had not previously seen: the judges, "three Beagles," all "yelped out with full mouth, No, no, no, not an inch of time," to which Lilburne replied "in a mighty voice," then "I appeal . . . to the righteous God of heaven and earth against you"; and immediately upon his words a scaffold of seats collapsed, in "great noise and some confusion," because of "the people's tumbling," so "terrifying the unjust judges, that for almost the space of an houre, they did nothing but stare one upon another. . . ." Elizabeth Lilburne would have known the Leveller reporter who wrote that last description. The same journalist claimed that during the hour of confusion John was busy with his papers, so that when order was restored and the judges ordered him to answer the indictment "he did confute them with good Law, and honest Reason (telling them, that they had prated like Fools, and knew no more Law than so many Geese)"; the reporter added that the judges were afraid before the militant crowd in the galleries, who "scoff'd, mock'd and derided them, Men, Women, and Children."[30]

But in fact the sources are silent about Elizabeth Lilburne at the end of the trial. Only John was observed, in a meditative pose which the court recorder found odd, though perhaps Elizabeth understood it. When the foreman of the jury read out "in a loud voice" the verdict of "Not Guilty," immediately "the whole multitude of people in the Hall, for joy of the Prisoner's acquittal, gave such a loud and unanimous shout, as is believed was never heard in Guildhall, which lasted for about half an hour without intermission; which made the Judges for fear turn pale, and hang down their heads"; but Lilburne "stood silent at the bar, rather more sad in his countenance than he was before."[31]

In January 1652 Lilburne was exiled, upon promise of death if he returned, by the Cromwellian Parliament (sitting unperturbed by the years of Leveller agitation as a Star Chamber-like court). In the two-year interim, while he tried to put together a "small estate" for his family, he had been expanding, and publishing, his files on the machinations of the new economic masters of England. John Lilburne needed no certificate of matriculation from the Inns of Court to establish himself as counsel for the "middle sort" of men ground down by the lords of land and commerce: "my interest," he said, was "amongst the hobnails, clouted shooes, the private souldiers, the leather and woolen Aprons, and the laborious and industrious people . . . as formidable as numerous. . . ."[32] That he persisted as infuriating gadfly against the new rich and powerful was cause enough for the

Cromwellians to watch for the moment to smash him; more, the revolutionary government was bedeviled by royalists on the one side and irreconcilable republicans on the other, and stories circulated that Lilburne conspired with the royalists (rumors which he publicly denied).[33] The parliamentary decree of banishment, its pretext another "libelous" pamphlet, descended upon him as a lightning shot: in forced haste, leaving his appalled wife and friends to attempt the political pleas (and Elizabeth to struggle with family finances encumbered now with a £ 7,000 Commons-imposed penalty), he was made to gallop to Dover and sail to a year and a half of isolated frustration in Holland and Flanders.

Elizabeth came to him in his unsettled residences in Bruges or Calais when she could. Left alone, pregnant of course, and miscarrying under the strain, surviving children ill, struggling with the weight of indebtedness, she seems to have retreated miserably into domesticity. But she took his "private case," as officials downgraded it, all the way to Oliver Cromwell. It was the Lord General, ever-courteous and sympathetic to her, so warm in his understanding of her desperate need of her husband, who gave her hope that John might be allowed to return; his pass home depended, she was told, upon the election of a new Parliament which would soon be done, and upon his being patient and *quiet*.

In that distant exhilarating beginning of his crusade for 'middle' England Lilburne had told a jailor that God had made him and his wife wonderfully willing "to help to bear one anothers burdens." What he had been saying was that Elizabeth, suppressing her apprehensions, had born the burdens he created for them with almost sublime willingness. But now, in John's exile, the "heartes and soules" of husband and wife were separated, unraveled, at cross purposes. Elizabeth came to Flanders imploring John to wait for Cromwell's promised pass, to yield, that is, to any conditions of political capitulation. John, astounded by his "poor credulous wife," her believing the General's "good words" and thinking him "infinitely to be her friend," was pounding to "chastize" Cromwell, that "bloody and devouring Wolf," to be "an actor or instrument" in the "downfall" of his "beastely and grosse Tyrannie." "Quiet"? Why should he promise to be quiet, he "as free born as any man breathing in England"? "Patient"? When he had "not a penny" to buy bread but what he was forced to borrow, when he already was hundreds of pounds in debt and "beholden to the charity or benevolence of friends," a state "so ugly" that he loathed the thought of it "more then death"?[34] Indeed, he swore "totally and positively" that he would never see England again "so long as *Cromwels* most hateful and detestable beastly Tyrannie lasteth, unlesse it be in a way to pursue him," and give him "satisfaction face to face. . . ."[35]

Lilburne had been alone too, in a "little Garden-house" in Bruges, passing the days by reading (Plutarch's *Lives* and "Machivell's *Prince*," the latter "more worth then its weight in beaten Gold") and writing violent letters to old friends and the looming foe (and let us note that he sent everything he wrote, including the blast against his wife, to be printed in Flanders and published in the practiced network in England). He was certain, with some cause, that would-be assassins tailed him in streets or to taverns, their bloody work hired by spies from both sides, Stuart and Cromwellian. Now, as he felt it, pressing him "beyond any bounds of reason" to return "in her way" to England, to "enjoy my company" and "live after that to eat or drink," his wife had joined the lists against him.[36]

Elizabeth *was* devious and disobedient in her determination to have John safely and quietly in England. When she was in Flanders she promised to send him the precious books and papers which he wanted to consult in composing a next thundering appeal to the nation against the Cromwellian dictatorship. But when she returned to England she refused to do so, though he "tooke so much paines," said Lilburne, "in reading, studying and writeing large Epistles to her, to satisfie her with reason," that he almost made himself "Blinde."[37] Of course he wrote the appeal despite the obstacles, and had it printed in Amsterdam and Paris with arrangements that it be sent on to London; there Elizabeth "having heard of it . . . most irrationally hindered it," so that he had to "take some other course to get it printed, whether she will or no. . . ."[38]

Lilburne's anger with Elizabeth was so high that he, the socially progressive Leveller, could handle it only by reminding himself (and hundreds of thousands of readers) what she was: a woman, unreasoning and unreasonable, weak, whining, and childish. The words were his: the wife whose "true masculine Spirit" he had relied on so proudly was essentially like all the others of her sex, motivated by "childishnesse, weakenesse, or womannishnesse." He had to concentrate all the 'progressive' qualities he possessed to deal with her, to show "tendernes" to a creature who had been through "so many miseries" with him in a way that became "a man of conscience, gratitude and humanitie." He had to force himself, he told a correspondent, to "deale with her," so "oppressed with sicknes, and the death of my little Babe," as if she herself "had been a Suckinge Babe. . . ." Not a semblance of equality remained: that they might "part with as little disgust of Spirit as possible could be" he had tried to "stoop to her as low as possible," and give her "all the satisfaction" he could muster of his "unshaken affection."[39]

But, declared Lilburne, Elizabeth, whether in pleading dependence of "womannish passion and anger," was "a burthen" which he "longed" to be "quit of." He informed her that he authorized her petition to Parliament on her own behalf and that of her children for his "small estate," that he would absolutely surrender it into her hands. He wanted now to be alone (even though he would rather "a thousand times over part with [his] life") to carry on his "present businesse": the "more masculinely to compleat" his address to England as a "master workman" or a "poore instrument" in the "hands of the Almighty," to "chastize that hypocriticall and Alchemy Saint Oliver *Cromwell.*"[40]

Finally the deterioration of Elizabeth Lilburne was a matter between man and man, yet another criminal act put upon the slate of Oliver Cromwell. In his published letter to the Lord General, Lilburne accused him of pursuing "the total destruction" of his family. You have "murthered and been the death of" three of my children, Lilburne charged in direct address; "you have deprived me of the company of my wife," she "whom I formerly entirely loved as my own life," the "greatest delight formerly to me in the whole earth," and have "exposed her" to "so much folly and lowness of spirit in my eys, in some of her late childish actions, as hath in some measure, produced an alienation of affection in me to her."[41]

Reconciliation of sorts came because Lilburne decided to end the exile. Without pass or authorization of any kind he crossed to England, Elizabeth waiting with horses at Canterbury, to face instant arrest and the preparation of another trial for his life. During the spring and early summer of 1653 the situation was too perilous for further revelation of the split between husband and wife. With old London Levellers by the thousands reorganizing in John's defense, petitions from far-out towns and cities bombarding Westminster, royalists poised for a restored monarchy, a shaky government was doubly more dangerous than in 1649. Lilburne's second trial, which lasted with intermission from July through August, was an international event threatening to topple the Cromwellian *haute bourgeoisie*. Once again, after brilliant courtroom tactics, he was pronounced by a jury of stout freeborn Londoners to be innocent of any crime deserving death; once again the onlookers' response, in the packed galleries, outside in jammed streets, from the official military guard itself, was a joyous affirmation "heard a full mile off."[42]

But steeled in that experience the Cromwellians were determined to finish John Lilburne. He was continued prisoner in the Tower "for the peace of the Nation," and in March 1654 ordered incarcerated on the isle of Jersey, where the writ of habeas corpus could not reach him. And here at last, more than figuratively chained to this rock-prison, in censored isolation from family and friends and the (floundering) Leveller movement, Lilburne knew himself beaten as political agitator. In his final two years, however, he would "mannage" his public demise in his own way: very different from that Elizabeth longed and worked for.

Toward the end of his term in Jersey Castle (Cromwell allowed him to be transferred to Dover Castle prison after a year and a half) Lilburne subsided into quiet and meditation. When he emerged publicly, in one last pamphlet, he had become a Quaker, committed to that pacifist, gentle, iron-hard sect of "Friends" whose advance groups wandered the counties and towns of England, gathering converts (many former Baptists, as Lilburne had been) to their certainty of the "inner light" within each person, and refusing meekly and absolutely to recognize the authority of magisterial or clerical officialdom. Reborn in Jesus, Lilburne categorically renounced his "politick endeavouring," declared that his "old bustling ways" and all "fleshly striving" were "dead or crucified" within him. Henceforth he would be "guided and directed by the heavenly wisdom of Jesus" to "redeem" his "lost, and misspent by-past precious time. . . ."[43]

Lilburne's conversion and political withdrawal stunned Leveller veterans: it was because, he acknowledged, his "old and familiar" friends were "much troubled and offended" with him that he wrote his final pamphlet, *The Resurrection of John Lilburne*. But Elizabeth seems to have been amazed too, and uncomprehending. She was busy with the double endeavoring she knew so well (or triple: she bore a son in 1654, and was pregnant again after Lilburne's transfer to Dover). With maddening complications frustrating the effort, she was scrounging for remnants of property formerly promised or assigned to John, or bought and indebted by him; and against all the odds she was petitioning and soliciting the Council of State for John's liberty.

Husband and wife were separated hereafter by more than water and walls. They quarreled about Elizabeth's estate negotiations: John was angry that she would accept as gifts from old enemies—tainted charity, as he saw it—properties which should have been his by legal right.[44] She was simply dense about the emotional power of his quakerism, continued to write him little homilies about retaining "a sober patient spirit," which would be of "more force to recover" him than all his old "keen mettal."[45] Or worse, she employed his conversion and declared quietism opportunistically, carried as pleading proof to Cromwell John's pledge that he would never again "draw the temporal sword against him."[46]

Lilburne tried distantly—from the non-fleshly serenity of his new faith—to overcome the alienation. He wrote Elizabeth that he rejoiced at reconciliation of their "late out-fall," and underlined, literally, the reassurance that the "old affection" he had for her was "of late in much sincerity . . . renewed." He urged her to join him in the Quaker faith, to "go cheerfully & willingly along hand in hand" with him; he instructed that Quaker literature be sent to her, with which he hoped she would "sit down a little," and "sequestered" from friends "behold the great salvation of the Lord."[47]

But he probably dug the out-fall deeper. Let alone the things he said in their private meetings, the words he published should have cut Elizabeth to the heart. He wrote her that as his faith had weaned him from "worldly or fleshly" desires he had come to "a final denyal of father, kindred, friends, my sweet and dearly beloved (by me) babes, or thy own self, who viz. thy self, for many years by past . . . hath been to me the greatest and dearest of all earthly delights and joyes." He ordered her to give up her "strong endeavours" to bring him back to England to an "outward liberty" he no longer wanted or needed. Instead, she was to seek the "heavenly strength and ability" to bear and "go through" his permanent exile.[48] He informed the world that he had not become a Quaker to "avoid persecution," nor to propitiate his "great adversaries," nor to satisfy "the carnal will of my poor weak, afflicted wife."[49] The only mitigation in that terrible last phrase was that it apparently held no intentional malice: Honest John was only stating the fact as he perceived it.

Lilburne, at least, found peace and some comfort in his final year. He was sometimes allowed a parole from Dover Castle prison to spend time with his family at a little house he rented in Eltham in Kent, "hired" it, as Elizabeth later related, so that she might be near friends at her lying-in,[50] and he occasionally preached at local Quaker meetings.[51] It must be assumed that Elizabeth had joined him in the Society of Friends; disloyalty in this would have been unthinkable. Faithful to the end, she was with him when he died in August 1657. His Quaker community organized the funeral. The body was taken to London, "conveyed to the house, called The Mouth at Aldersgate . . . the usual meeting place of the people called Quakers," where a "medley" of mourners assembled. It was a plain and private affair, barely noticed in the (government-controlled) newssheets, though the reports related one moment of "controversy" when a man outside the house tried to cover the coffin with a velvet cloth; but the Quaker majority forbad it and with the unadorned box on their shoulders continued on to the burial at the "new Churchyard, adjoining Bedlam."[52]

Obviously it would be absurd to enlarge the rich marital experiences of Elizabeth and John Lilburne into some general statement about the like affairs of even their Leveller peers. On the other hand it is equally absurd to deny them as particular examples of relevant values and perceptions of middle England. A writer identifying himself as "your present Christian friend" was motivated to an open letter to Lilburne in 1653, after the publication of the latter's fury with Elizabeth's attempts to silence him in Bruges. "You also blame your wife," admonished the anonymous lecturer, who as "all sober and moderate men must judge" is "more prudent" than you, and "I heartily wish you had been ruled by her, both for your own quiet, and your friends comfort."[53] To that most readers would have said, "Amen!" Elizabeth Lilburne's counterweight to John's volatility comforted even Oliver Cromwell; she was a mainstream woman who never lost sight of who she was and what she was *supposed* to be doing. John then was the complete maverick? Manifestly he was nobody's Everyman. How much he expected of Elizabeth as he dragged them both aloft, ignoring her reluctance and fear. And how hard he was with her when she refused any longer even to try to fly. Lilburne's intense convictions and positions emerged from selective use of the fertile material available in his social environment. *He* located the rock-foundation for his crusade for individual rights in medieval common law; to the twentieth-century historian Brailsford he was a Chartist born before his time, plucking from the revolutionary rhetoric of the bourgeois of great property the *implications* of equal rights and political democracy.[54] Perhaps in his relations with Elizabeth we should see him with feet fixed in seventeenth-century bourgeois England, but looking both ways, pulling forward, drawing out the implications. He expected her to be his assistant, his faithful steward, as the preachers urged it, the extension of his working, committed self. And he expected her to be more than, better than, what he knew and accepted as typical, 'natural'; he demanded that she transcend what, as social reflex, he perceived as the "womanish" essence, the female weak, unreasoning, materialistic, "carnal."

The Widow Lilburne survived upon what one assumes was a joyless practicality. Her postscript consists of two petitions, the first to the Lord Protector, Oliver Cromwell, a few weeks after Lilburne's death. She told Cromwell the circumstances of John's dying on the last day of a ten-day parole from Dover Prison, "leaving me," she continued, "with 3 children and his estate under a fine of £7,000, so that I dare not administer to the little that is left, and therefore I cannot have the £15 arrears due of his allowance." She requested that the Protector "obtain the repeal of the Act which destroys the fatherless and the widow," and that John's allowance on which he had lived while he was in prison be continued. Cromwell ordered the payment of the arrears and the continuance of "the 40s. a week granted to her late husband."[55]

The second petition was dated January 1659 and addressed to a new Lord Protector, Cromwell dead the year before. To his son Richard, Elizabeth Lilburne recapitulated the whole of her financial dilemma. As follows:

> . . . Having long suffered heavy afflictions, I hoped that my husband's death would have been the last of my piercing sorrows. But I find the means for my children's maintenance perplexed by an unexampled Act of Parliament of 30 January 1651-52, fining my husband £7,000—£3,000 assigned to the State and £4,000 to 5 gentlemen,—viz. £2,000 to Sir Arthur Heselrigg, £500 each to Messrs. Winslow, Russell, Squibb, and Mullins,—when, his debts duly weighed, he was not worth £500. The only provocation for such a fine was his delivering a petition for Josiah Primate, for whom he was counsel, about a colliery which Sir Art. Haselrigg would have had sequestered. The Commissioners for Compounding gave the case against Primate, and he petitioned Parliament for relief. My husband did not draw the petition, but only delivered it. Primate was fined £7,000 and sent to the Fleet, but he soon got out, and gained his colliery, and this adds to my vexations.
>
> Your late father professed very great tenderness to me, and persuaded Sir Arthur to return the estate he had taken from me, and this he lately did (though the perverseness of tenants prevent my having much profit from it). His Highness also remitted the part allotted to the State, and willed the Commissioners to remit the other parts allotted them. He also granted me a pension, which by your great favour is continued, or I and mine might have perished. Sir Art. Haselrigg has relinquished £2,000, and Mr. Squibb £500, their shares of my husband's fine, but the other assignees will not follow their example. I was advised to address Parliament to repeal the Act, but omitted it in your father's lifetime. I beg you to discharge the £3,000 due to the State, and to recommend Parliament to repeal the Act, that after 17 years' sorrows, I may have a little rest and comfort among my fatherless children. . . .

Upon the advice of the Attorney-General and Solicitor-General the Lord Protector Richard Cromwell could discharge the £3,000 owed the State in Lilburne's old fine, but, Elizabeth was informed, unless the other "parties concerned will discharge the other parts of the fine, they can only be discharged by Parliament."[56]

NOTES

1. *The Humble Appeale and Petition of Mary Overton*, 24 March 1646, E.381(10).

2. Antonia Fraser, *Cromwell, The Lord Protector* (New York, 1973), pp. 311-12.

3. *Mercurius Militaris*, 17-24 April 1649, E.551(13), pp. 13-14.

4. Pauline Gregg, *Free-born John: A Biography of John Lilburne* (London, 1961), p. 163.

5. J. Lilburne, *Englands Weeping Spectacle*, pp. 2-4.

6. See Gregg, *Free-born John*, pp. 6, 360, for the genealogy provided by a descendant, Ian R. Lilburne.

7. Lilburne, *Legal Liberties*, p. 22.

8. Lilburne, *Lt. Colonel John Lilburne Revived*, March 1653, "Letter to a friend in Scotland," E.689(32), p. 1.

9. Lilburne, *Anatomy of the Lords Tyranny*, 1646, E.362(6), p. 17.

10. Lilburne, *Englands Weeping Spectacle*, p. A2.

11. Clarendon, *History*, 5: 305-6.

12. Lilburne, *Englands Weeping Spectacle*, p. 5.

13. Lilburne, *Legal Liberties*, p. 23.

14. Ibid., 24.

15. Lilburne, *Englands Weeping Spectacle*, p. 5.

16. *Mercurius Elencticus*, 29 October-5 November 1647, E412(30).

17. Lilburne, *Legal Liberties*, p. 26.

18. Lilburne, *Jonahs Cry out of the Whales belly*, 26 July 1647, E.400(5), p. 4.

19. Lilburne, *Legal Liberties*, p. 26.

20. Lilburne, *Anatomy of the Lords Tyranny*, pp. 16-17.

21. Lilburne, *The Resolved Mans Resolution*, April 1647, E.387(4), pp. 2-12.

22. Lilburne, *A Whip for the Present House of Lords*, 27 February 1647-48, E.431(1), p. 26.

23. Lilburne, *Legal Liberties*, pp. 42-60.

24. Ibid., p. 65.

25. *L. Colonel John Lilburne His Apologetical Narration*, April 1652, E.659(30), p. 14.

26. See *The Humble Petition of the Well-affected in and about the City of London, Westminster, and parts adjacent; Presenters and Approvers of the late Petition of the 11 of Sept.*, October 1649, E.579(9).

27. Lilburne, *Apologetical Narration*, p. 14.

28. *A Preparative to An Hue And Cry After Sir Arthur Haslerig*, 13 Sept. 1649, E.573(16), pp. 38-39.

29. *Cobbett's Complete Collection of State Trials*, 4: 1379-80.

30. *Truths Victory over Tyrants, Being the Tyrall of that Worthy Assertor of his Countreys Freedoms, Lueftenant Colonal John Lilburne*, "Printed in the fall of Tyranny, 1649," E.579(12), pp. 6-7.

31. *State Trials*, 4: 1405.

32. Lilburne, *The Upright Mans Vindication*, August 1653, E.708(22), p. 15.

33. Lilburne, *A Defensive Declaration*, June 1653, E.702(2), p. 19. See Pauline Gregg, *Free-born John*, pp. 315-19.

34. Lilburne, *Upright Mans Vindication*, pp. 5-6, 14, 18; *L. Colonel Lilburne Revived*, March 1653, E.689(32), pp. 2-3.

35. Ibid., p. 3.

36. Lilburne, *Upright Mans Vindication*, p. 5.

37. *L. Col. Lilburne Revived*, p. 3.

38. Lilburne, *Upright Mans Vindication*, p. 26.

39. *L. Col. Lilburne Revived*, pp. 3, 1, 22.

40. Ibid., pp. 2-3.

41. Lilburne, *Upright Mans Vindication*, pp. 25-26.

42. Gregg, *Free-born John*, p. 332.

43. Lilburne, *The Resurrection of John Lilburne*, 16 May 1656, E.880(2), pp. 9, 14, 7.

44. See Gregg, *Free-born John*, p. 340; also *State Papers Domestic*, 1658-59, pp. 260-61.

45. Lilburne, *Resurrection*, p. 5.

46. Ibid., p. 9; *SPD*, 1655, pp. 263-64.

47. Lilburne, *Resurrection*, p. 5.

48. Ibid., pp. 4-5.

49. Ibid., pp. 4-5, 14.

50. *SPD*, 1657, 2: 148.

51. Gregg, *Free-born John*, p. 346; Anthony Wood, *Athenae Oxonienses*, 3: 357.

52. *Mercurius Politicus*, 3 Sept. 1657, E.505(18); A. Wood, *Athenae Oxonienses*, 3: 357-58.

53. *A Letter to Leiutenant Collonel John Lilburne now Prisoner in the Tower* (London, 1653), E.712(14).

54. Brailsford, *Levellers*, p. 217.

55. *SPD*, 1657, 2: 148.

56. *SPD*, 1658-59, pp. 260-61.

5

Sectarians, Fearless for the Lord

In the political earthquakes of the 1640s how many women had shifted it well enough to venture into centers of upheaval? Tens of thousands signed parliamentary or Leveller petitions; inestimable numbers of others made their mark in the "pillow talk" of marriage or by being remarkably useful in public defense and solicitation; a few momentarily came crashing through the loophole to the "affaires of State" in disguises not unworthy of a Middleton-Dekker heroine. But an enlargement of a female 'role' in politics was scarcely perceptible.

The point need not be labored. How could women have done more than they did when male democrats—and Digger communists—had been brutally shut outside the political fortress of the rich and the great? In any case, women (and after the "demoralisation and despair"[1] of the Leveller defeat in 1649 the male radicals too) had the alternative in religious sectarianism to express their political passions. Women made their political statements in the byways open to them, in denying the right of the state church to dictate to their consciences, in acting as equals in the sects, in calling down divine judgment upon tyrannical kings, priests—and husbands.

And here to the historian's eye were the numbers, in the public ventures of women in civil war and commonwealth religious sects. As against the names of less than a handful of political women we have a long list of sectarian writers and activists. Contemporaries claimed that in many Independent congregations, particularly Baptist and Quaker, women members outnumbered the men, and modern historians have tested and corroborated the assertion: after one weighs the evidence it "remains true," wrote Keith Thomas in his important article, "that in the sects women played a disproportionate role," and that they received thereby "correspondingly greater opportunities."[2] Although forbidden to preach in most congregations women could "prophesy" (which "often came to much the same thing," Thomas observed); the female prophets now have their historian, who has found over three hundred of them, as she explores the "visionary writings by women," and "accounts of women prophecying in public."[3]

No barriers had ever separated women from religion. 'My mother/wife was a godly home-bound woman,' went the familiar male eulogy; she "very seldom was seen abroad, except at church."[4] Church was a stimulating place. In the reformed Church of England several generations of women had been taught their spiritual equality with men; through the 1630s Puritan ministers told them of their equal responsibility to resist 'papist' corruptions in the Anglican service; in the 1640s "seditious" Independent preachers enticed them by droves into separatism, welcomed them in sectarian 'congregations of saints'; and in the progressive democratization of the sects they were expected to seek and to follow their own "inner light" to the discovery and knowledge of God's truth.

Many women, then, seized upon this permissible outlet in the 1640s and 1650s, in a marvelous variety from the occasionally sane Lady Eleanor Davies to the most gullible illiterates who testified to the semidivinity of a male companion.[5] But the focus of this bright picture requires refinement. Relevant question: if a freed John Lilburne had taken the itinerant path of Quaker preacher and gatherer George Fox would Elizabeth have marched by his side, dodging the cudgels and stones of mobs and submitting to the judicial savagery and filthy jails of small-town magistrates? It is just as well that she did not face that prospect (that we know of). Elizabeth Lilburne is conceivable in the mostly background role of Fox's supporter and late-life wife, the undeniable gentlewoman and landed heiress, Margaret Fell. But she was no kin to Elizabeth Hooton, preacher, disturber of the "priests" of parish churches, and regular resident in the common prisons of the northern counties.

Religious activities as well as mysticism had traditionally been an outlet for the most energetic, committed, forceful, articulate, and imaginative women. But in the tightly defined bourgeois domestic role descending how did such qualities exist other than in identification of the unseemly, the rebelliously misfit? And further, the women who persisted in nourishing such quirks in the 1650s were caught in association with Seekers, Ranters, and (early) Quakers, even with the stubbornly revolutionary Fifth Monarchists, all beyond any shade of respectability. Keith Thomas finished his article with the balancing conclusions that despite all, "the sectarian insistence upon women's spiritual equality" does not "seem to have been of very great importance in the later history of female emancipation in general." It is "probable," he said, "that the more exotic and extravagant of these female prophets and preachers only served to do harm to their own cause, since for most people they illuminated by contrast the virtues of the Marthas who stayed at home."[6]

Most English women did not become sectarian spectacles, would not have considered speaking out in church or Independent gathering; their views were both shaped by and reflected in the old, well-known sources of thunderous male disapproval of any such behavior. Behind the principled flamboyance of the prophetesses was the murmuring and clucking of the stay-at-home Marthas, the harried Elizabeth Lilburnes, and the legion of Lucy Hutchinsons. Mrs. Hutchinson, we remember, was intellectually convinced of the error of the tradition of infant baptism, but instead of joining the Nottingham Baptist group of the 'middling' sort of folk she handled her anabaptist conviction privately and remained within the parish church; it was a matter of propriety, of class ambition, reputation, and self-image.

In reading the records of female religious enthusiasm, then, one needs double vision: one eye on the intrepid women themselves; the other watching, with more difficulty, the variegated chorus of naysayers all about.

One of the earliest of the seventeenth-century women preachers and writers was Katherine Chidley, a person of dignity and educated intelligence, of both blazing commitment and unassailable sobriety. Katherine Chidley was of sterner stuff, even, than the colonial Pilgrims. Like her social superior Lucy Hutchinson she was impelled to be a witness to the godly society emerging; but while Mrs. Hutchinson remained in her private closet, Mrs. Chidley went public. She might have gone, probably considered going, to Holland with the separatist Brownists, or with the associated group determined to raise the new Jerusalem in America. She did not. With her "faithfull yoake-fellow" she stayed in England, "persecuted" by the "Hyrarchy" of Bishops-Priests," driven from one "place of abode" to another, but for more than two decades organizing and preaching to separatist congregations so that, she said, "people rightly informed will not have their necks captivated, under *Jewish yoakes of tithes paying*, to maintaine a *popish-ordained Clergie*."[7] She raised a worthy son, the Samuel who traveled with her, and who emerged in secular rebellion with the Levellers. (A strong voice for civil rights beyond Independency, Samuel Chidley spoke for "the poor and the women," for widows "required by the Law, to deliver up all to the Heir," and "forced to borrow & pawn, yea and sometimes to begg their bread.")[8]

Of the host of enemies Mrs. Chidley made in her twenty-odd-year ministry none was more persistently implacable than the Reverend Thomas Edwards. Edwards was a Presbyterian divine (with his own history of being persecuted, under the Laudian discipline of the 1620s and 1630s) who so hated the Independents that his published fanaticism caused contemporaries, ordinarily hardened to verbal violence, to "stand and wonder."[9] His most sensational work, which sold out three rapid editions in 1645-46, was *Gangraena*, subtitled "a Catalogue and Discovery of many of the Errours, Heresies, Blasphemies and pernicious Practices of the Sectaries of this Time." The book—or books, for Edwards kept adding things—was a nonstop, furious encyclopedia of over two hundred "heresies" of sixteen sectarian groups (the sixteenth he identified as "Scepticks and Questionists, who question every thing in matters of Religion"), embellished with anecdotal, purportedly eyewitness evidence on the activities and behavior of the sectarians. The heretical error which most incensed Mr. Edwards, however, was the sectarians' denial of the ministers of the Church of England as the supremely chosen Elect of God, their refusal to admit "the calling and making of Ministers of the Word and Sacraments" as "*jure Divino*." For it was this central defiance which was opening the abyss of social revolution: any sort could be ministers, merchants, booksellers, tailors "and such like"; "mechanicks taking upon them to preach and baptize, as Smiths, Taylors, Shoomakers, Pedlars, Weavers . . . also some women in our times, who keepe constant Lectures, preaching weekly to many men and women."[10]

Katherine Chidley was so prominent on Thomas Edwards's list of horrible sectarians that he referred to her without introductory pause in his text. "Katherine Chidley about August last," began one entry, "came to Stepney (where she hath drawn away some persons to Brownism) and was with Mr. Greenhill [that is, she debated with Greenhill, the local Anglican minister], where she with a great deal of violence and bitterness spake against all Ministers and all people that meet in our Churches, and in places where any Idolatrous services have been performed . . . she was so talkative and clamorous, wearying [Greenhill] with her words, that he was glad to go away, and so left her."[11]

The Reverend Edwards collected and printed stories, unverified and unverifiable, from clerical correspondents about the country dramatizing the consequences of permitting women to speak out on religious matters. In some of the tales women appeared as mere simpleminded dupes; in others they were sexually promiscuous and morally evil. The one led to the other, of course: "When Women Preach, and

Coblers Pray / The fiends in Hell, make Holiday."[12] The stories could not have been wholly fabricated, only embellished, since Edwards had no scruples (nor fears of libel) in naming his victims, from Katherine Chidley to William Walwyn. In any case, noting the verisimilitude, we can thank him for a richly detailed narrative about a preaching lace-woman and her on-the-job trainee, the major's wife.

The setting was London, in the mid-1640s: there were "women who for some time together, have preached weekly on every Tuesday about four of the clock, unto whose preachings many have resorted." The described session was led by two of them, one a "Lace-woman, that sells Lace in Cheapside, & dwells in Bel-Alley in Colemanstreet," and the other "a Majors wife living in the Old Baily." It was held in a chamber at the Bell-Alley address, before "a great company both men and women."

A little flurry of indecision delayed the start of the meeting. As the two women took their places at a table at the front of the room the lace-woman, obviously the more experienced, wanted the major's wife to begin. That "Gentlewoman"—in "her hoods, necklace of Pearle, watch by her side, and other apparrell sutable"—shyly demurred, instead "falling into a commendation of the gifts of the Lace-woman." Perhaps as yet unprepared the latter "turned herself to the company . . . excusing herself that she was somewhat indisposed in body, and unfit for this work, and said if any one there had a word of exhortation let them speake; but all the company keeping silent, none speaking . . . the Lace-woman began."

She made a little speech about the days coming to pass that God had poured out "his Spirit upon the handmaidens, and they should prophesy," and then she prayed "for almost halfe hour," and "after her Prayer took that Text, *If ye love me, keep my Commandments.*" For "the space of some three quarters of houre" she "laboured to Analyze the Chapter as well as she could. . . ." When she was done she again asked the company if any wanted to speak, or make objections, "but all held their peace."

> "Then the Gentlewoman that sate at the side of the Table began to speake, making some Apologie that she was not so fit at this time in regard of some bodily indisposition, and she told the company shee would speake upon that matter her Sister had handled, and would proceed to the Use of Examination, whether we love Christ or no; . . . and as she was preaching, one in the company cryed, *Speake out*, whereupon she lifted up her voice; but some spake the second time, *Speake out*, so that upon this the Gentlewoman was disturbed and confounded in her discourse, and went off from that of love to speake upon 1 *John* 4. *of trying*

the Spirits, but shee could make nothing of it, speaking non-sense all
along; whereupon some of the company spake againe, and the Gentlewoman went on speaking, jumbling together some things against those
who despised the ordinances of God, and the Ministry of the Word; and
upon that some present spake yet once more, so that shee was so amazed
and confounded, that she knew not what she said, and was forced to
give over and sit down; The Lace-woman who preached first, seeing all
this, lookt upon those who had interrupted her Sister with an angry bold
countenance, setting her face against them, and she fell upon concluding
all with prayer, and in her prayer she prayed to God about them who
despised his Ambassadors and Ministers that he had sent into the world
to reconcile the world; where-upon some fell a speaking in her prayer;
Ambassadors, Ministers, you Ambassadors! with words to that purpose;
and upon those words she prayed expresly that God would send some
visible judgement from heaven upon them; and upon those words some
of the company spake aloud, praying God to stop her mouth, and so shee
was forced to give over: In briefe, there was such laughing, confusion,
and disorder at the meeting, that . . . never saw the like; . . . the confusion, horror, and disorder . . . was unexpressible . . . ."[13]

The last mention of the Tuesday-Thursday meetings reported that
they were moved from the Bell-Alley house to Old Bailey because the
"multitude" became too large. Whatever their initial gifts as ministers
of the Word the "Sisters" continued in experience and fortitude.[14]

Gripped by religious faith and apocalyptic convictions women
emerged from, turned their backs upon, lives of respectable obscurity,
and stubbornly exposed themselves to ridicule and abuse. There was
Elizabeth Avery: born-again sectarian, Fifth Monarchist, prophesying
writer; behind her was a Puritan life so exemplary that she had been
in New England, where her brother, Thomas Parker, was "Pastor of
the Church of Newbury," and colleague of "Mr. Cotton, Wilson, and
Noyes."[15] In desolation after the successive deaths of three children,
and in a torment of perceiving "Gods wrath in everything against
[her]" Elizabeth Avery became a seeker in the religious maelstrom
of the late 1640s. She was in Dublin in 1650-51, a convert to the
mixed congregation of anabaptists and millenarians led by John Rogers. It was Rogers who wrote that he saw "no warrant for" traditions
of male "Soveraignty," nor the robbing "Sisters" of "their just rights
and priviledges" as equal members of godly congregations (and split
the congregation on the issue),[16] and who recorded and published the
individual members' testimonies of religious awakening, giving equal
time to sisters and brothers.[17]

Elizabeth Avery was moved to write a book of ecstatic vision of the
second coming of Christ and the Day of Judgment, with heaven "pass-

ing away with a great noise, and the elements . . . melting with fervent heat, and the earth and the works thereof . . . burning up, . . . all accomplished in the Saints . . . to appear with him in Glory . . . ten thousand of his Saints, to execute judgement. . . ."[18] Her closest reader may have been her brother, the New England minister. Thomas Parker was appalled by his sister's "Heretical opinions," by her blasphemous rejection of "Ordinances," the "Word" and the "Sacraments," by her disavowal of her "own Husband." You have written a book, he said in outraged conviction, which is "beyond the custom of your Sex," is "above your gifts and Sex," and "doth rankly smell." You say, Reverend Parker quoted, "that Christ hath no humane body," that "his second coming is in his Saints, whereby they . . . are as truly Christ as Christ . . . yea, their very being is God," and that if "Saints are Christ you are without sin"? "I will spit at this," he concluded, "and say no more." Except that he added, "you are a weak woman, and ignorant of the wiles of Satan"; at bottom was the "Pride of Women, or Spiritual Pride," through which "dear Sister" had shamed the "Reason" that she herself lacked, had given over "at the first push" her "Parents, Friends, Church, Christ, God, and life Eternal."[19] Elizabeth Avery was if not serene untouched by this brotherly appeal. "I fear not the prison," she wrote," I fear not reproach; for I can wear it as my Crown: I fear not want, in that I do enjoy all in God: and though I may be counted mad to the world, I shall speak the words of sobernesse: and if I am mad, as the Apostle saith, it is to God; and if I am in my right mind, it is to the benefit of others."[20]

Women were prophesying, that is, preaching as the Spirit moved within them, before the biblical license was publicly bestowed upon them by male sectarians. But the new stress, as it were the rediscovery, of the words of the Book of Joel, "and your Sons and your Daughters shall prophesie . . . upon the Handmaids . . . will I poure out my spirit," illuminated alike the printed pamphlets of female millenarians[21] and the public appearances of female mystics. Of the latter none was more strange than the coming of Elizabeth Poole with a "divine revelation" to the army's self-appointed Council of State in December/January of 1648-49.

Elizabeth Poole twice brought the details of her "Vision" to the Council, to the army grandees wrestling—politically, intellectually, emotionally, spiritually—with the central revolutionary dilemma of restructuring the state, and disposing of a king whom they deemed criminal. Did Elizabeth Poole know what was going on behind the somber faces of her hosts on those winter days, the drive and determination, the uncertainty of the will of a majority of the country (and

thus of God's), the apprehension of the Levellers with their alternative constitutional Agreement of the People, the fear, the need, the
inevitable opportunism? In her vision, she told the Council, she had
seen a woman and a man: the woman was "crooked, sick, weak and
imperfect in body," unmistakably representing, to Mistress Poole,
"the weak state of the Kingdom"; but the man was "a member of
the Army," and he swore his "diligence" for the "cure of this woman,"
pledged to "be a sacrifice for her." Enlarging grandly upon this clear
directive for army leadership, Elizabeth Poole added, "I have considered the agreement of the people that is before you, and I am very
jealous that you should betray your trust in it. . . . the Kingly power
is fallen into your hands [and] in giving it up to the people . . . you
will prove your selves more treacherous then they that went before
you. . . ."[22] By now transfixed, listening with "great gravity," some
of the "chief officers" (Commissary General Henry Ireton, Major-
General Thomas Harrison, and Colonel Nathaniel Rich)[23] put the key
questions. We are not, then, to "deliver up the trust," they asked, "to
Parliament or people?" And if we do not how "shall we be free from
aspersions of the people, who will be ready to judge that we improve
this interest for our own ends?" Elizabeth Poole replied, "Set your
selves, as before the Lord, to discharge the trust committed to you
. . . [not] that you should bee exalted above your bretheren, but that
you might stand in faithfulnesse to discharge your duty"; of the Parliament and people, "take them with you as younger bretheren who
may be helpfull to you . . . ," but "Betray not you your trust."[24]

In this moment of official approbation Mistress Poole was heard
with the closest attention and perfect credulity: Colonel Rich observed
that by her vision God had been "manifested heere by an unexpected
Providence"; and Ireton thought that there was in her words "nothing
. . . butt those [things] that are the fruites of the spiritt of God. . . ."[25]
Providence indeed: the Lord's intent descending through the "gentlewoman" Poole to His chosen Saints, who were intrusted out of the
several millions of their countrymen with "the cure of England." But
then a revealing thing happened, revealing, that is, that Elizabeth
Poole was on a solitary and, given her audience, entirely apolitical
mission. Her parting message to the Council, and to be sure, she
thought it might not find "acceptance" among its officers, was about
the "tyrant" king. Charles was king by "divine pleasure," she an-
nounced, and as a husband to the nation: and "you never heard that
a wife might put away her husband, as he is the head of her body,
but for the Lords sake suffereth his terror to her flesh, though she be
free in the spirit to the Lord"; accordingly "you may hold the hands

of your husband that he peirce not your bowels with a knife or sword to take your life," but "neither may you take his. . . ."[26]

The credulity was fading fast among Council members, where at the front of every mind were exactly these crucial issues. Elizabeth Poole was asked if she spoke "against the bringing of [Charles] to triall, or against their taking of his life." She answered "Bring him to his triall, that he may be convicted in his conscience, but touch not his person."[27]

Poor Elizabeth Poole. She had been a member of a Baptist congregation "in fellowship with Mr. Kiffin"—William Kiffin, so much Cromwell's supporter that he had rushed into print to smear and deny another former member and old friend, John Lilburne (who rejoined that Kiffin and his ilk were "fauning daubing knaves").[28] Kiffin and his saintly associates disavowed both Elizabeth Poole and her vision, effectively worked, as her lone defender put it, "to weaken the Message by scandalising and reproaching the Messenger, charging her with some follies committed many years ago, and long since repented of, and with other things she knew not," like Jesus accused of "being a glutton, a wine bibbar, a friend of Publicans and Harlots. . . ."[29] Elizabeth Poole fought back against the "pursuit by them that are called Saints" in a double reprint of her vision, with pointed addenda about the grandees doing "wickedly" in killing the King, and about the "vengeance" that God prepared for their "evill party."[30] But she only added to her punishment.

Her one Baptist friend, female, identified as "T.P.," told the story of what happened when an insignificant woman crossed the saints in 1649 by contradicting politics with religion. "T.P." said that Elizabeth Poole had been "cast out" of the congregation for proposing that the execution of the king was a measure of "selfe-love," and that it would be a "great stop and let to the Independent design." The pretense that she had been guilty of "scandalous evils" in the "long time past" was "killing all the day long." For "you cannot be ignorant," T.P. charged, "that she hath no livelihood amongst men, but what she earns by her hands: and your defaming her in this manner cannot in an ordinary way but deprive her of that and so at last bring her blood upon you: if you say, you acquaint none but the Saints with it, that is evident to the contrary, for your open publishing it in the Councell of War, caused the world to take notice of it. . . ." So deeply distressed about Elizabeth Poole's treatment in presenting what the congregation judged "a delusion for a vision of God," Mrs. T.P. pleaded that "mercy" was "required of toward our Sister. . . ."[31] In the blackout of further information about Elizabeth Poole we do not know whether she received the forgiveness of the saints, or whether she remained an outcast, deprived of livelihood and a caution to those females who might want to be both prophetesses *and* respectable bourgeoises.

To go on, or return, to the Quakers, where strong women abounded: in the 1650s and 1660s Quaker women defined the qualities of exalted piety, strength, singleness of purpose, and social heedlessness. The early Society of Friends was the most egalitarian of the sects; the women stood up with the men in their meetings as in Commonwealth and Restoration prisons. "Let all your mouths be stopt forever," George Fox cried, "that despise the spirit of prophesie in the daughters. . . . Christ be in the same in the male, & in the female which cometh from Christ. . . ."[32]

Certainly it was possible to be a visible female Friend *and* respectable. From the top of the bourgeois social scale came Margaret Fell, mistress of Swarthmoor Hall in Furness, near Lancaster. Born Margaret Askew, of an old Lancastershire landed family, she brought to her first marriage a large portion and an estate of her own. Her husband was Thomas Fell, a justice of peace in Lancashire during the civil wars and an Independent member of the Long Parliament, and a circuit judge and chancellor under the Commonwealth. With her "tender and loving" husband Margaret Fell supervised a large household, bore eight children, and quietly "sought after God." Swarthmoor Hall was open to "serious godly men," the touring lecturers of the Independent ministry; Mistress Fell had been "inquiring and seeking about twenty years" when George Fox first visited in 1652, held meetings in the Hall and spoke at the local parish church. Listening to Fox speak of the "inner light" in each person, Margaret Fell wrote, "opened me so, that it cut me to the heart; and then I saw clearly that we were all wrong." So "I sat down in my pew," she said, "and cried bitterly; and I cried in my spirit to the Lord, 'We are all theives; we are all theives; we have taken the Scripture in words, and know nothing of them in ourselves.' "[33]

The Fells' Swarthmoor Hall became a sanctuary for itinerant Friends and the north-county refuge of George Fox and his companions. Judge Fell, though "favourable to their views," did not join the Friends, sometimes complained of his house and stables bulging with guests and their horses. His wife told him that "charity doth not impoverish," and was pleased to note that their hay crops were usually large enough for the needs of both family and guests, with surplus to sell.[34]

Such private support was Margaret Fell's Quaker commitment until the Judge died in 1658. Clearly this estimable lady had considered first the duties of her marriage. Her public debut (and the assumption of the role which a future generation would remember as the "Mother of Quakerism") was forced by fearful challenges. In the political shock waves of the restoration of Charles II the Quakers were caught in sweeping persecution, associated in the mind of the court with the real antimonarchical rebels, the Fifth Monarchists. Quakers, of course, would take no oaths, a position the state found subversive enough: Quaker meetings were invaded, members beaten and jailed; and in 1663 Margaret Fell too was convicted for refusing to swear the oath of allegiance to the monarchy, with a sentence of Praemunire, the forfeit to the king of all her property, real and personal, and life imprisonment. By 1668 she was released, and the sentence lifted; she spent the rest of her life working in behalf of George Fox and other Friends still intermittently jailed, and as Mrs. Fox (from 1669) being a solid center of organizational activities of the rapidly expanding Quaker societies.[35]

Margaret Fell-Fox testified that she was never "terrified" in her travails. Her Quaker faith sustained her, obviously, but also an unshakable social assurance. Her appeals and protests were addressed not to minor magistrates but to the "Great": her call was "to plead the cause of the persecuted and oppressed before the rulers of the land"; thus she "fearlessly approached the monarchs, and those in power," spoke "often with the King" and "writ many Letters and Papers" to Charles, to the Duke of York, the Duke of Gloucester, to the Queen Mother, even the queens of Orange and Bohemia. "I was mov'd of the Lord," she said, "to lay the Truth before them, and did give them many Books and Papers, and did lay our Principles and Doctrine before them, and desired that they would let us have Discourse with their Priests, Preachers and Teachers. . . ."[36]

The other many thousands of activist Quaker women did not speak to kings and queens and dukes. Informed in their meetings of equality of all in Christ they might have imagined doing so, but the opportunity would not readily have arisen. They did a lot of speaking out, however, which made them notorious to conforming folk, and compelled them to communicate further with the judges of county courts. Here, an excerpt from one of the many, is a Quaker "list of imprisoned" in 1653:

Yorkshire: Elizabeth Hooton, committed for "disturbing a Priest";

                           Mary Fisher, committed for "disturbing a Priest";

                           Jane Holmes, as a "wanderer".

Elizabeth Hooton	for speaking to the
Mary Fisher	Judge, each fined
Jane Holmes	£200.

Westmoreland: Margaret Gilpin, committed, for speaking in the Steeple-house;

Mary Collison, committed, for saying (while the Priest was speaking) "Tremble before the Lord";

Margaret Smith, committed, for speaking to the Priest;

Dorothy Waugh, committed, for speaking to the Priest;

Agnes Wilkinson, committed, for speaking to the Mayor;

Mary Dodding, committed, for speaking to the Priest.

In Kendal ten women and one man went before the justice of peace, to protest his persecution of their friends and to warn him "of the evil to come." The J.P. ordered them to jail. Why? "They speak out in public assemblies"; they will not "put off their hats"; they will not find "sureties," that is, admit their guilt.[37] In Bristol, a city with a large Quaker group and thus much tension with the conforming, one Elizabeth Marshall "being moved of the Lord" made a habit of interrupting local ministers in mid-sermon: the "multitude" of parishioners would drag her outside, "crushing her Arms, pinching, and thrusting," and there "violently" assault her "with staves and cudgels"; but it was she who was taken by the constable to the mayor, accused of causing "tumults in the streets" and hustled away to Newgate prison "without a *Mittimus.*"[38] Troublemakers and brawlers they were to the ordinary onlooker. The estimate in the 1660s was that "above 8,000" Quaker women and men were in prisons.[39]

Christopher Hill and others[40] have abundantly documented the common roots in apocalyptic popular radicalism of Quakers and Ranters. Wrote Hill, "the whole early Quaker movement was far closer to the Ranters in spirit than its leaders liked to recall." The Quaker preacher, as Friends themselves admitted, was considered "a sower of sedition, or a subverter of the laws, a turner of the world upside down, a pestilent fellow"; even George Fox had contributed warnings that the "great men and rich men" would "Weep and howl" for their "misery" coming on "the day of the Lord."[41] To outside opinion both

Quakers and Ranters would have "no Christ but within; no Scripture to be a rule; no ordinances, no law but their lusts, no heaven nor glory but here, no sin but what men fancied to be so, no condemnation for sin but in the consciences of ignorant ones."[42]

In the 'world of the Ranters' some—males—explicitly asserted the right, without sin, of desertion of wives and sexual freedom. It was "perfectly simple," Hill thinks, "for any couple to team up together and wander round the country, preaching and presumably depending on the hospitality of their co-religionists or those whom they could convince."[43] The certainty of such irregular coupling, of course, had been at the tip of the pen of hostile reviewers since the preaching days of the impeccably monogamous Katherine Chidley. The Reverend Thomas Edwards fixed his points in appendices to his 'eyewitness' stories of female ministers. Thus it was "given out" about a preacher named Mrs. Attaway that she met "a Prophet here in London, who hath revealed to her and others that they must go to Jerusalem, and repair Jerusalem, and to that end Mrs. Attaway hath gotten money of some persons . . . [and] run away with another womans husband . . . who used to hear her preach"; Mrs. Attaway "left her children behind . . . at six and seven," and the man too left children and a wife "distracted" and "great with child. . . ."[44]

Quaker leaders, Christopher Hill observed, would spend "many weary hours differentiating themselves from Ranters and ex-Ranters," and, he added, "Anabaptists, Antinomians, Socinians, Familists, Libertines, etc.," for in the early 1650s the Quakers inherited them all.[45] Among them was a yeasty mass of stories of female saints fit to scandalize, or titillate, the Reverend Edwardses. Sarah Wight or Anna Trapnel, in the trances of month-long fasts (feeding only "on Jesus Christ"), were absorbable because of their "great interest," a sort of freak appeal, to crowds of ministers, doctors, and "great ladies" who came to marvel at their bedsides.[46] But what to do with women like the "Anabaptistical" Anne Wells, who had "revelations," and because of them took up with two male faith-healers, married one and slept with both?[47] Or with Jane Holmes, probably the same "wanderer" on the arrest list of Quaker women of 1653 (and diagnosed by a modern Quaker writer as "exceptionally unbalanced mentally")? Jane Holmes was a member of the Friends' society in Malton in Yorkshire where she was "ducked as a scold" for "crying her message" through the streets. In her hearing for "Abusing ministers," she was cited as "an immoral person" who enticed local wives to Quaker meetings from which they "did not come home any night until 12 o'clock, and some nights not at all"; Jane Holmes, it was charged, was an "instrument" for the desertion of wives. Clearly her behavior was a "cause of criticism" of Quakers "in Malton and the district."[48]

If the famous story, the tragic and still almost unbearable story of James Nayler was "a parting of the ways for the Quaker movement" and, Hill continued, "for the English Revolution as a whole,"[49] it was a watershed too for forward women saints. Interwoven with the details of Nayler's "symbolic entry" into Bristol in 1656 was a female presence no contemporary account passed over or underplayed. Nayler, "deluded and deluding Quaker and Imposter," rode into the city, a woman leading his horse/donkey and others "lovingly" marching on each side, "deep in the muddy way then to the knees," strewing "their garments" before him and singing "a buzzing mel-ODIUS noyse. . . ."[50] "I did ride into a Town," Nayler testified at his examination, "and by the Spirit a woman was commanded to hold my horses bridle; and some there were that cast down clothes, and sang praises to the Lord, such songs as the Lord put into their hearts; and its like it might be the Song of Holy, holy, holy, &c."[51] Bristol magistrates straightaway arrested the party, to begin the desanctification of James Nayler. They had this time the man who, rather than George Fox, was the leader of residual Leveller radicalism: for key example, John Lilburne, in frustrated torment on the Isle of Jersey, found his converted solace in Nayler's tracts (and had them sent to his wife Elizabeth for her enlightenment).[52] As Nayler was sentenced to savage punishment—beatings, branding, mutilation—for blaspheming the Christian religion, George Fox (not to mention the future generations of Quakers) disowned him: he was Trotsky, in Hill's striking analogy, to the official 'Stalinist' historiography.[53]

Nayler suffered hideously in this episode; but he had an atonement of sorts, even in his own lifetime, and surely in the narratives of some later historians. The women who accompanied him, though, remain at best "holy imbeciles"; to the seventeenth-century orthodox (and Quaker respectables) they were a sum of feminine stupidity and evil— "silly women," a "company of wretches" of a "filthy spirit," strumpets, whores, "deceitful Trull[s]," sorcerers and witches.

Two women were arrested with Nayler, Martha Simmonds, who held the bridle of the horse, and Hannah Stranger, who had walked at the side. Martha Simmonds, of a family of "some standing" in London, was the wife of Thomas Simmonds, "Stationer," and sister to Giles Calvert, publisher and bookseller of radical literature from Quakers and Fifth Monarchists to Gerrard Winstanley, and whose address at "the Blackspread-Eagle at the West end of Pauls" was the regular meeting and contact shop for radical sympathizers. Hannah

Stranger, "also respected" in the City, was the wife of John Stranger, whose occupation was listed as "Combmaker."[54] A third woman was implicated and interrogated, Dorcas Erbery, daughter of William Erbery, sectarian minister, chaplain in the New Model Army, friend of the Levellers, "champion of the Seekers."[55] None of the women had deserted their husbands: Dorcas Erbery was unmarried, and the husbands of the others were "disciples" of Nayler.[56]

By everyone's account, implied or explicit, Martha Simmonds was the "villain,"[57] the ringleader of the whole sad affair. Surely James Nayler took the force of the wrath of sober and conservative Christians for his manifestation of the 'inner light,' for acting it out, as he said in interrogation, as the "Son of God" because "the ever-lasting righteousnesse is wrought in mee." George Fox sternly told him that he had "trained up a company" against the "power and life of truth." Ralph Farmer, the Bristol Presbyterian minister who published and editorialized on the transcript of the trial, pointed out that Nayler had parted his hair and trimmed his beard to look like descriptions of Jesus, and had used this "amongst simple clowns and silly women, who are easily drawn to believe any story that is seriously told them."[58] But Farmer named Martha Simmonds as the "chief leader" (and as Nayler's "very baggage" of a "spouse").[59] Quaker correspondents told one another that she had made Nayler a cult figure—out of "an exceedingly filthy spirit . . . got up in her."[60] In the letter in which he turned his back on Nayler, Fox referred scathingly to "Martha Simmonds, which is called your Mother."[61] And punctuation of the culpability of Martha Simmonds was the implication of black magic: she had gotten Nayler in her "power"; she had "betwitched" him; she had lured simpleminded females into "idolatrous" postures before him; she was herself a witch.[62]

It may be that George Fox and other Quaker leaders really believed that the "filthy spirit" in Martha Simmonds was of the devil. But they knew very well the chronology of her relationship with James Nayler. She had been one of a "clique" of women, some of them "tainted with Ranterism," powerfully attracted to Nayler's charismatic preaching in London: the familiar and continuing pitfall, a Quaker historian pointed out, of popular ministers.[63] Mrs. Simmonds and her friends were constantly with Nayler, praising and flattering him, quite turning the head of this simple Yorkshire countryman. And then the women became so openly partisan that they talked critically and contemptuously of the work of the other two Quaker ministers in the London area, Edward Burrough and Francis Howgill. They made themselves "an intolerable nuisance" at meetings: Mrs. Simmonds, said a Friend, "labours to break and destroy the Meetings if it were possible";[64] another bluntly charged that she "strove" to set Nayler against his "bretheren," and "make a party within the movement."[65]

Martha Simmonds added to this that she had been so moved by Nayler's work that she too wanted to "declare" to the world, that is, to become a prophetess. But "they," the two other Quaker ministers, forbade it, told her, she said, "that I was too forward to run before I was sent." Thus she was resentful, angry, and admittedly disruptive in congregation. So she went to Nayler to ask his help in obtaining "justice" from his fellow preachers. He was at first "harsh" with her, she testified. Undaunted, she searched for the words to reach him, and when "at length" they came, they "struck him down": *"How are the mighty men falen,"* she exclaimed, *"I came to Jerusalem and behold a cry, and behold an oppression"*; Nayler was "pierced," and lay "in exceeding sorrow for about three daies" in the Simmonds home, a further imprudence, during which time "the power arose" in Mrs. Simmonds.[66]

The version of the Brethren has it that Martha Simmonds exerted her power over Nayler by "a kind of hysterical moaning and weeping," in a performance which "so affected James, that he became dejected and disconsolate."[67] Nayler's mental and emotional state baffled and disturbed the Friends (Martha Simmonds noted that he did "sweat exceedingly");[68] a later Quaker writer diagnosed him as "utterly passive" as "two forces" fought for "his soul and his sanity."[69] Friends took him away to the west counties, but the temptress Simmonds pursued him with the lure of her exalted adoration. Finally in his pit of weakness Nayler yielded, to become the center of a brief 'party' within the Quaker movement (which declared, we remember, that Christ was in everyone), the leader worshipped by the few who cast him as the "King of Israel," the "Son of God," the "Prince of Peace" and "Righteousnesse."[70]

All of this, in the understatement of a later Quaker, "had a very sobering effect on the Friends."[71] Well before the Act of Toleration which legalized the Quakers' journey to prosperity and perfection as *bons bourgeois*, they had discarded the excesses of the 1650s. After Nayler's "Fall," wrote a Quaker historian, "high language about personal infallibility," with its "special dangers" of "attended enthusiasm," was "abated."[72] The problem, of course, was the special enthusiasm of a special sort of people, "shallow and flighty women and men," in the later Quaker's phrase.[73] Women *and* men, the writer admitted. Men adored James Nayler too, and one of them walked bare-headed before his horse in the procession into Bristol. But who got the blame for fanaticism/blasphemy, and the sequential destruction of Preacher Nayler?

The story is well-known of Quaker organization from the 1680s, and within it the subordination of women's activities. It is, though, the obvious and fitting finale to a chapter on "forward" females in the civil war sects. In William Braithwaite's much-cited discussion of the "position of women" in *The Second Period of Quakerism* there is double finding. On the one hand, women themselves sensibly kept a low profile in public meetings. Braithwaite's quoted evidence about a "typical" woman of "ripe experience" bears repeating in full: "She had wisdom to know the time and season of her service, in which she was a good example to her sex; for without extraordinary impulse and concern it was rare for her to preach in large meetings; and she was grieved when any, especially of her sex, should be too hasty, forward, or unseasonable in their appearings in such meetings."[74] On the other hand, at the turn of the century, between 1697 and 1701, women ministers seem to have had a flurry of ambition: sitting with brethren ministers at the Yearly Meeting; planning a separate Meeting of women; speaking up in the public meetings. In 1701 the Yearly Meeting "suppressed" separate meetings of women ministers (and not until 1784 would an English women's Yearly Meeting be allowed). As for female speaking in public sessions the "Minutes reveal somewhat crudely the attitudes of the men": "This meeting finding that it is a hurt to Truth for women Friends to take up too much time, as some do, in our public meetings, when several public and serviceable men Friends are present and are by them prevented in their serving, it's therefore advised that the women Friends should be tenderly cautioned against taking up too much time in our mixed public meetings."[75] Pulling away and pushed at the same time, modest women withdrew and a lingering few had to be tenderly urged: comparatively seen it was not at all crude, but rather bourgeois civilized.

NOTES

1. A. L. Morton, *The World of the Ranters* (London, 1970), p. 16.

2. Keith Thomas, "Women and the Civil War Sects," *Past & Present* 13 (April 1958): 45.

3. Ibid., p. 47; Phyllis Mack, "Women as Prophets during the English Civil War," *Feminist Studies* 8, no. 1 (Spring 1982): 24, 41n.22.

4. Nehemiah Wallington, *Historical Notices*, vol. 1, Introduction, ix-xi.

5. See Theodore Spencer, "The History of an Unfortunate Lady," *Harvard Studies and Notes in Philology and Literature* 20 (1938): 43-59; and, as a

sampling, *All the Proceedings at the Session of the Peace Holden at Westminster* (London, 1651), E.637(18).

6. Thomas, "Women and the Civil War Sects," p. 56.

7. Katherine Chidley, *A New-Years Gift, or a Brief Exhortation to Mr. Thomas Edwards*, Epistle to the Reader (London, 1644).

8. Creditors of the Common-Wealth: *Concerning the Publick Faith . . . and Grievances of the Nation* (London, 1653), E.711(6).

9. Jeremiah Burroughes, *A Vindication of Mr. Burroughs against Mr. Edwards his foule Aspersions in his spreading Gangraena* (1646).

10. Thomas Edwards, *Gangraena* (London, 1646), Bk. 1: 15, 29, 84.

11. Ibid., Bk. 1: 79-80.

12. *Lucifers Lacky, or the Divels New Creature* (1641), E.180(3).

13. Edwards, *Gangraena*, Bk. 1: 84-86.

14. Ibid., pp. 87-88.

15. Thomas Parker, *The Copy of a Letter Written by Mr. Tho. Parker*, 22 Nov. 1649 (London, 1650), E.584(3).

16. John Rogers, *Ohel or Beth-shemesh, A Tabernacle for the Sun* (London, 1653), pp. 463-64.

17. Ibid., pp. 402-16, and passim.

18. Elizabeth Avery, *Scripture-Prophecies Opened, which are to be accomplished in these last times, which attend the second coming of Christ* (London, 1647), E.413(4).

19. Thomas Parker, *Copy of a Letter*, pp. 5-17.

20. E. Avery, *Scripture-Prophecies Opened*, To the Reader.

21. Cf. Phyllis Mack, "Women as Prophets"; and Ethyn Morgan Williams, "Women Preachers in the Civil War," *Journal of Modern History* 1 (1929): 561-69.

22. Elizabeth Poole, *A Vision, Wherein is manifested the disease and cure of the Kingdom* (London, 1648), E.537(24), pp. 1-3.

23. *The Clarke Papers*, ed. C. H. Firth (London, 1894), 2: xix, 151-54; Harrison and Rich, of course, became prominent Fifth Monarchists.

24. Poole, *A Vision*, pp. 2-3.

25. *Clarke Papers*, 2: 152-54.

26. Poole, *A Vision*, pp. 3-5.

27. Ibid., p. 6.

28. John Lilburne, *Picture of the Council of State*, E.550(14), p. 24.

29. Elizabeth Poole, *An Alarum of War, given to the Army*, 17 May (London, 1649), E.555(23).

30. E. Poole, *An Alarum of Warre, given to the Army, and to their High Court of Justice (so called) by the Will of God; revealed in Elizabeth Poole* (London, 1649), E.555(24), pp. 2, 9, 13.

31. Poole, *Alarum of War*, E.555(23), pp. 7-9, 13.

32. George Fox, *The Woman Learning in Silence* (London, 1655), E.870(8), p. 5.

33. *The Life of Margaret Fox . . . compiled from her own narrative, and other sources* (Philadelphia, 1859), pp. 6-11; *A Brief Collection of Remarkable*

Passages and Occurrences . . . of Margaret Fell (London, 1710), p. 2; also, Isabel Ross, *Margaret Fell, Mother of Quakerism* (London, 1949), pp. 5-7.

34. *The Life of Margaret Fox*, pp. 14-15.

35. Ibid., pp. 35-48; and *Remarkable Passages*, p. A2.

36. *Remarkable Passages*, p. 4.

37. *To the Parliament of the Commonwealth of England* (London, 1653), E.714(10), pp. 2-7.

38. *The Cry of Blood* (London, 1656), E.884(3), pp. 19-21.

39. *A Short Relation of some of the Sad Sufferings and Cruel Havock and Spoil, Inflicted on the Persons and Estates of the People in God, in Scorn called Quakers* (London, 1670), p. 74.

40. Hill, *The World Turned Upside Down*, chapter 10; A. L. Morton, *The World of the Ranters*, pp. 17-18; Mabel Brailsford, *A Quaker From Cromwell's Army: James Nayler* (New York, 1927), pp. 93-95.

41. Hill, *World Turned Upside Down*, p. 187; also cited (Edward Burrough) in Ibid., p. 197, and (George Fox), p. 188.

42. Cited in Ibid., p. 190.

43. Ibid., p. 255.

44. Thomas Edwards, *Gangraena*, Bk. 1: 121.

45. Hill, *World Turned Upside Down*, pp. 187, 192-93; or in Ra. Farmer, *Sathan Inthron'd in His Chair of Pestilence, or Quakerism in its Exaltation* (London, 1656), E.897(2), p. 28: Quaker doctrines were "a mixture and medly of Popery, Socinianisme, Arrianisme, Arminianisme, Anabaptisme, and all that is nought."

46. See Geoffrey F. Nuttall, *James Naylor, A Fresh Approach* (Philadelphia, 1954), p. 10.

47. *A Brief Representation and Discovery . . . The Substance of the Information and free confessions of . . . Anne Wells* (London, 1649), E.559(8).

48. Ernst E. Taylor, "On the Great Revival at Malton in 1652," *The Journal of The Friends' Historical Society* 33 (1936): 29-31.

49. Hill, *World Turned Upside Down*, p. 201.

50. *The Grand Imposter Examined* (London, 1656), E.896(3), pp. 1-3.

51. Ibid., p. 5.

52. *The Resurrection of John Lilburne*, p. 5.

53. Hill, *World Turned Upside Down*, p. 186.

54. *Grand Imposter Examined*, p. 3.

55. Hill, *World Turned Upside Down*, p. 154.

56. Thomas Simmonds seems to have dropped out after the Bristol disaster (*Sathan Inthron'd*, p. 20).

57. Brailsford, *James Nayler*, p. 97.

58. Farmer, *Sathan Inthron'd*, pp. 14, 9, 26-27.

59. Ibid., pp. 22, 29.

60. Ross, *Margaret Fell*, p. 102 (in a letter from Richard Hubberthorne to Margaret Fell).

61. Farmer, *Sathan Inthron'd*, p. 9.

62. Ibid., pp. 10-11; *Grand Imposter Examined*, pp. 22-23.

63. Brailsford, *James Nayler*, p. 94-95.

64. Ross, *Margaret Fell*, p. 102 (Hubberthorne to Fell).

65. Charles Evans, *Friends in the Seventeenth Century* (Philadelphia, 1876), pp. 136-37; also, W. C. Braithwaite, *The Beginning of Quakerism*, 2nd ed. (Cambridge, 1955), Chapter 11.

66. Farmer, *Sathan Inthron'd*, pp. 10-11.

67. Evans, *Friends*, p. 137.

68. Farmer, *Sathan Inthron'd*, p. 11.

69. Brailsford, *James Nayler*, p. 100.

70. Farmer, *Sathan Inthron'd*, pp. 14-16, and passim; *Grand Imposter Examined*, p. 6, and passim.

71. George Fox, *An Authobiography*, edited, with an introduction and notes, by Rufus M. Jones (Philadelphia, 1919), p. 273n.

72. William C. Braithwaite, *The Second Period of Quakerism* (London, 1919), p. 250.

73. Evans, *Friends*, p. 137.

74. Braithwaite, *Second Period*, p. 286.

75. Ibid., p. 287.

6

Elizabeth Cellier, Misfit

Catholic midwife

It is irresistible to append to a collection of 'public' bourgeois women in the turmoil of the English Revolution the story of Elizabeth Cellier. Professional midwife, turncoat Catholic, Cellier is the odd woman out, fittingly nowhere, impossible to categorize, except as a person to whom the stirring times had dealt such a strange hand that she had no alternative (given her obvious gifts and competence) to be a very special case. Perhaps this in itself is a pattern in middle-class culture.

So many things are there to savor in the career of Elizabeth Cellier that it is a challenge to tell it properly or carefully enough. She had a minor if dangerous role in the "Popish Plot" with which the scoundrel Titus Oates bewitched a credulous English populace; but her place there was in a "sham" plot within the supposed plot, and *that* affair, the "Meal-tub Plot," in which she was in fact the star, was so labyrinthine that a contemporary well-informed royal minister pronounced it "an intrigue, which he could never make anything of."[1] Rather than risk the perplexity of Sir William Temple with the internal complexities of Elizabeth Cellier's meal tub we had better survey the violent and perilous scene in which she played a part.

Fundamentally, during the last years of the reign of Charles II the lid was coming off the Restoration settlement. Once again, a Stuart monarch sparred with many of the most powerful monied interests of land and city; Charles tried to manipulate hostile parliaments, supporting his rule with secret subsidies from Louis XIV of a France feared and detested by mainstream Protestant England, and finally, from 1681 to his death in 1685, would govern without Parliament entirely. Political and economic conflicts were, of course, religious as well, and indeed the religious issue was the most explosive: Charles having no legitimate progeny was to be followed by his brother, James, Duke of York; and James, even more endowed with the Stuart knack

Ch.1

of infuriating most of the English nation, was an open and aggressive Catholic (while Charles was a secret sympathizer who would reconcile with Rome on his deathbed). The political opposition, the core of the emerging Whig party, wanted to handle the problem directly, by denying James the succession: "Exclusionists" in Parliament, the City, and the counties were mobilizing Protestant England to a new confrontation with the Stuart monarchy; in short, the Glorious Revolution of 1688 was an inevitability for a decade before.

In the summer of 1678 a self-seeking drifter named Titus Oates began noising about London tales of a popish plot to kill the king, put York in his place, and in armed uprising restore England to the Catholic faith. In command performance before the king's privy council, where in effect he waved lists of the names of card-carrying papists, Oates was plausible enough to silence a skeptical Charles, and to earn himself a guarded apartment at Whitehall with a monthly salary of forty pounds.

From start to finish the Plot was a lie. Oates, who had been ousted from Cambridge with the reputation not only of a shady fellow but a "great dunce," who after he had managed to "slip into orders" had been dismissed from every clerical post he held, and had even been imprisoned for scandalous perjury,[2] was the only plotter: he intended to make his fortune by stretching the tensions of the Exclusionist controversy. He had done an impressive amount of preparatory research for several years, professing himself a Catholic convert to the underworld of the London faithful, journeying to study at a Jesuit seminary in Spain (from which he was expelled in disgrace, though the London priests did not know that), regularly visiting the closer Jesuit English college at St. Omer, south of Calais. Thus his stories were convincingly embellished with close details of Catholic intrigue and Jesuit machinations at the highest level of English government.

In October 1678 the justice of peace to whom Oates had first given his evidence of a popish plot was found mysteriously murdered (it is still a mystery: perhaps Oates and his accomplices were responsible). Everywhere it was believed that vengeful Catholics had done the deed and the witch-hunt was on. Parliament officially proclaimed the existence of the "damnable and hellish" Plot to destroy the Protestant monarchy; the Exclusionist faction in the House of Commons tried to indict the Duke of York for covert encouragement of "the present Conspiracy and Design of the Papists against the King and Protestant Religion"; a petition from the "Lord Mayor, Aldermen and Commons of the City of London" informed the king that "the whole protestant Interest" was imperiled by the papists "all about Your Royal Palace and this City."[3] As constables, courts, and hangmen swung into action the secretary to the Duke and Duchess of York was among the first to die by the fury of Protestant England; in the next two years five Catholic lords were imprisoned and seven Jesuit priests executed along with more than a score of laity implicated by Oates and copycat informers—in all about thirty-five men.

In the frenetic months of 1679-80 official panic was transferred to London taverns, streets, and dwelling places by rumor-fed hysteria. An unlucky goldsmith named William Stalay of the parish of St. Giles in the Fields was overheard in a pub conversing in loud French with an "Outlandish Man"; Stalay was seized, tried as a traitor, convicted by a jury of "persons of quality," and hung, drawn, and quartered, all in little over a week.[4] Informers jostled to assist the magistrates in enforcing the king's command that all Catholics depart from the City; persons identified as papists were ferreted out of their hiding places and bundled off to prison amidst popular relief and rejoicing. Charles dissolved the Parliament which had sat since 1660, hoping that new elections would return a more manageable Commons and Lords, and suggested that his brother withdraw quietly to Flanders. Just then the king took suddenly and seriously ill, and the response in the City to his actions and his sickness was a flood of terrified apprehension: "People are saying," as the authorities' report put it, that "Popery and arbitrary government are coming again," that the "nation is sold to the French," that "a Parliament is not to come again."[5]

Into this tense and violent scene came Elizabeth Cellier, Catholic midwife "intimately acquainted" with "many considerable families," including those of court—papist—aristocrats,[6] married moreover to a French merchant. Why should she have chosen to make herself conspicuous in this perilous London climate? Her judges would take it as a matter of fact that she was an agent, paid by the Countess of Powis, whose husband became one of the five accused Catholic lords, to assist in mounting a counterattack upon the Oatesian tormentors. A close associate of the Duke of York, Lord Peterborough, remembered that his friend the Countess of Powis had introduced him to Mrs. Cellier; he was told that she was an "ingenious Woman" with such intimate contacts with important Londoners that she might help soften a few virulent anti-Catholics, who could possibly be brought into "the King's service," that is, paid off with a place at court.[7] Cellier herself firmly denied that she had had money from the Countess of Powis, at least in her initial efforts to succor the persecuted papists; it was out of love and charity, she insisted, that she brought food and money out of her own pocket to the Jesuits and others held in Newgate Prison.[8] Whatever the reality—probably a mixture of Peterborough's and Cellier's versions—London authorities were watching Elizabeth Cellier as early as the fall of 1678: every day she appeared at Newgate, carrying baskets and cash for her inmate friends, pumping employees for information about their welfare, arguing with already irritable officials.

Only the sketchiest information is available about Cellier's background. Antiquarian genealogies say that she was a member of the "noble family" of Dormer, who "became possessed of extensive landed property" in Buckinghamshire "very soon after the reformation," which indicates an old and well-placed family doing even better by gathering in monastic lands put on the market by Henry VIII.[9] In her trials of 1679-80 Cellier gave bits of autobiography she considered relevant to her case. She said she had been born to a Protestant family, no name or date given; that her family had been loyalist during the civil wars; that she had lost her father and brother "both in a day" and that her family had been "stripped and plundered," utterly "ruined."[10] (The genealogies refer to the eldest son of Baron Dormer of Wing who was created Earl of Carnarvon in 1628, and died fighting for Charles I at the Battle of Newbury in 1643.)[11] Her "education being in those times," Cellier said, she had learned to hate the Protestant "murderers" of the king; and as she "grew in understanding" she had turned to the religion to which the detested Protestants "pretended the greatest antipathy." She had a son and a daughter of a previous marriage, a fact she revealed in complaining of her inability in prison to manage their inherited estate. Of Peter Cellier, her French husband, there is almost nothing, except that she had met him in England (for she testified that she had never been abroad) and that because of his unfamiliarity with English law she represented him in contractual matters in London.[12] It is not much of a biography, but the bits correspond nicely to the Cellier we see in the brief glare of publicity in Restoration London: a mature and seasoned woman, accomplished, prosperous, self-assured, self-created.

The immediate result of the capable Mrs. Cellier's foray into the politics of the Popish Plot was that she was 'conned,' used by a temporary Newgate prisoner named Thomas Dangerfield (alias Willoughby, as she first knew him). Cellier was convinced at the jail of mistreatment of Catholic prisoners, including what she thought was the use of the rack, forbidden by common law, for a man implicated in the famous murder of the Justice of Peace. Dangerfield/Willoughby became her productive informant, bringing her written testimonies of people claiming to have been hideously tortured. And then he added more irresistible informational bait. He had evidence, Dangerfield said, that the whole of the Popish Plot had been fabricated by leaders of the Protestant (Exclusionist) party, that the Earl of Shaftesbury, chief of the party, was promising thousands of pounds to those who would falsely swear that the Duke of York and the Catholic lords in the Tower had plotted to kill the king and restore England to the Catholic religion.[13]

That the Popish Plot was a "Presbyterian" invention was exactly what Elizabeth Cellier wanted to hear. She paid Dangerfield's fines and got him out of Newgate (he told her he was there by mistaken identity), fed and clothed him, and set him to the gathering of more rumors about town. Certainly he earned his keep: the talk of the coffee houses, he reported back, was the mobilization of the Presbyterians and all the nonconformist sects, with the "Old Rump officers" (i.e., Cromwellians) handing out commissions to disbanded soldiers or to any burning to serve the Good Old Cause; indeed, he said he had himself been offered a captaincy. In any case, people were saying that "there would be a rebellion before Michaelmas."[14]

Mrs. Cellier wasted no time in contemplation of these stories. They must go to the king, she said, and warn him that "that Gang" and the "Rabble of Westminster" were planning to seize his throne, to dispose of the son as they had the father. She instructed Dangerfield to write down the details of the 'Presbyterian Plot,' and she put the papers he gave her into her *meal tub* for safekeeping. Then she called upon the Earl of Peterborough, who related the information to the Duke of York, who passed it on to the king, who turned it over to his secretary—and the last paid Dangerfield forty pounds to more generously cover his continuing spying costs.[15]

Contemporary comment on Thomas Dangerfield has him a "subtle and dexterous man," a "handsome, proper young fellow," a "versatile rogue."[16] One courtwatcher (Roger North, brother to a Lord Chief Justice) found it "pleasant" to observe how he "deluded the midwife Mrs. Cellier,"[17] though by that time the facts, at least some of them, were known, and it was sure that he had fooled a lot of people, many of them with less reasons for credulity than the midwife Cellier. Apparently he had three schemes ongoing in the six or seven months he spent in her employ. The first, obviously, was to cut himself into the Titus Oates rewards by ingratiating himself with Cellier, pretending to papist sympathies in order to collect profitable evidence of the Popish Plot. Next he circulated among the disorganized groups of the old dissenters, picking up news of real discontent, embellishing it grandly with names of Exclusionists such as Shaftesbury, and tying it all together as an anti-royal, 'Presbyterian' uprising: more saleable goods, to Catholic lords (Powis, Peterborough) *and* to the court of Charles II. Third, he was in contact with the Exclusionists, probably in the pay of Shaftesbury, who was delighted to trumpet the charge that the Duke of York, with the king's tacit approval, was trying to take the heat off the Catholic party with charges of a Presbyterian rather than a Popish Plot. A "fine fellow," an exasperated judge would finally say of him, "first to come to his majesty with one story, then to the lord Powis, and from him to lord Shaftesbury, discovering to one what discourse he held to another."[18]

It was the second of Dangerfield's schemes which unraveled. Needing more and richer material on a Presbyterian conspiracy (and this is what became known as the "sham-plot," or the "Meal-tub Plot") he wrote his own, planted it in incriminating places and 'found' it himself; the papers were exposed as forgeries, and Dangerfield was in prison once again.

Back in Newgate, and for the moment lacking alternatives, Dangerfield turned on Elizabeth Cellier. Not only did he implicate her as his accomplice in the forgeries of the meal-tub papers; he accused her, the Countess of Powis, and others as traitorous conspirators in the Popish Plot. Cellier's house was ransacked by the Middlesex justice himself, Sir William Waller, friend of Shaftesbury, and a public servant "distinguished," in the neat phrase of the *DNB*, in "catching priests, burning Roman Catholic books and vestments, and getting up evidence." Sir William found the notorious papers in their homely hiding place, as well as a ream of others equally interestingly filed "between the Pewter in my Kitchin," Cellier recalled: the testimonies of supposedly tortured Catholic prisoners, correspondence with various imprisoned "Traytors," records indicating that Cellier had "harboured the St. Omer Youth" (English students at the Jesuit college across the Channal). She was arrested, to the accompaniment of lively and articulate resistance, and sent to be "close confin'd" in Newgate Prison.[19]

The foregoing relates as faithfully as possible a complex set of events, but at this point Elizabeth Cellier must take over herself. Her version of the subsequent story could not, of course, have been objective, but her self-serving was neither whining nor, given her injuries, blindly vindictive. She wrote and published her book after her acquittal in unforgiving fury with young Thomas Dangerfield; this competent and worldly-wise woman (surely her self-view) was not accustomed to being used and betrayed by anyone, and she was going to ruin Dangerfield if she could. But *Malice Defeated, Or, a brief Relation of the Accusation and Deliverance of Elizabeth Cellier* was a controlled and calculated rebuttal, sometimes coldly factual, sometimes slyly, mockingly humorous. And Cellier used a direct-dialogue format through much of it, an excellent technique to puncture pompous judges sitting upon their monopoly of the law, self-appointed investigators selling 'truth' to the highest bidders, or a society in which every man was on the make and instantly ready to do in every other fellow. It is a brilliant narrative.

Here from *Malice Defeated* is Cellier's account of the first days of her imprisonment in the fall of 1679 (the emphases are in her text):

> *Friday* the last of *October*, I brought myself to the *Kings-bench Barr*, in hope to be Bail'd; but then at the Barr, *Church* opposed it, saying, *His Worship* had sent in an accusation *of high Treason against me*, though I had as yet no Accuser; *And by the Law, no person ought to be committed for Treason, till accused by two honest, sufficient, lawful, and credible Witnesses, witnessing one and the same Individual Fact.*
>
> *November* the first, I was examin'd before His Majesty and the Lords of the Council, where the Fable of *The Husband-man, and the starved Snake, was proved a Truth*; For *Willoughby* [Dangerfield] accused me of all the Forged Stories he tells in his Lying Narrative; and I unfeignedly told the Truth, and the whole Truth, and nothing but the Truth. But the Lord Chancellor told me, no body would believe a word I said, and that I would Dye.—To which I replyed, *I know that my Lord, for I never saw an Immortal woman in my life*: And then kneeling down, said,
>
> *Cellier.* I beseech your Majesty that I may not be Tortur'd.
>
> *The King.* The Law will not suffer it.
>
> *Cellier.* Such things are frequently done in *Newgate*; and I have more reason to fear it than any other person, because of what I have done against the Keeper, and therefore I beseech your Majesty, If at any time I should say any thing contrary to what I have now said, that you will not believe me, for it will be nothing but lies forc'd from me by *barbarous usage*, what I have now told you, being the truth, and the whole truth, to the utmost of my knowledge.
>
> Then I was sent away to Newgate, and the next day was brought again before the Councel, and than a lord said, *Turn up your hoods, Mrs. Cellier*, I did so;[20] The Lord Chancellor ask'd me, if I had not been at the *Tower* to tell of *Willoughby's* Commitment, and bring instructions for him.
>
> *Cellier.* I protest I have not been at the *Tower* Since.—Then the Lord Chancellor Interrupted me, saying *She cannot speak three words of Truth.*
>
> *Cellier.* Pray my lord be pleased to hear me out, *and do not Judge me till then*, I have not been at the *Tower* since *Thursday* was seven night.

Lord Chan. That was the Time, what did you there?

Cellier. I Din'd there.

Lord Chan. Had you no talk concerning Willoughby? tell us the Truth, for the Countess of *Powis* hath told us all.

Cellier. My Lord, nothing of Truth can do me any harm, and I am sure her Ladyship will tell nothing else. . . . Then I was commanded to withdraw.

And understanding, soon after, that I should be Close Confin'd the dread of being lock'd up on the top of *Newgate*, and attended on by Fellons, as Mrs. *Prescick* had been, though big with Child. . . ; [and] some had been locked up there a full year, and kept in Irons above Six months of the time, the fear of this, or worse usage, did so oppress my spirits, that though I be not the most timorous of my Sex, and never had any kind of Fit before, I fell into such Convulsions, that I had like to have died at *White-hall* Gate. Then I was carried to the Keepers House, and laid upon a Couch, and being a little come to my strength and senses, I told Captain *Richardson*, that if I should die in that desolate place, as it was like I might that very Night, most persons would believe that he had caus'd me to be Murthered, in revenge of the Articles I put into Parliament against him; whereupon he bid me be of good Comfort, for I should not be carry'd to the top of the Goal, but lye in his own House, which promise so revived me, that within an hour, I was able to go up into the Garret, where I had a very Good Bed, and a Maid ordered to lye in the Room by me; she tended me very diligently, and seem'd very much to Commiserate my Condition, *being, I suppose, set on to do so, that she might the more easily betray me*: I had brought Pen, Ink, and Paper from the Gate-house, and easily prevail'd with her *for money*, to carry a Note home to my House, in *a Bottom of Thred*, she carried and recarried three or four, shewing them first to the Jaylors Wife and Sister, and they took Copies of them, and sent them to the Councel, perswading themselves they should make strange Discoveries, but I had Committed no Crime, and therefore *nothing but Innocence would be found in my Letters*. . . .[21]

Elizabeth Cellier's inquisitors next sent Dangerfield to talk with her. He appeared at a "Window over against mine," she wrote, "with yet another Rogue behind me, to hear what I said." Along with his other skills Dangerfield had acting talent; he wept in feigned contrition, "shewed his Arms, and Howl'd, saying he had been so miserably Tormented, that he was not able to bear it" and had made the false accusations in fear of death. Cellier lashed at him, "Ah Villain, will you bely the Innocent, to save an Infamous Life? . . . Do you think to wipe off your other sins, by committing Perjuries and Murthers?" He responded with a moment of candor, "No, but God is merciful, and if I live, I may repent. . . . But since no body took any care of me, I had reason to take some of my self, which I will do." Back in form, he went on to tell her that those he belonged to now were "very kind" to him and that he would have a "Pardon" in two or three days. He was on the track of his third scheme now: he wanted Cellier (so that she "not ruin" her family) to become "Kings Evidence," to "come in now whilst it is time, and *joyn with the most powerful.*" And to hasten this turnabout he transmitted the promise of a huge and temptingly packaged bribe. "If I would say," Cellier summarized it, that the Duke of York "gave me the Original of those Papers that were found in my *Meal Tub*, and bid me cause [Dangerfield to] . . . Kill the Earl of Shaftesbury, then I should have a Pardon, and more Mony than all the Witnesses had had together, for the Earl of *Shaftesbury* and the rest of the *Confederate Lords* would raise *The Thousand Pounds* among them. . . . And I should have Twenty Pounds per Week setled on me by Act of Parliament as long as I liv'd: And if I would do it, some Persons of Honour should come and treat with me; for though I were confin'd, *there was Lords that were Privy to all*, that would come on pretence to Examine me, and settle things to my satisfaction."[22]

Mrs. Cellier's account steadily surpassed itself. Her answer to Dangerfield: "Repent you Rogue, and *tell the King who set you on*, for you will certainly be Damn'd if you do not." And "I shook him so," she said, "that he Howl'd like a Dog that had the Tooth-Ach." She told him that he was a "Cowardly wretch" who thought only of saving his miserable life. And "he howl'd again, and wrung his hands, pretending Repentance," and promised her that "against to morrow he would write down all the Intrigue, with the Names of *those Lords and others*, that set him on." Cellier shut her window on him, but next day he was there again, "hancred about," and "shedding Crokadils tears, holding up his hands, and making beseeching signs. . . ." Presently the windows were nailed shut and Dangerfield came no more; thought Cellier, the Shaftesbury party had "more fears" that "I should Convert him, than hopes he should Pervert me."[23]

Elizabeth Cellier was held from her arrest in November 1679 until her trial in June 1680. She had many fencing interrogations, with Sir William Waller, for one, in which they quarreled about the events of the civil wars, she accusing him of being party with the *"Murtherers of his Majesties Royal Father, and many of his Loyal Peers and Gentlemen."* In interesting insight of the perils of even well-paying female inmates, Mrs. Cellier was wary of Sir William: *"indeed I durst not trust my self with such a* Doughty Knight *as* Sir William *was, lest he should make Romances of me, as he has done of others. . . .*" And regularly, rather than the formal trial she agitated for, she was questioned by the King's Council, in sessions which always began, in her telling, with an unnamed lord requesting, "Turn up your Hoods, Mrs. Cellier." In one of them she was quizzed about a casual conversation she had had at the "Devil-Tavern" with a Mr. Adams, the latter brought in to testify to her subversive opinions. Mrs. Cellier, said Mr. Adams, had ordered him to drink to the health of the Duke of York, and had talked largely about a Presbyterian plot against the government of Charles II. This interchange with the Council resulted:

> Cel. *My Lord, of all this fine Story there is nothing true, but that I was at the Tavern, but it was three weeks before the time he mentioned, and I did Pledge the D's Health, and say, I believed there was a Plot among the Presbyterians, to play their old Game over again, but I hoped God would bless the King and his Royal Brother, and that their Affairs would go well, and God would destroy their Enemies, and send quiet Times.*

> Adams. She did say she had been beyond Sea, and *Mr. Petly* will swear she said had been in *Flanders.*

> Cel. *If I did say so, I lyed.*

> L. Presid. If you Lyed then, how shall we know you tell Truth now?

> Cel. *My Lord, there is a great deal of difference between what I say at a Tavern, to a Man of his Understanding, and what I say here, where every Word ought to be equal to an Oath.*

> Adams. Your bawdy Story I left out of the Depositions, I was asham'd to speak it.

> King. What, can she speak Bawdy too?

> Adams. Yes, indeed she did.

> L.C. I, she's fit for anything.

> Cel. *My Lord, I never spoke an immodest word in my Life.* [Mr. Adams,] *though you strive to take away my Life, do not take away my Honour; What did I say?*

> King. What did she say? come tell us the Story.

> Adams. She said—She said—that—She said—That if she did not lose her Hands, she could get Mony as long as—

> King. As long as what? out with it.

> Adams. made as if he were asham'd, and could not speak such a word.

> Cel. I said, if I did not lose my Hands, I should get Mony as long as Men kissed their Wives.

> Adams. By the Oath I have taken she said their Mistresses too.

Cel. *Did I so, pray what else do they keep them for?*

L. *Chan.* That was but witty.

King. 'Twas but natural to her Practice.

Cel. Mr. Adams *I am sorry for your Ignorance,—I beseech your Majesty let me be inlarged.*

L. *Chan.* You are an obstinate Woman, and will tell us nothing we ask you.

Cel. *My lord, I tell Truth to all you ask.*

L.C. Here's no body believes you, you will trifle away your Life.

Cel. *My Lord, I will not belye my self nor others to save it, but I will assure your Lordships, never man that came before you, feared Death, nor valued Life less than I do.*

L.C. I, she's fit for them, Withdraw, Withdraw. . . .[24]

Her prosecutors kept a tight watch and heavy pressure upon Elizabeth Cellier through the months of her imprisonment. She saw even her husband with a jailor present, and only for a few minutes. She had no legal or financial help, she said, from her beleaguered friends. "*Singly and Alone,*" she wrote, "without the Advice or Assistance of any Catholick breathing *Man or Woman*, I was left to study, manage, and support my self in all my troubles to my Expence and Loss *much above a thousand Pounds*, never receiving one penny towards it, directly or indirectly, but ten pounds given me by the hands of a condemn'd Priest, five days before my Tryal; nor have I since received any thing towards my Losses, or the least civility from any of them."[25] But then of course, as her friends must have pointed out, her defense, and hope of acquittal, lay in her story of having acted alone.

In any case, Mrs. Cellier was not idle in prison. She did considerable brooding about Thomas Dangerfield, who was out of Newgate, and, as she imagined him, strutting about with a fine coat and a full purse. She knew he had been "visited by and from Persons of considerable Quality, with great Sums of Gold and Silver, to encourage him in the *new Villanies* he had undertaken, not against Me alone, but Persons in whose Safety all good Men (as well Protestants as others) in the three Kingdoms are concern'd."[26] But her dark thoughts about Thomas did not trail off into impotent rage: she was doing the research which would exonerate her and expose to the public the evil that Dangerfield was.

Cellier's trial for high treason was scheduled first for May 1680. The state had two witnesses against her, Dangerfield and another former friend, the astrologer John Gadbury. The latter was ill, however, and the lord chief justice (the notorious Sir William Scroggs who had presided over the "judicial murders" of the Catholics the year before) ruled a postponement until June. "It is," he informed Mrs. Cellier, "but a little while to it." In Cellier's transcript a testy dialogue ensued:

> Cel. *My Lord, my Husband will think it a great while*; at which the Court laugh'd.

> Cel. *My Lord, he hath a great cause to think it long, for he is already a Thousand pounds the worse for my Imprisonment; I have lain two and twenty weeks close confin'd, During which time my Husband put in near 20 Petitions before the Lords of the Council; to speak with me before a Keeper; but they were all rejected: and he then had a suit in Chancery to a considerable value, which had been heard before the Master of the Rolls, . . . a good part of the Money lay in the Court of Chancery, but my Adversary taking Advantage of my confinement, Petitioned for another Hearing; and my Husband not knowing how to defend the Cause, was forced to discharge seven hundred and odd pounds, for sixty one, because he could not be permitted to speak with me.*

> L.C.J. You arraign the Councel.

> Cel. *No, my Lord it is not to Arraign them, but to make it known how I have been used, and pray redress.*

> Serj. Maynard. Why could not your Husband follow his Law-Suit without you?

> Cel. *Because he is a Stranger, and does not understand the Law.*

> Serj. Maynard. Then you do Gentlewoman.

> Cel. *No Sir, but I have got enough to make a Country Justice, and pray that I may be tryed, And if I be Guilty, punished; and if Innocent, acquitted. And that my Husband and Children may not suffer as they do by my Imprisonment.*

> L.C.J. You shall be tryed the first day of the next Term, and it is in compassion to you that we appoint that day.

> Cel. *My Lord shall I be discharged, if I be not Tryed then?*

> L.C.J. You shall.

> Cel. *My Lord, the Laws I am to be Tryed by have sufficiently compensated their denying me other Councel by allowing me you my Lords that are my Judges, for Councellors, and I will depend upon your Faithful advice with confidence, and humbly pray fair play for my life.*

> Judges. You shall have fair play.

> Cel. *I thank your Lordships.*

> L.C.J. Keeper of *Newgate*, take her back, and use her with respect.[27]

The trial in June proceeded with almost anticlimactic ease and speed. (One important point: Scroggs had been ordered by the King to cool his antipapist zeal; Cellier, in short, was luckier than the early Catholic defendants.) Mr. Gadbury was trotted out and surprised the court with testimony which established nothing more than that Mrs. Cellier believed in astrology, was a loyal subject of both Stuarts, king and duke, and had in the past two years worried about the unrest in the country. "Brother," Scroggs observed to the attorney general, "you are mistaken in your Evidence."

Then Dangerfield was called, he to save the day for the state. Acting without counsel, the law in treason cases, Mrs. Cellier immediately objected that he was incompetent to testify, that she had evidence and would call witnesses to prove her charge. *"My Lord,"* she told a dismayed Scroggs, *"Witnesses for Treason ought to be Honest, Sufficient, Lawful, and Credible; And I will prove that he hath been Burnt in the Hand, Whip'd, Transported, Pillorie'd, Out'law'd for Felony, Fin'd for Cheating, and suffer'd publick Infamy for many other notorious Crimes."* She documented it all: Dangerfield had had a criminal career since early adolescence, and a trail of offenses that crisscrossed southern England. It was a sweet final scene for Elizabeth Cellier: Dangerfield blustering that he had been pardoned (another lie); the court forced to forfeit him as a second witness (in fact, he was taken back to jail); and, since two witnesses were required for conviction for treason, the jury necessarily declaring her not guilty.[28]

In the afterglow of her triumph Mrs. Cellier was told by the jury members that she owed them "a Guiny a man" because, they said, had they convicted her the king would have paid them that tip. She searched out the legality of the matter since, she said, "I have cost my Husband a great deal of Mony already, much more than my Person was worth," and refused them with a polite note which concluded with the alternative offer of her "most humble Service" to themselves and their "Several Ladies." And, she wrote, "if you and They please, I will with no less fidelity serve them in their Deliveries, then You have done me with Justice in mine, and thereby preserv'd Liberty and Property. . . ." The jurors were neither appeased nor amused: their spokesman went away "expressing his resentment in such language" as Mrs. Cellier would "not spoil Paper with."[29]

In the best of all possible worlds Elizabeth Cellier's story would have ended with her expensive victory at the King's Bench. But she had made too many enemies, too many powerful Protestant enemies. Roger North, the court-watcher, remarked that her "tongue, which was not tied, would be very foul upon the Evidence," by which he

meant the evidence against the Catholic lords in the Tower.[30] Whatever the complexity of their reasons, the enemies found the material
to silence Mrs. Cellier in *Malice Defeated*, which she had rushed into
print bare weeks after her trial. So in September 1680 she was at the
bar again, this time at the Old Bailey, on the lesser charge of libel.
As intoned by the clerk of the court she had "falsely, maliciously and
seditiously" written, "imprinted and published a scandalous Libel,
intituled, 'Malice Defeated: Or, a brief Relation of the Accusation and
Deliverance of Elizabeth Cellier: Wherein her Proceedings, both before and during her confinement, are particularly related, and the
Mystery of the Meal-Tub fully discovered: Together with an abstract
of her Arraignment and Trial: Written by herself for the satisfaction
of all lovers of undisguised truth.'"[31]

The prosecuting attorney was one "Robert Dormer, esq. of Lincoln's Inn": a distant relative? In his opening remarks he referred to
the defendant as "the gentlewoman at the bar, the wife of Peter
Cellier of the parish of St. Clement-Danes in the county of Middlesex,
gentleman," a more formal recognition of her social status than she
was accustomed to in court. But then he continued in his remarks to
the jury: "Gentlemen, this is a Libel so complicated and general, that
within this book are contained as many libels of several natures, and
against different persons and orders of men, as there are paragraphs;
his majesty, the Protestant religion, our laws, government, magistrates, counsellors of state, courts of judicature, the king's evidence,
and the public justice of this kingdome are all aspersed and defamed,
by the virulency and malice of this woman's pen."[32]

Mrs. Cellier had once again pleaded not guilty to the charge. She
had counsel but did the talking herself, protesting that she was "sur-
prized" and had not had time to collect her witnesses. Her initial
defense, which certainly surprised the Court, since she had admitted
the responsibility earlier, was a Lilburne-like stalling about the authorship of *Malice Defeated*. It was a shaky start, for the prosecution
was prepared with printer and bookseller, name, date, and manuscript. And from there her trial, with the Lord Mayor of the solidly
Whig establishment of London presiding, went as badly as imaginable
for Elizabeth Cellier. The proceedings came to such a pass that, pinned
down and at a loss for words, Cellier appealed for outside help:

> *Cellier.* May not counsel speak for me? I desire you would hear him.
>
> *Mr. Collins* [her counsel]. I have nothing to say for her.
>
> *Baron Weston* [chief judge]. He says, he hath nothing to say for you.
>
> *Mr. Collins.* And if you had said less for yourself, it had been better.[33]

Surely it was not naiveté which led the shrewd Elizabeth Cellier to the surprise and fluster of her trial for the 'libelous' assertions of *Malice Defeated?* Would social 'estrangement' be the better explanation? She was pinioned for assault upon two of the most sacred canons of emerging English Whiggery. First, she had insisted in print and in repeated interrogations that all Protestants were rebels and regicides, so that the only recourse for a person like herself, with "innate loyalty" to the "lawful king," was to convert to Catholicism. If she had not understood before that she had cut to a sensitive nerve of the 'Thermidorians' of Restoration England probably she did as she listened to Baron Weston counter this slander in his summary to the jury. "Now this libel," began Weston, "branches itself out into several parts; the first whereof is a very fine insinuation, as though her leaving the protestant religion was, because those that murdered the king, and made that very great subversion that was made in the government by the late Long Parliament, and the army that succeeded them were protestants. . . ." Mrs. Cellier, alerted, interrupted to say, "Pray, my Lord, I say, called protestants." Weston continued angrily, working himself to higher and more general levels of Protestant patriotic fury. The passage is a striking history lesson:

> . . . . she pretends it was by those that were called protestants; but if they were only those that were called protestants, and not protestants, what reason had she to go off from the protestant religion, to turn papist, when there was such a body of loyal protestants that did adhere to the loyal party? Therefore that was as villainous an insinuation as could be; as though the protestant religion did nourish and teach seditious principles, which in the consequence of them tended towards the subversion of the government and order, which certainly it does cherish in the highest degree of any religion in the world, and hath the most peaceable principles in matters of duty, both in subjection to our superiors, and of a charitable deportment of men one towards another: And the practice of those principles hath been seen amongst protestants, especially amongst English protestants, as much as any nation in the world; this may be said of it to this day, for the reputation of the English nation, that there is more fidelity, honesty, and generous trust amongst them, than among all the nations of the world besides; so that if a man were to go out of England to any other part of the world, he might well use the words of Demosthenes, upon his going out of Athens, at his banishment; 'Farewell, beloved city, I am going into a world where I shall not find such friends as I have had enemies here.' Friends in other places will be no better than our enemies here; the carriage of Englishmen is so much beyond all others, except the Germans, who, I must confess,

are famed for their honesty and integrity one to another; but if you take the French, the Italian, the Spaniard, or any Levantine people, they live like so many wolves, especially in those places where the popish religion is professed.[34]

Elizabeth Cellier's second unpardonable slander was her accusation of torture of Catholic prisoners in Newgate. The prosecution prepared its case carefully with this: the very people Cellier cited as victims appeared as government witnesses to testify that they had been marvelously well-treated. Baron Weston was again moved to a lecture on the general principle that hideous torture machines were relics of the dark, papist, past. "You must first know," he said, "the laws of the land do not admit a torture, and since queen Elizabeth's time there hath been nothing of that kind ever done. The truth is, indeed, in the 20th year of her reign, Campion was just stretched upon the rack, but yet not so that he could walk; but when she was told it was against the law of the land to have any of her subjects racked (though that was an extraordinary case, a world of seminaries being sent over to contrive her death, and she lived in continual danger), yet it was never done after to any one, neither in her reign, who reigned 25 years after, nor in King James' reign, who reigned 22 years after; nor in king Charles the first's reign, who reigned 24 years after; and God in heaven knows that there hath been no such thing offered in this king's reign; for I think we may say, we have lived under as lawful and merciful a government as any people whatsoever, and have had as little bloodshed, and sanguinary executions as in any nation under heaven."[35] Cellier, who had been convinced throughout her first imprisonment that she might be tortured, was apparently silenced by this outburst.

With neither case nor counsel she could hope only for the court's leniency. Rather halfheartedly she tried an unfamiliar excuse: her female insufficiency. "I desire you to consider," she said, "I am a poor ignorant woman and have erred out of ignorance: I thought nothing, but that I might publish what others had said and told me; and so I have offended in ignorance if I have offended . . . my lord, then I beseech you consider me, I am a woman, and deal with me in mercy, as well as justice." But when the unrelenting Baron Weston seized this sign of weakening to demand her admission that some of her "wicked priests" were the real authors of *Malice Defeated*, Mrs. Cellier fast dropped the poor-little-woman line. Her last ploy was a reminder that she and her family had "suffered" for the king, that she had ventured her "life through a sea and an army to serve him," and her "loyal parents" had "lost their estates for him." Baron Weston replied that His Majesty would not fail to "recompense" Cellier her due; but here, he concluded severely, "we are to proceed according to the rules of law."[36]

Elizabeth Cellier's sentence was not light. The Recorder[37] read it out:

> "Mrs. Cellier, the court doth think fit, for examples sake, that a fine of 1,000£ be put upon you; that you be committed in execution till that thousand pounds be paid; and because a pecuniary mulct is not a sufficient recompence to justice, which you have offended, the Court doth likewise pronounce against you, That you be put on the pillory three several days, in three several public places; in the first place, in regard her braided ware received its first impression and vent at her own house, it is thought fit that she stand (as near her own house as conveniently can be) between the hours of twelve and one, for an hour's space, at the May-pole, in the Strand, on the most notorious day; I think there is a market near that place, let it be on that day. At another time, that she stand in Covent-Garden on a public day the like space of time; a third time, that she stand at Charing-Cross on the most public day, for the space of an hour. And in the next place, that she find sureties for her good behavior during her life; and in every place where she shall stand on the pillory, some parcels of her books shall, in her own view, be burnt by the hands of the common hangman, and a Paper of the cause to be put upon the pillory."[38]

It had not been a good year for Elizabeth Cellier. She must have tallied up the account in her several unpleasantly inactive hours: betrayed by a scoundrel like Dangerfield; testified against even by her own maids; patronized by her old friend Gadbury (who made "all the company laugh" when he told the Court that in conversing with her he "only smiled to hear a woman's discourse");[39] deserted by the Catholic party; lectured by Protestant bigots; heavily fined (to put it in perspective, Samuel Pepys, conspicuously consuming on his way up the social ladder in the 1660s, was both gratified and appalled when he spent a thousand pounds in one year); publicly humiliated and doubtless jeered by the "Westminster rabble" she so despised.

She was now a notorious woman, and so free game for all kinds of crude sexual raillery. During her first trial the court simply assumed she had been intimate with Dangerfield, put loaded questions to her frightened maids, and left the aspersions of adultery unexplored in the record. Dangerfield himself answered *Malice Defeated* with a scurrilous pamphlet in which he described Cellier as a regular adulteress through *two* former marriages. Dangerfield liked a riot of detail: he had Cellier a whore and the madam of a whorehouse until she persuaded an elderly French merchant to be her third husband; and then nice old Peter Cellier was constantly cuckolded, with Elizabeth having an eye especially for handsome young Spaniards.[40] By this time Dangerfield was branded as an inveterate liar, but in the Restoration London of merry King Charles this sort of scandalous trash was a delight to the leering locals. Another anonymous pamphlet about the trials, though not unfriendly to Cellier, displayed her on the title page as "Midwife and Lady Errant," and had great fun with her professional self as "a Brokeresse of Buttocks":[41] a challenge surely to tavern wits for further inventiveness on the theme.

But even while she was, in Roger North's phrase, the "Entertainment of all Coffee-Houses,"[42] no one needed (or needs) to feel sorry for Elizabeth Cellier. "I know I am the talk of the Town," she wrote Gadbury (she must have reinstated him as friend), "but what do the Judicious say of me, for it is that I value, and not the prate of the Rabble."[43] Through all her "Clamor of her ill Usage"[44] she had gotten her due for "Wit and Courage": even the dangerous inquisitor Sir William Waller had granted her that; "I have as much respect for you," he told her, "as if you were my Sister, and had rather take your counsel, than any Woman's I know." To that she had replied, "I'll assure you Sir William, I will never take yours. . . ."[45]

Mrs. Cellier moved in and about the male world clear-sighted and unimpressed. Men, so wrongheaded and innately wicked as to have killed a blameless king, did not inspire her involuntary confidence. Her (fitting) profession was an important equalizer: the angle of vision of midwifery, like that of the valet, did not encourage reverential admiration. In her adolescent defiance she had chosen to be a Catholic; and though she had no choice in being a woman she elected her sex defiantly too. Or rather, she *used* it: the little-womanly-me-routine in court. And she "counterfeited a Labour," said Roger North in obvious relish;[46] in any case she employed the ultimate female weapon of pregnancy (when she had to be in her late thirties or early forties) in her legal battles. In one of her interrogations before the King's Council this exchange occurred:

A Lord. Are you with Child, Mrs. Cellier?

Cel. *Truly, my Lord, I know not certainly.*

Lord. You say so in your Letter, and that it will keep you from any Stricter examination.

Cel. *No my Lord, I have no reason to think so, this is a time in which no Compassion is shown to Sex, Age, nor Condition.*[47]

She used her sex too, more precisely her legal nonexistence as wife, in a prime comedy scene when badgered by Sir William Waller to take the Oath of Supremacy and Allegiance, that is, not only to the king but to the Anglican church. Mrs. Cellier said: "Have you any Authority to offer it to me? . . . I am a Foreign Merchants Wife, and my Husband, both by the General Law of Nations, and those of this Kingdom, ought to remain unmolested both in his Liberty and Property, till a breach happen between the two Crowns, and the King hath declared as much in his Royal Proclamation, and if you violate the Priviledges my Husband ought to have as a Merchant-stranger, the King of *France*, whose Subject my Husband is, has an Ambassador here, by whom we will complain to His Majesty, and I hope we shall obtain Redress."[48]

Is it 'and yet' or 'because of' her assertion of her femininity that Elizabeth Cellier took one of the first positions of feminism before Mary Astell? She was a contemporary of Pepys's wife (bored, tearful, jealous Elizabeth Pepys) and of Aphra Behn. She spoke to them both in the postscript to *Malice Defeated*:

> And as to my own Sex, I hope they will pardon the Errors of my Story, as well as those bold Attempts of mine that occasion'd it, since in what I meddled with . . . though it may be thought too Masculine, yet was it the effects of my Loyal (more than Religious) Zeal to gain Proselites to his [Charles's] Service.
>
> And in all my defence, none can truly say but that I preserv'd the Modesty, though not the Timorousness common to my Sex. And I believe there is none, but had they been in my Station, would, to their power, have acted like me; for it is more our business than mens to fear, and consequently to prevent the Tumults and Troubles Factions tend to, since we by nature are hindered from sharing any part but the Frights and Disturbances of them.[49]

The last we hear of Elizabeth Cellier was her proposal to her proper king, James II, published and presented to him in 1687 and found later in his papers. In a professional and wholly apolitical spirit she urged the royal foundation of a training and lying-in hospital. Thousands of women and babies had died in the last twenty years, she wrote, "for want of due skill and care, in those women who practice the art of midwifery." Hers was an enlightened viewpoint, but she did not suggest turning obstetrics over to male specialists: in fact, male physicians were to enter the hospital only as irregular and controlled consultants. She wanted to create under government supervision a corporation of the "whole number of skilful midwives," who would staff the establishment and train girl-apprentices, perhaps

"Foundlings," until the age of twenty-one and a licensed medical proficiency.[50] But that is a different chapter in the life of the intriguing and independent Cellier.[51]

NOTES

1. *Cobbett's Complete Collection of State Trials* (London, 1810), 7: 1184.

2. *Dictionary of National Biography* (hereafter *DNB*).

3. *The Popish Plot, Taken out of Several Depositions Made and Sworn before the Parliament* (London, 1680); *Reasons for the Indictment of the Duke of York, Presented to the Grand Jury of Middlesex* (London, 1680); *The Humble Relation and Address of the Rt. Honourable the Lord Mayor, Aldermen and Commons of the City of London* (1681).

4. *The Tryal and Condemnation of William Stalay for High-Treason* (London, 1678).

5. *Calendar of State Papers Domestic* (1679-80), p. 21.

6. Robert Halstead, *Succinct Genealogies of the Noble and Ancient Houses* (London, 1685), pp. 434-35.

7. Ibid.

8. Elizabeth Cellier, *Malice Defeated, Or, a brief Relation of the Accusation and Deliverance of Elizabeth Cellier* (London, 1680), p. 2.

9. Daniel Lysons, *Magna Britannia* (London, 1806), 1: 468, and "Additions and Corrections," 695.

10. Cellier, *Malice Defeated*, p. 1; *State Trials*, 7: 1198, 1203.

11. Lysons, *Magna Britannia*, 1: 665-66.

12. Cellier, *Malice Defeated*, p. 31; but some of the Dormers must have been Catholics during the civil wars: see Rushworth, *Historical Collections*, 5: 42, for mention of "Mr. Dormer, a professed Papist"; and *Exceeding Joyfull Newes from Varley* (London, 1642), E.118(13), about "Master Dormer, a great Papist. . . ."

13. Cellier, *Malice Defeated*, pp. 8-12.

14. Ibid., pp. 12-14.

15. Ibid., p. 14.

16. *State Trials*, 7: 1055, 1063-64.

17. Ibid., 1064; Roger North, *Examen, or, an Enquiry into the Credit and Veracity of a Pretended Complete History, shewing the Perverse and Wicked Design of it* (London, 1740), p. 260.

18. *State Trials*, 7: 1063.

19. Cellier, *Malice Defeated*, pp. 15-18.

20. Mrs. Cellier apparently wore to her interrogations a cloak or tippet with face-concealing hood, or a "loose limp hood." One can only guess her reasons: for dramatic effect, perhaps, or to emphasize the discomforts prison life imposed upon a gentlewoman. In any case the headgear was unfashionable: "To go bare-headed out of doors as well as in was much the fasion" (C. Willett and Phillis Cunnington, *Handbook of English Costume in the Seven-*

teenth Century (London, 1955), p. 179); see also, F. M. Kelly and R. Schwabe, *Historic Costume* (New York, 1968), p. 175; and *Life and Letters in Tudor and Stuart England*, ed. L. B. Wright and Virginia A. LaMar (Ithaca, N.Y., 1958), pp. 392-93.

21. *Malice Defeated*, pp. 18-19.
22. Ibid., p. 21
23. Ibid., pp. 21-22.
24. Ibid., pp. 23, 28-29.
25. Ibid., p. 32.
26. Ibid.
27. Ibid., p. 34 (misnumbered).
28. Ibid., pp. 39-41; *State Trials*, 7: 1054.
29. Cellier, *Malice Defeated*, p. 42.
30. North, *Examen*, p. 264.
31. *State Trials*, 7: 1184.
32. Ibid., 1188.
33. Ibid., 1191, 1203.
34. Ibid., 1204.
35. Ibid., 1205.
36. Ibid., 1203.
37. This was Sir George Jeffreys, soon to be the Hanging Judge of Monmouth's rebels.
38. *State Trials*, 7: 1208-9.
39. Ibid., 1046.
40. Thomas Dangerfield, *Answer to a Certain Scandalous Lying Pamphlet Entituled Malice Defeated* (London, 1680).
41. *Modesty triumphing over Impudence, or Some Notes upon a late Romance published by Elizabeth Cellier, Midwife and Lady Errant* (London, 1680), p. 129.
42. North, *Examen*, p. 264.
43. Cellier, *Malice Defeated*, p. 24.
44. North, *Examen*, p. 264.
45. Cellier, *Malice Defeated*, p. 26.
46. North, *Examen*, p. 264.
47. Cellier, *Malice Defeated*, p. 24.
48. Ibid., p. 16.
49. Ibid., p. 32.
50. E. Cellier, "A Scheme for the Foundation of a Royal Hospital," *Harleian Miscellany* (London, 1809), 4: 142.
51. It might be useful, or at least tidy, to report the fate of Mrs. Cellier's rascally enemy. Her other opponents are well enough known: Sir William Waller, implicated in the Rye House plot in 1688; Scroggs, who as Lord Chief Justice turned the king's man and so angered the Exclusionists that they tried to impeach him; Sir George Jeffreys, the recorder who had read out Mrs. Cellier's pillory sentence, and the scourge of the west county Monmouth rebels in his "bloody assizes," who after riding high as James's Lord Chan-

cellor died an alcoholic death in prison in 1689. But the passing of the common felon, Thomas Dangerfield, is a bit of historical trivia, worth a line in the *DNB*, but only barely.

Dangerfield's end was gruesome and painful. If Mrs. Cellier was the "magnanimous midwife" Roger North jestingly called her, she would not have wished it for him. He had been tried and convicted of libel against the king immediately upon James II's accession to the throne in 1685: final unraveling of the schemes of 1680. He had been whipped from Newgate to Tyburn, and was being returned in a coach when a pedestrian, Mr. Robert Frances, barrister of Gray's Inn, stepped alongside and asked Dangerfield "in a jeering manner, whether he had run his heat that day?" Understandably touchy, Dangerfield answered, you "Son of a whore." Whereupon Mr. Frances, "having a small cane in his hand, thrust it into his eye with all his force"; in hideous suffering Dangerfield lingered either two hours or two days—the sources do not agree on the time. And the postscript to *that* story was that Robert Frances was tried for murder, with witnesses testifying at the trial that Dangerfield and Mrs. Frances had been having an affair; though the king was urged to clemency in the case of so loyal a subject, the piteous Frances was convicted and hung. See *Howell's Collection of State Trials* (London, 1811), 11: 503-10.

PART 3

Of Private Lives

7

"Happy" Women, Extraordinary Models

Upon the death in 1658 of Mrs. Mary Bewley, an "eminent Gentle-woman," though "not generally known," the Reverend Doctor (Ed-ward) Reynolds published a short eulogy. Dr. Reynolds "recom-mended" his *Imitation and Caution for Christian Women* to the reader with the observation that "Reverend Divines" in England elsewhere had long "judged it expedient and useful to propose some women as patterns to others." Therefore his eulogy was offered to "publick view" not "so much out of private affection" for the obscure Mrs. Bewley, "but chiefly to illustrate the glory of God, and to edifie the living . . . so many of her sex as shall find leisure to read this short narrative. . . ."[1]

Dr. Reynolds's lesson of inspirational reading for Christian women began with bibliography. On page 2, prefacing his text, was this list of suggested works: the Rev. Samuel Clarke's "Examples, and second vol. of lives"; "The womans glory by Mr. [Samuel] Torshel"; *The English Gentlewoman*, by Richard Brathwaite; "Opera Anna Maria Aschurman . . ."; "The Ladies vindication by Mr. [Charles] Gerbier"; "Mrs. Bretterghs life and death subjoyned to the Two Funeral Ser-mons preached at her burial, by Mr. Harrison, and Mr. Leigh"; "The holy life and Christian death of Mrs. Stubs"; "Two Funeral Sermons of Mr. Gataker, the one at the Funeral of Mrs. Rebecca Crisp, the other at the Funeral of Dr. Featlies wife"; "Mr. Nicholas Guy, his Narration of the life and death of Dr. Gouges wife"; "Mrs. Drake revived, showing her strange case and cure, printed 1647"; "Mr. Josselin at the Funeral of Mrs. Harlakenden"; "The life and death of Mrs. Ratcliffe of Chester, by Mr. Ley, one of the Assembly"; "Mr. Robinsons Sermon, at Mrs. Bernidistons Funeral . . . Mr. Mantons at Mrs. Blackwels . . . Mr. Calamies at Mrs. Moors . . . Mr. Roberts at Mrs. Jacksons of Bristol"; "Mr. Shawes Narrative of his wifes life and death, recommended to the Reader by the Epistles of Mr. Manton, Mr. Heathcoat, Mr. Pool, and the consolatory verses of Mr. Jenkin";

"Mr. Thomas Goodwins Sermon at the Funeral of Lady Barrington";
"Mr. Greenhill on Ezekiel, vol. first, his Epistle Dedicatory to the
late Princess Elizabeth . . . and the many Epistles Dedicatory to Ladies
and Gentlewomen in his Epistle before Mrs. Shawes life."

Dr. Reynolds's pamphlet, with its additional teaching aids, is very
interesting. Here in 1658, after a century of work of the great "domesticall" clerics—Thomas Becon, William Perkins, Robert Cleaver,
William Gouge, Matthew Griffith—successor divines were still hard
at it, still endeavoring to shape the female for the glory of God. Dr.
Reynolds's list of further reading has, however, some special features.
Apparently the older books for the instruction of women, the 'bokes'
of matrimony and *Christian Oeconomie* and "Domestical Duties,"
were too familiar to require citation. And only three of the cited works
were abstract treatises. Two of those were slanting reminders of the
'Great Debate,' the "Popular Controversy over Women,"[2] which had
raged intermittently (and entertainingly) for a hundred years: the
Reverend Samuel Torshell's *The Womans Glorie*, in second edition
by 1650; and Charles Gerbier's *The Praise of Worthy Women*, first
published in 1651. (The debate was hardly over, given the ancient
roots of the notion of the inherent wickedness of the daughters of
Eve; one of the most furious misogynist expressions, Joseph Swetnam's *The Araignment of lewd, idle, forward, and constant Women*,
thrived in new editions, seven, perhaps eight, into the eighteenth
century.)[3] The third, Richard Brathwaite's *The English Gentlewoman*,
stands oddly alone on the list: a sort of recipe-guide to virtuous success
and successful virtue, it was the profitable pamphlet of a secular and
popular essayist. The rest of the works in Dr. Reynolds's bibliography
were about real people, or more precisely, about recently living women
"eminent" in that they were gentlewomen of middle-class respectability and as otherwise generally unknown as Mrs. Mary Bewley (the
wife of a rich London merchant, both wife and husband members of
the church of Samuel Clarke, author of the cited "Examples, and
second vol. of lives," and Pastor "in Bennet Fink, London").[4]

Dr. Reynolds seems to have been saying that in this second century
of social reformation 'ordinary' women had achieved the self-gen-
eration of models, and further that any woman with "leisure" (a
loaded word implying the status of Anglican/Presbyterian families
and the privileged access to bookshelves well-stocked with serious
literature) could emulate them. The seeding work of the Reverend
Divines was now fruitfully multiplying in the heart and minds of
women themselves. The ideal had descended to the mundane, and

was producing a saintly succession of women whose lives radiated fulfillment, and even, in this 'vale of tears,' happiness.

When we go (dutifully, as instructed) to the cited eulogies and funeral sermons, we find them a male medium, morality plays produced and staged by the divines. In the first survey we find in them a structural sameness: the soaring point is always the "coelestial Felicity," the "Triumphs in Glory," of the dear Departed Ones.[5] Sometimes we find the ministers taking over entirely: the renowned Thomas Gataker (himself an expert 'domesticall' teacher) in one of the cited "Two Sermons" filling pages with a text on "Deaths Advantage," the "Benefit of Death," and the "good cause and great cause" of every Christian "to desire death"; and compressing the living years of his subject, his kinswoman Mrs. Rebekka Crisp, into a few phrases about the "Piety and Patience" which made her end "so sweet, so cheerfull, so comfortable."[6] Never will we find unguarded revelation of petty details in the life of the deceased, most especially from husbands who were also preacher-eulogizers: the Good was always the True. (Had he survived Elizabeth, his wife, the Manchester minister Henry Newcome might well have preached a moving tribute to her almost fifty years of marital perfection. To his diary he had confined the blemishes: "I was exceedingly perplexed about my wife," he wrote in 1652, "God knows what I should do. These four years have I now lived with her, and do not know how to humour her. When she is angry, I do aggravate her passion by saying anything. . . . When she is patient, peace is so sweet to me that I dare not speak lest I should lose it. . . . I must confess I think all women to be thus weak. . . .")[7]

Men talking about women, defining female goodness and happiness through selected parts of the lives of the holy corpses before them, such in content and in form are the funeral sermons and eulogies. There is no reason to suppose, of course, that had they been able to memorialize one another women would have done it differently. The females so chosen for distinction were cultural heroines because they had in their individual circumstances attempted to live (or at least to die) in undistracted consciousness of the mercy of God; so long as religion was in fashion, to paraphrase Lucy Hutchinson, other women of their class and status could ignore them only at the cost of emotional and mental peace. What is impossible to know is from what perspective, with what mediated personal experiences, unmarked and indistinguishable women readers both interpreted and internalized the male-framed examples of these Protestant "patterns."

The Mrs. Shaw whose eulogy Dr. Reynolds cited toward the end of his reading list (the proper title was *Mistris Shawe's Tomb-stone, or the Saints Remains*, published in 1658) was Dorothy, "dearly beloved wife of Mr. John Shaw, Preacher of the Gospell at Kingstone upon Hull." Mrs. Shaw "sweetly slept in the Lord, Decemb. 10th, and was interred at Trinity Church, in Hull, Decemb. 12, 1657." She was mourned by husband and six daughters, and by family and friends all over the Midlands; her husband addressed her eulogy to kindred and acquaintances "in Kingston, Derbyshire, Cutthorp, Somersall, and in Yorkshire at Penistone, York, Sickhouse, Hal-broom, Brom-head, Rotherham, and in Lancashire, Manchester, Alding-hum, &c." Mr. Shaw added to the publication as well letters of condolence from brother ministers in London: the "Epistles" of Mr. Manton, "Mr. Heath-coat," Mr. Pool, Mr. Jenkin, Mr. Thomas Goodwin. The wide lamentation upon Dorothy Shaw's death was testament to her strength and purpose, to what must have been a 'happy' life as a doing, sharing, engaged minister's wife.

Dorothy Shaw was eldest of the eight children of Mr. George Heath-cote of Cutthorpe-Hall in the parish of Brampton in Derbyshire. She was early such a seeker that she ignored the "reading Minister" in Brampton and went every Sunday two miles to Chesterfield to hear a "faithful Preacher" at a "private house"; it was her pressure upon the spokesmen of the godly community which brought a "faithful and powerful Preacher" to Brampton. She married John Shaw in 1632, and journeyed with him as he made his name as a dissenter from Ripon to Rotherham in Yorkshire. When the civil wars began Shaw was hunted as a traitor by the king's forces. His church in Rotherham was invaded by royalists; Mrs. Shaw was "hurried towards prison" while her husband, the enemy searching for him "narrowly," hid in the steeple, their house being "plundered" to "the full." Through it Dorothy Shaw was "a special help to her Husband, for saving his life and liberty" in those "troublesome times," and a "chearful sufferer with him, to the hazarding of her health, liberty and life. . . ."[8]

"She was a knowing Christian," John Shaw said, "for her Sex." Mrs. Shaw had decided opinions on the battles of the 1640s and 1650s, a Lucy Hutchinson-like keenness about religious disputes and factionalism. "She could never like of womens preaching," wrote her husband, "and yet her life was a continual Sermon." She was "sound in the doctrine of Religion," which meant that she rejected Independency, was sharp with Anabaptists, and "sore grieved at the dangerous errours lately spread in these Nations." A good Presbyterian, she was suspicious of "men out of their place." She "was clear for a needfull seperation in a Church, but not, for a needlesse seperation from a Church," and would "often say, that if those who seperated from us, (some of whom she had dear affection to . . .) would have joyned with us, to have purged out the cursed errours that broke in upon us . . . we might have been much purer and more reformed ere now. . . ."[9]

Mr. Shaw did not remember that in twenty-five years of marriage Dorothy "did ever do any thing that she thought might offend him"; whatever his "just desire" she fulfilled it, and "if she at any time saw him displeased, she would meekly hold her peace, till she saw a fit opportunity, to give him all just satisfaction." And yet: "She would oftentimes presse her Husband to act vigorously for God, and to go boldly, and thorough-stitch in Gods work." Shaw consulted her about his professional affairs, for example, "desired (as usually) to know her mind" when he was offered "a place of very great preferment" away from Hull where he had "much work, and very little pay." Mrs. Shaw's advice, which he took, was to remain in Hull: "I will go with you any where chearfully," she said, "as I have hitherto done, through Darbishire, Devonshire, Yorkshire, &c, but I mainly desire, that you would only look herein at this end, where you think, that God may have most honour by you, and let no other by-end whatever, move you at all, God having never put us to any straits, for temporal estate." She was "a great Comforter," Shaw observed, and "would quickly so cheer up his spirit" that he would find "his muddy bitter waters, turned into wine."[10]

Dorothy Shaw was the devoted mother of six daughters, but no special point was made of her domesticity or home confinement. She much "rejoyced" in the "Company" of people, even "the poorest godly man or woman." In Hull she was "most tender" of the "poor people in the Charter-house, both for their bodies and souls, and was daily conferring with, and inviting of them, and seeing them supplyed." She was a woman of sympathy and warmth who gave love, one would guess, unstintingly, even though it pricked her conscience. She spoke to her husband "often" to "this purpose": "I am afraid that we do too much love one another, and take from God, that which is due. . . ."[11]

Most of the women eulogized in sermons on Dr. Reynolds's list were mature, at least one dying after late childbirth, a few apparently old, succumbing to long and painful illnesses.[12] The youngest were both Elizabethans: Katherine Stubbes, who died at age twenty in 1591; and Katherine Brettergh (or Bretterg or Brettargh), dead at twenty-two in 1601. Both were thus special models, appealing to succeeding generations of the very young. Mistress Stubbes's eulogy—not precisely a sermon—written by her husband as *A Chrystal Glasse for Christian Women*, had seven editions by 1647. Dr. Reynolds considered the story of Katherine Brettergh so important that he listed it twice: in Samuel Clarke's "Examples" (from his *Second Part of the Marrow of Ecclesiastical History*), and in the published funeral sermon by "Mr. Harrison and Mr. Leigh" (which was in its fifth edition by 1617).[13]

Katherine Stubbes was the "rarest Paragon in the world," according to her husband, Philip Stubbes, one of the fiercest Puritan writers of the turn of the century, author of the famous and fiery *Anatomie of Abuses*. In that work, Stubbes censured along with other detestable abuses in "Ailgna" (i.e., Anglia) the "apparell" of women, "wearing dublets and Jerkins," their faces bedaubed "with certain oyles, liquors, unguents and waters made to that end," fingers "decked with gold, silver, and precious stones," and "holes in their eares, to hang rings and Jewels by"; their "soules," he was sure, were "thereby deformed."[14] The thirty-year-old Stubbes could be content that his fifteen-year-old bride Katherine indulged in none of these vices.

In Philip Stubbes's "Glasśe" Katherine glowed with youthful purity and innocence. Daughter of rich Londoners, "honest and wealthie parents" who were "zealous in the truth, and of a sound religion," she had been a Puritan prodigy, seldom found "without a bible, or some other good booke in her hands," indeed "ravished" she seemed in her thirsting after God's word.

As wife Katherine Stubbes surpassed mere goodness. She never lied, scolded or "brawled," nor was her "conversation" other than sweet. She "utterly abhorred all kinde of pride both in apparrell, and otherwise." She "rarely went abroad with any, either to banquet or feast, to gossip or make merry." And when Philip was away "not the dearest friend she had in the world" could entice her out "to dinner or supper." Uncaring for "things of this lyfe" Katherine Stubbs concentrated upon God—and her husband. If she saw the latter "to be merry, then she was merry"; if "he were heavy or passionate, she would endeavour to make him glad . . . if he were angry she would quickly please him"; she "would never contrary him in any thing, but by wise counsell and sage advice with all humilitie and submission seeke to persuade him."[15]

The Stubbeses had one baby, a boy, after whose birth Katherine pronounced that she would "never beare more children." Speculation is useless: no explanation was given about the pregnancy, the lying-in, the health of the child, the mother's pain, joy, whatever: only the familiar and ominous words that in days she was ill of an "exceeding hot and burning quotidian ague."

Kindred and friends gathered at the request of the dying girl, barely twenty, to hear her confession of faith. She directed her own death scene in a rapturous state, "smiled and laughed" at her visions of "heavenly sights." But she was marvelously rational as she spoke of her belief in the Father, Son, and Holy Ghost, and meditated upon the predestination of the "Soules of all the Elect children of God." In choosing some for salvation, she was sure, God shows his "unspeakable mercie, grace, favour and love"; and in damning the rest he shows "his power, his justice and judgement." If "two debtors owe me a thousand pounds," she said, "I can release one and make the other pay"; this was as the "justice of God."[16]

Mirrored in seven editions of Philip's eulogy Katherine Stubbes might have been the focus of thousands of adoring and teary young faces, model of, model for, the romantically religion-struck.

Katherine Brettergh was a virtuous young woman too, "blameless in her whole course," said the ministers at her funeral. Perhaps the feature that Dr. Reynolds, from the distance of fifty-odd years, liked particularly in her short story was that she and her husband had to live as Calvinist pariahs on the family estate in Lancashire, near Liverpool, surrounded by "ignorant, and brutish Papists" who were "always doing some wrong, and injury" to their parks and livestock. Or perhaps he found instructional in Katherine Brettergh's "pattern" the fact that before she died in glory she had moments of doubt of God's mercy and grace.

From our very great distance Katherine Brettergh's sparse biography has several intriguing points. Like Katherine Stubbes she was a prodigy: the studious daughter of "Master John Bruen, of Bruen-Stapleford" in Cheshire, she had so early "walked before [God] with an upright heart" that at her marriage she was well prepared in "knowledge, patience, mildness, and constancy for the Truth." As with Katherine Stubbes her husband was chosen for her, but she did not approach him in humility and submission. "Sin was so hatefull to her," said her funeral sermonizers, "that she would grieve for it, both in her self and others," including Master Brettergh. One Sunday riding to church with her husband, she heard him "angry with his man"; she said to him, "Alas Husband, I fear your heart is not right towards God, that can be thus angry for a trifle," and, weeping, added, "you must pray against your passions, and always be sure your anger be for God, else how dare you appear this day before his Minister, and offer up your prayers in the publike Congregation before God?" On another occasion a tenant of her husband's was tardy with his rent: Mistress Brettergh prevailed in granting the man "a quarter of a year longer" and when the tenant brought the money Katherine "with tears" told her husband, "I fear you do not do well to take it of him, though it be your right, for I doubt he is not well able to pay it, and then you oppress the poor."[17]

In her second year of marriage Katherine Brettergh took violently ill (she had had a baby but the illness does not seem to have been puerperal fever). The sickness came unpredictably in "fits" during which she talked "idlie"; by "Satans subtilty," said her clerical biographers, "she began to fall into an heavie conflict of Spirit." The biographers almost identify the cause of Mistress Brettergh's distress: her illness she felt a sign of the "severity of Gods justice," that is, a withdrawal of God's grace from her. Bitterly, she blamed herself: accused herself of "pride," that she had "delighted in herself, and her beauty too much"; then "she thought that she had no faith, but was an hypocrite, and one that had not imbraced Religion so sincerely, nor glorified God so carefully, especially with her tongue, nor loved him so fervently as she should have done." In her sinfulness, she cried, she was "a disgrace to Religion, and a shame to her Husband, Kindred, and all true Christians." She dwelt upon "the originall corruption of her nature . . . She wished that she had never been born, or that she had been made any other Creature, rather than a woman . . . a weak, wofull, a wretched, a forsaken woman. . . ."[18]

With the help of husband and friends Katherine Brettergh recovered, not from the illness, but from the satanic lure of loss of faith. She lingered briefly in blissful belief, lay with "a cheerful countenance, as one ravished in her spirit," her tongue overflowing "with the praises of God": "I confess before the Lord his loving kindness," she avowed, "and his wonderful works before the sons of men, for he hath satisfied my soul, & filled my hungry soul with goodness. . . . now I perceive, and feel, that the countenance of Christ my Redeemer is turned towards me, and the bright-shining beams of his mercy are spread over me. . . . happy am I that ever I was born to see this blessed day. . . ." And "presently" she "fell asleep in the Lord, passing a way in peace, without any motion of body at all."[19]

Perhaps it was her youth (or her intelligence) which made Katherine Brettergh question God's purposes in sending her sickness and creating her female. If Dr. Reynolds's readers preferred examples of perfect acquiescence through a longer life they found a lovely model in Elizabeth Gouge. Of course, nothing less than female perfection would have been expected in the wife of that towering Puritan divine, Mr. (Dr., after 1628) William Gouge, pastor of Blackfriars in London and author of many works, including his summary of key sermons,

Of Domesticall Duties. Upon her death of the "Dropsie" after "travail and weakenesse in Childbed," Mrs. Gouge's domestical qualities were given public acclaim in the funeral sermon preached by the Reverend Nicholas Guy.

Elizabeth Gouge too came from a family of "very good note and name," her father a "Mercer and Citizen of London of good worth." She was raised, after the death of her parents, in the "pious, painfull, faithfull" house of a minister in Essex, growing there in "pietie" and "modestie." Her guardians and William Gouge's father arranged her marriage, in 1603, but she and William took "a liking one of another." By the only words directly attributed to her in the funeral sermon Elizabeth Gouge was pleased with her assignment to a student-divine: "as of all other callings," she had said, "I most desire an Husband, being otherwise well qualified, of that function."[20]

Elizabeth Gouge "did much grace her Husbands vocation." Her marital life was apparently unruffled by the gathering storms in Stuart England. (Though a thundering Puritan in the pulpit William Gouge was only briefly at odds with Archbishop Laud in the 1620s; even as "father of the London ministers" and a declared Presbyterian in the 1640s he took no political stand in the civil war divisions.)[21] In obedience to Saint Paul and in "all dutiful respect" to her husband Elizabeth Gouge exhibited the "commendable vertues of keeping at home, and keeping silence," unlike those Mr. Gouge "sharply" reproved for "wandering about from house to house, and for being not only idle, but tatlers also and busie-bodies." She was a woman of "retirednesse, and taciturnitie."[22]

Necessarily the Revered Guy dwelt upon Mistress Gouge's homely preoccupations. She spent time reading—and had a "pretty Library"—and supervising the devotional exercises of her children and servants, all of whom she kept "in dutiful awe." She displayed "indefatigable sedulity" in the tasks of "good house-wifery": with "her owne fingers" she made all the "Vallances, Cup-bord cloathes . . . besides all her owne, husbands, and childrens wearing linnen"; and if the days were short she and her maids stayed at their work in candlelight. In ordering the affairs of her house "prudently and providently" she observed the natural and godly division of marital responsibilities. She was "very careful" over Mr. Gouge, "that both well to nourish and cherish him, and also to free him from the trouble of all those things which shee in her place could manage"; accordingly the Reverend Gouge "had the more leisure to attend his publicke functions." Exhausting such biographical data, Nicholas Guy resorted to appropriate adjectives: Elizabeth Gouge was a "pious, prudent, provident, painfull, carefull, faithfull, helpfull, grave, modest, sober, tender, loving Wife, Mother, Mistris, Neighbour." And almost needless to add, she stretched "out her hands to the poore."[23]

Mrs. Gouge produced thirteen babies in twenty years of marriage. In his authoritative work on "Domestical Duties" her husband obliquely discussed sexual relations. The "marriage bed" was "undefiled," he said, and activities there, while not to be "in excesse," were a "debt" to be paid, husband to wife, wife to husband, "readily and cheerefully," in "delight" and "goodwill."[24] Elizabeth Gouge paid her debts. She also nursed "with her owne milke" seven of her children, "as many as she could," as another "bounden dutie." And after the thirteenth birth, afflicted with the "Dropsie," she died, apparently as silently as she had lived. Nicholas Guy preached that her end was an "honour." Elizabeth Gouge died "in her calling," as a "Souldier" in "battell," even as "a Preacher in the Pulpit." It was recorded in the Scriptures, Pastor Guy concluded, that women who die in childbirth "dye as Saints," and so "undoubtedly did this pious Matron."[25]

Certainly the imitable Elizabeth Gouge was everything that a woman should be; and her virtues could not too often be held high, to those City wives, for example, who sometimes "murmured" and shifted in their seats when the Reverend Gouge lectured them on their domestical duties (to "subject themselves to husbands as to Christ," as the start).[26] But if his own contribution is suggestive evidence, Dr. Reynolds favored the stories of women who had struggled with temptation, with weakness or sin, before crossing over to transcendent saintliness, as had his "pattern," the London merchant's wife, Mary Bewley.

Until her final months Mistress Bewley had lived as blameless a life as the best of women, sound in religion, a loving and obedient daughter, a conscientious, devoted, and submissive wife; she gave respect to her friends and charity to the poor. But unseen she had allowed to swell in herself a fault: an excessive love for her only son, Thomas, Jr. In 1658 eighteen-year-old Thomas did not survive an attack of smallpox. His mother was devastated: she "lost appetite to her food, and sleep departed from her eyes, and by day she neither could nor would use any diversions"; she "pored" over her son's death, and "the small circumstances thereof," imputing it "one while to this, another while to that omission. . . ." Thus she became a "warning to Christian members"; she "did not speedily and chearfully submit to the will of God," and acquiesce "in his declared good pleasure." Worse, in the selfishness of her grieving she did not "withstand" the "subtle and cruel Adversary," who "play'd his game" with her through "his injections and phantasmes. . . ." In such wickedness Mary Bewley "made way for her sicknesse and death," contracting a "malignant feaver, and vapours of the mother, followed with convulsion fits."[27]

But "Imitation" as well as "Caution," Mary Bewley's story had a holy conclusion. Her family and friends about her in her illness, in her "great bodily pain," she was able to turn back the "slie, roaring and cowardly Divel," to overcome him with "the Lamb of God." She "freely confessed all her sinnes," made her everlasting peace in earnest prayer, and finally rested, "satisfied in great calmnesse of minde." Her death followed that of son Thomas by two months, and she was buried beside him in his grave.[28]

The foregoing eulogies pale as mere sketches in comparison with one last cautionary tale from Dr. Reynolds's bibliography. Published in 1646, *Trodden Down Strength, or Mrs Drake Revived* was a book-length narrative, that space necessary to describe, in the words of the subtitle, the "strange and rare Case" of the subject's journey to her sanctified end. Frequently apologizing for his care, the writer felt compelled by bafflement to set down everything he knew about Mrs. Drake; and as he was an "eye-witnessing Actor in all her Tragick-Comedy" that was a lot. The story he told was on its high pitch a spiritual drama, a contest between divinity and darkness, with the purposeful point of the eulogy. And it was a history of an unhappy woman, "for tenne years together" on the edge of mental breakdown, frequently self-destructive and alternating between depressed withdrawal and aggressive hysteria.[29]

The writer of *Trodden Down Strength* cloaked himself as the "Relator," Joan Drake's "sometimes unworthy friend," or in title page signature, "Hart On-hi." His identity has been murky, the second edition of the book in 1654 attributed to a John Hart, perhaps the "obscure Scottish divine." Recent research persuasively proposes him as Jasper Hartwell, a barrister of the Middle Temple who had rooms, as the Relator did, in White Friars, whose letters to various eminent ministers about Mrs. Drake have survived, and who had close friendships with some of the clerics brought into the "Case."[30] But we will keep him the "Relator" in the following reproduction, recalling less his personal identity than the fact that he was a male—a sensitive male—observing and interpreting the prolonged "distemper" of a woman, prescribing and helping other males to carry on her treatment, and cataloguing his male perceptions of her "cure." It will be worth remembering too that his "little book," though "almost forgotten" now, still impresses male-historians for its selected em-

phases, its observation and interpretation, its "psychological perception."[31]

The Relator began his narrative with unusually fine details of Joan
Drake's life and personality. She was the daughter and "only Heire
apparent" of "that worthy Gentleman" William Tothill, Esquire, pur-
chaser of prime manors in Amersham, Buckinghamshire, and "one
of the six Clerks of Chancery," holding that lucrative office (it sometimes sold for £6,000 in the seventeenth century) from 1598 until
his death in 1626. Her mother was Catherine Denham, sister of the
Sir John Denham who became lord chief justice of the king's bench
in Ireland, and aunt of the poet of the same name.[32] Besides "excellent
breeding" and the expectation of "very great fortune" Mistress Joan
had a "too great indulgence" from her parents in her youth, by her
"own confession," said the Relator; this permissiveness "occasioned
so much sorrow unto her in her riper years," he added, "receiving
then no correction at all"[33] (that remark left to the reader's imagination).

Yet about 1605-6 these too-indulgent parents arranged a marriage
for daughter-heiress Joan without her consent, "against her will," the
Relator wrote, appending his opinion that this was "a great over-sight
in Parents." For this it was, he declared, "which first bred in her the
foundation of those stormes and tempests, which in time were in
danger to have overthrown her."

As a healthy young woman Joan Tothill was "of a low well com-
pacted stature, of a lovely browne complexion," and "a full nimble
quick Sparrow-hawk eye." She had "a naturall joviall constitution"
only "accidentally melancholy"; she was "full of love, curtesie, mercy
and meekness." Her "wit" was "nimble quick . . . tender-hearted,
free and bountiful . . . the freest alive from all hypocrisie." She wore
"her worst side outmost, being plaine, true and tender open-hearted,
modest, easily drawn with love and good words; but if opposed, stour,
stern and inflexible . . . resolute in her undertakings, valewing even
then reall goodnesse where shee saw it in any without hypocrisie,
detesting shewes without substance. . . ."

The marriage negotiated by the Tothill parents was with Francis
Drake, Esquire, of Esher in Surrey, "a worthy fine Gentleman," said
the Relator, "of good birth, parts and fortunes."[34] Perhaps the parents'
eyes were on the parts and fortunes. Francis Drake was then or soon
would be "a gentleman of the Privy-Chamber of James I"; he had
inherited from his father, a Richard Drake who was an equerry of
Queen Elizabeth, the rich manor of Esher (the Duke of Newcastle
would own it in the eighteenth century, then Lord Clive; Princess

Charlotte and Leopold of Belgium later possessed it, and ex-King Louis Phillippe of France lived there, post-1848).[35] But Mistress Joan "could not affect" Francis Drake, possibly saw in him show without substance.

Though "obedient and dutiful" her forced marriage "stuck close" with Joan Drake. For a decade she tried to conceal her unhappiness: in her "strength of spirit and joviall temper" she distracted herself with "merry company" and "divers journeyes." Distraction was futile: "secretly" a "habit of sadnesse" grew in her, persisting even in "midst of her mirth with her friends."

Joan Drake was not then, observed the Relator, "acquainted with the power of godliness," though unconsciously she had it "in admiration." That is to say, she did not in her silent despair turn to God; in fact casting about for relief she would "jest" with the "worser sort" of people, making fun of sound and sober Christians. But the Relator had heard that she would sometimes "open her selfe" to her waiting women "in this strange presaging manner": "Doest thou see these people, some of whom I doe so jeare at and vex? of my conscience I shall one day ere I die, bee one of them; for those of them who are right, are the only happy soules."[36]

In the Relator's somewhat confusing chronology, "not long after her marriage "Joan Drake was "brought to bed of a daughter." Rather, this was after ten years of marriage, during which she had born two sons.[37] But the delivery of the girl-child was traumatic: "being much wronged by her Midwife, shee was ever after troubled with fumes and scurvie vapors mounting up unto her head, which bred in her for the most part a continuall head-ach, like unto a megrum, together with somewhat like unto a fire continually burning at her stomack, which no physick could remove, or was not Gods pleasure it should. . . ." She seemed to recover, and with her "usuall strength of spirit and chearefull disposition" pretended that all was well; but weakness and pain worked explosively upon her "sad thoughts."

Mrs. Tothill (mother and father had come to Esher to be with their daughter in her lying-in) told the Relator of Mistress Joan's first hysterical episode. The mother was wakened at night by "terrible shricks & out-cryes," and her daughter's voice screaming that *shee was undone, undone, shee was damned, and a cast-away, and so of necessity must needs goe to Hell"*; when Mrs. Tothill rushed to her Joan was "dropt down with sweat," trembling and weeping wildly. Not all the mother's "skill" could comfort or quiet the daughter, who continued through the night "shaking exceedingly and crying out, *That now shee was a forelorne creature, being assuredly damned, without hope of mercy*," in fits so violent that the whole chamber seemed to "rock and reele."[38]

For a time Joan Drake's condition worsened alarmingly, "some out-rage" being "joyned with her sadnesse and distemper," as the Relator put it. She turned away food, was "unruly" and talked in "strange desperate speeches," inexplicably "slighting and laughing at all said unto her." When "by their authority" her husband and parents "prevailed" with her to come to the table she ate "sparingly, very musing and silent." She became cunning: "she swallowed down many great pins" which "by Gods mercy without hurting passed through her"; once she bribed a maid to bring her "forty" oranges because that fruit had been forbidden "as naught for her" (though this time merely proving that even in excess oranges were "excellent medicines," for they purged her of "abundance of black ugly filthy matter, which made her to look much better"); yet again she hid a knife in her sleeve and smuggled it to her room. In fear that she would hurt herself the family had her constantly tended by "two Gentlewomen by turns," never left alone but "over-awed with Overseers who were jealous of her ruine." Such behavior continued "untill she had in a manner wearied out everybody. . . ."[39]

In *his* supreme anatomizing of melancholy Robert Burton wrote that "we must first begin with prayer, and then use physick."[40] Joan Drake was a sad, sick woman whom physic did not help, or it was God's pleasure that it should not; and in any case she was "averse" to it. The Relator never mentioned the word "lunatick" though clearly the family was contemplating her as that gentry misery, the madwoman locked in an upstairs chamber. Trying to sooth her hysterical daughter out of the terror of that first post-natal nightmare Mother Tothill had told her that "the Devill was a liar," and "so fell a praying with her" to drive out the satanic "illusions." From that moment prayer was to be the sole treatment.[41]

Francis Drake and the Tothills called in the "spirituall Physitians" (or perhaps it was Francis Drake alone, for all we know of the Tothill's religious depth was that they had allowed their daughter to neglect devotional studies). And remarkable was the number, the nonconformist eminence and training of the ministers who traveled to Esher to conduct the struggle for Joan Drake's mind and soul. It was as though the entire educated Puritan community of southern England (or at least a hard core of the graduates of Cambridge, especially of Emmanuel College) found irresistible the case of this daughter of a senior legal bureaucrat and wife of a rich landed gentleman. The Relator himself was introduced to it at a dinner party in Isleworth with the "worthy Minister Dr. Burges the Elder." The latter was John Burgess, nonconforming divine who had been ejected from his living soon after the accession of James I, and had—interesting point—spent several subsequent years earning a "doctor of physic" degree in Leyden; he was in Isleworth between 1613 and 1617, having there a "large and lucrative practice." The conversation at dinner came round to "Mrs. Drakes great distemper" and "how desperate it was." Dr. Burgess had dire insights because he had already been summoned to Esher, in his clerical capacity, and had failed to calm the distraught matron. The people at dinner were so involved that it was "concluded by all" to entreat into the case "Mr. John Dod of Ashby," who "with his so milde, meek and merciful spirit" might have more success with Mistress Drake than "any one they could then think of."[42]

From Canons Ashby, Northamptonshire, John Dod came, a man well over sixty, former fellow of Jesus College, Cambridge, venerated for his learning and his integrity, "silenced" (but irrepressible) by episcopal order in 1611 for his nonconformist preaching. He lived at Esher months at a stretch, for three years Joan Drake's chief "helper" and supporter in many "hot skirmishes with Satan"; thereafter he returned from time to time, and was a beloved witness of her end.[43] In and between Dod's residences other divines shouldered the problem: the Scotsman John Forbes, a "wise, acute, learned, discreet man," in the Relator's precis, drawn to it in a brief return from his ministry in exile in the Netherlands; James Ussher, renowned preacher and professor at Trinity College in Dublin and later "primate" of Ireland, whose triennial journeys to Oxford and Cambridge were deliberately structured to keep him in touch with English Puritans; the "worthy powerful late thundering Preacher, Mr. [John] Rogers of Dedham," another Cambridge product, who "would have entertained her at his house" (with Joan Drake anxious to go, and angry when her family thought it beyond her capacities); Ezekiel Culverwel, his degree from Emmanuel College and his vicarage in Felstead, Essex, volunteering to accompany Mistress Drake wherever she might find clerical expertise; Robert Bruce, minister in Edinburgh, writing long letters of advice about his own "terrors of conscience" (which had "forced" him to "settle into the Ministry") and assurance that with Mrs. Drake rejecting the "Devils counsell" all would "shortly bee well"; John Preston, D.D., fellow at Queens College and later Master of Emmanuel, present with John Dod at Joan Drake's final declaration of faith. And out of the "many" other worthy clerics there was Thomas Hooker, who replaced Dod as primary helper about 1618; he was a "good acute, smart Preacher," said the Relator, "newly come from the university" (Emmanuel) with a "new answering method," though "the same things." When old Mr. Dod left, "lovingly dismissed, and rewarded largely" by the Tothills, Thomas Hooker accepted the Drake's donative "Cure" at Esher, though it was a "poore Living of 40 per annum" plus his "dyet and lodging"; his stay pleased Joan Drake because after Dod's course of instruction she had become "covetous of knowledge."[44] (Hooker's biographers see his stay at Esher from 1618 to the early 1620s as a critical influence upon him, formative for his life-ministration to the "poor doubting christian"; he married there too one of Mrs. Drake's waiting women, altogether an important stop on his way to confrontation with the Anglican establishment and resulting resettlement in New England.)[45]

Certainly with all of these consultants come to do battle with the devil within her Joan Drake was a difficult patient. Old John Dod especially got the worst of her "distemper." Upon his first appearance she "flung up staires" and locked herself in her room, opening it sullenly when her husband threatened to break the door with a "great iron forke." When Dod knelt to pray at her she "hid her selfe over head and eares in the bed," and it was after his initial interviews with her that she swallowed the pins and stuffed herself with the oranges. His incessant praying one day so infuriated her that she "took a bed-staffe, and threatened to knock him on the head" (though "did not").[46]

But in body language and in speech Joan Drake was always consistent and 'rational' about the source of her disturbance. She told Dod at the start and she told the Relator at her end that her problems emerged with the marriage without love, by implication on the part of both partners, imposed upon her by (unloving) parents. Within it she could find no joy, none in children unlovingly conceived and hideously born, nor in superficially merry friends, nor in rich, beautiful Esher which she could not "endure" because of its associations. "Shee was quite destitute of all naturall affection unto Husband, Father, Mother, Children, and every body else," she informed John Dod, "having in briefe no love either to God or man"; furthermore "shee could not grieve, nor be sorrowful for that wofull estate she was now in. . . ." And thus honestly facing the evidence of her "hardened" and locked heart she concluded that she was "a damned Reprobate," marked to "goe unto Hell to live forever."[47]

The not-so-strange thing is that the men did not listen to her. The Relator who set down her words did not actually hear them, nor did John Dod and the many other ministers to whom she must have said them a thousand times. They were there to argue her out of her self-evaluation, to "correct" her "private vision of reality," in the words of Hooker's recent biographer.[48] Like Dod's prayers their messages were aimed at and through her. It is not you thinking these wicked things, they told her, but the Devil implanting his lying words in your mind. From his first day at Esher, Dod addressed the Third Person in the room; as he prayed, Joan Drake stiff and non-participating, he asserted that "the Devill was afraid, run away, and durst not stand to it." Satan "malicious, violent, subtile, various in his temptations, changing shapes, by all means striving," he cried, had in this "good womans case" urged and persuaded her to make "mountains of mole-hills, and of mole-hils to make mighty mountaines." John Forbes declared that Mrs. Drake's insistence on her position was beyond the "skill or strength of her own spirit or wit." Hooker's "strong disputes" with her were intended to "discerne and catch Satan in all his soph-isms." The "Devills rhethorike" had taught Mistress Drake "against her selfe," the clerics agreed, had "corrupted her judgement."[49]

Joan Drake might have melted into mindless relief—or really gone mad—under this ministerial invasion and denial of her feelings. That she did not is corroboration of the strength and nimble wit the Relator had noted in her youthful self. The clerics would not let her withdraw into her despair (good enough therapy, one supposes) because they knew that the devil worked in the silence of his victims. She was defiant and rude: go away, she would order the divines, "it was in vaine, and too late for her to use any meanes"; she "would use none, nor ever goe to Church againe. . . . all her comfort and portion being in this life, shee was resolved to spend the remainder of her time in all jollity and merriment, denying her selfe of no worldly comforts." But early during the efforts of John Dod she entered into the theo-logical spirit of the thing. She started with the rather crude tactic of "tumbling and rolling over" the pages of the Bible "to finde places against her selfe," and "hit upon many," and soon moved up to "toughly dispute the businesse," to argumentation which so "wearied out" the ministers that they had to tackle her in relay. It was better distraction than empty mirth or suicide attempts; clinchingly, when the wearied-out Dod and others left her she relapsed into melan-choly.[50]

Thus on their parallel and separate lines Mistress Drake and the ministers fenced for ten years, she defending her self-consciousness, the clerics assaulting the Cruel Adversary who directed her thoughts. Joan Drake 'theologized' her defense with the assertion that she had committed the "unpardonable sin against the holy Ghost." Through months of discussion John Dod "proved" to her the "delusion" of her claim of this most terrible offense: people so sinning, he said,

were those who having had "inward illumination" of the word of God
later "maliciously and purposely" rejected and opposed it; Mistress
Drake was not "qualified" in this since she was still in "her naturall
estate, by her own confession being farre from this enlightening,
never having tasted of this heavenly gift. . . ." Well, she said, she had
"other sinnes enough to damne her," which were manifest precisely
in her lack of enlightenment. That she had "no heart or power to
performe any holy duty, but was like a creature starke dead, yea twice
dead," did it not mean that "the Decree of God against her was past"?
And this was her "stronghold" conviction from which she "flung off
all with seeming assurance of her knowledge. . . ."[51]

The cum laude graduates of Cambridge University exhausted themselves in trying to correct Mistress Drake. After obtaining her promises on critical issues—that she would no longer "meddle" with the
decrees of God which no mortal or devil could know, that she would
attempt the "meanes" for salvation, that she would give up "tumbling" the pages of the Bible and foreswear suicidal dramatics—John
Dod retired to ponder and restore himself. Explicit where others
mutely shook their heads, John Forbes "confessed she was too hard"
for him, that though he might have "the better of her in a discourse
of Faith" he would have to "study how to answer" her "sophistically
applyed" scriptural objections; he would no more "come to visite
her," he said, nor be "drawn into it."[52] Thomas Hooker was the man
who could "rough hew" her because she was delighted with the new
answering method of the same old things which he had mastered at
Emmanuel: trained as he was in "the sermonic use of Ramist logic,"
wrote his recent biographer, Hooker separated and "analyzed" Mrs.
Drake's arguments in order "to correct her faulty notions of Christian
doctrine," and also "to clear her conscience so that *her judgment of
herself truly accorded with God's judgment*" (my emphasis).[53] But if
Hooker did not give up on her he clearly slid as gracefully as possible
from the case: he had "done his best," he declared, "to comfort,
uphold and rectifie her spirit, so fitting her for mercy, as nothing
remained to bee done but a full gaile of spirituall winde to blow upon
her, to bring forth her fruit." In sum, the clerical consensus was that
"the Lord had some strange work to doe by her," for in her "stout-
nesse and stiffnesse" she was the "strangest" that had been "seen,
heard or read of."[54]

Joan Drake 'cured' herself. Through the years of preoccupation
with her certain damnation her "weaknesse and indisposition of body"
and the "heart-burning and in a manner perpetuall megrum" had
persisted (perhaps after all physic should have been the primary treat-

ment). Though so "tormented" in body that she lay "much of the day upon her bed," she was increasingly "chearefull in minde," becoming "in her thoughts a woman in some sort of another world." In 1625 she decided that she was "neare unto her last," and she resolved in her "unremoveable" way to die in her father's house in Amersham. Her husband stood "much wondering" but did not hinder her as she departed with "two of her men." Her parents wondered too at her unannounced appearance without Mr. Drake, and at her stark declaration of approaching death. Mistress Drake's behavior continued to astonish, she "being in a surpassing extraordinary strange humor of talking of the best things perpetually night and day without intermission, not having any jot of sleep almost night or day." People had time to gather: the Relator arrived, and John Dod, Thomas Hooker, and John Preston; Francis Drake followed in "a week or ten dayes"; and in a constant flow her chamber was full of friends amazed to see her here "fraught with joy, after so many sorrowfull dayes."[55]

No one was unmoved by Joan Drake's finale. In a "fit of sudden, extreame, ravishing unsupportable joy" she experienced her enlightenment, her "illumination." With "uncouth out-cry" she cried, *"what's this, what's this? I am undone, undone, undone, I cannot endure it . . . the Angels are come, they wait, they stay for me."* In rambling vision she told the company that she had been "like a piece of knotty timber," absorbing "knocks with strong wedges," but at last God had heard her prayer and revealed Christ unto her. Mistress Drake had been "saved," in so "heavenly" and "rational" a revelation as to bring "contentment" to all her observers. Rousing on the next day she dressed herself all in white; radiantly happy she instructed her mother that this costume was to be her apparel in her grave, for she was "a Bride now trimmed for Christ the Bridegroome." In utter peace she called servants to her individually for goodbyes, conversed an hour alone with her father about the "ordering of his estate and family," and granted "a sort" of leave-taking to her mother and husband (the Relator said that Mr. Drake was grieving excessively, "weeping and wringing his hands").[56]

At last Joan Drake spoke with affection and gratitude to John Dod, and then turned to the Relator. "I have been so unkind to you," she said to the latter, "for I have not loved you by the hundred part, in that measure I ought to have done. . . . But will you know the cause? I could love no body as I should so long as I was not assured of Gods love to me (for that onely sets our love a fire to runne strongly the right way) I could untill then neither love you nor any body else, during so much distraction and diversion as I should have done: And now that my love is thus kindled, this is my sorrow (my time being short) that now I can no otherwise expresse my selfe then by this poor acknowledgement. . . ."[57]

Could some female someone have failed to interpret Joan Drake's speech—her mother, her waiting women, the readers of *Trodden Down Strength*? She could not repent, Mistress Drake had once argued with Thomas Hooker: could she "goe to Heaven without Repentance?" Hooker had replied that God "at his pleasure . . . did not tie salvation unto any measure of repentance."[58] The dying Joan Drake had deserted husband, children, and Esher, and *then*, yet unrepentant at her Sharedeloes estate in Amersham, she was assured of God's love; a "happy soule," she could allow a final expression of love for mortals. And thus she died: her eternally youthful self pledged to her true husband Christ, she slept sweetly in the Lord.

The future master of Emmanuel College, John Preston, preached Mrs. Drake's funeral sermon: voicing the reverent wonderment of his brethren at her conversion he offered her as a "matchless monument of Gods unspeakable mercy, unto all stout, stiffe, and hardhearted sinners."[59] We cannot know what women witnesses or readers made of Mistress Drake as Caution and Imitation on her strange and rare road to happiness.

NOTES

1. Rev. Doctor Reynolds, *Imitation and Caution for Christian Women, or the Life and Death of that Excellent Gentlewoman, Mrs. Mary Bewley* (London, 1658), E.968(10).

2. See Louis B. Wright, *Middle-Class Culture in Elizabethan England* (Ithaca, N.Y., 1958), chapter 8.

3. Swetnam's *Araignment* was reprinted in 1619, 1628, 1634, 1690, 1702, 1707, 1733, 1807.

4. See Samuel Clarke, *An Antidote Against Immoderate Mourning For the Dead. Being a Funeral Sermon Preached at the Burial of Mr. Thomas Bewley, Junior, Dec. 17, 1658.* (London, 1659), E.1015(5).

5. Francis Roberts, *The Checquer-Work of God's Providence* (London, 1657), p. 39.

6. Thomas Gataker, *Two Funeral Sermons, Much of One and the Same Subject; to wit, The Benefit of Death* (London, 1620).

7. *The Autobiography of Henry Newcome, M.A.*, ed. Richard Pardinson, 2 vols. (Manchester, 1852), 2: 296.

8. *Mistris Shawe's Tomb-stone, or the Saints Remains* (London, 1658), E.1926(1), pp. 12-13, 24, 19.

9. Ibid., pp. 31, 16, 39, 40-41.

10. Ibid., pp. 17, 22, 29-30.

11. Ibid., pp. 25-26, 29-30.

12. Probably Rebekka Crisp and Joyce Featley, in Gataker's *Two Sermons*, Mrs. Elizabeth Moore, in Edward Calamy's *The Godly Mans Ark* (6th edition, 1669), Mary Jackson, Francis Roberts's *Checquer-Work of God's Providence*.

13. Samuel Clarke, *The Second Part of the Marrow of Ecclesiastical History* (London, 1650), E.611; William Harrison, *Deaths Advantage little regarded, and the soules solace against sorrow, Preached in two funerall Sermons at the burial of Mistris K. Brettergh*, 5th edition (London, 1617).

14. Philip Stubbes, *The Anatomie of Abuses* (London, 1593), pp. 31-38.

15. P. S. Gent, *A Christal Glasse for Christian Women*, (London, 1591), pp. A2-A3.

16. Ibid., 4-11.

17. Clarke, *Second Part of the Marrow of Ecclesiastical History*, Bk. 2: 107-12.

18. Ibid., 112-13.

19. Ibid., 116-20.

20. Nicholas Guy, *Pieties Pillar: or a Sermon Preached at the Funeral of Mistresse Elizabeth Gouge, late Wife of Mr. William Gouge, of Black-friers, London* (London, 1626), pp. A, 38-39, 40-41.

21. Ibid., p. 42; *DNB*.

22. Guy, *Pieties Pillar*, pp. 41-42.

23. Ibid., pp. 47-49, 42, 43-44, 41.

24. William Gouge, *Of Domesticall Duties* (London, 1622), pp. 218-25; see also Daniel Rogers, *Matrimoniall Honour* (London, 1642), pp. 178-79.

25. Guy, *Pieties Pillar*, pp. 45, 49-52.

26. William and Mary Haller, "The Puritan Art of Love," *Huntington Library Quarterly* 5: 249; Gouge, *Domesticall Duties*, pp. 345-48.

27. Reynolds, *Imitation and Caution*, pp. 14-15, 17.

28. Ibid., pp. 16-17; and see also Clarke, *An Antidote against Immoderate Mourning*, for a portrait of Mrs. Bewley's son Thomas.

29. *Trodden Down Strength, by the God of Strength, or, Mrs. Drake Revived* (London, 1646), E.1156(1).

30. George Huntston Williams, "Called by Thy Name, Leave Us Not: The Case of Mrs. Joan Drake, *Harvard Library Bulletin* 16, no. 3 (July 1968): 278-88.

31. Frank Shuffleton, *Thomas Hooker, 1586-1647* (Princeton, 1977), p. 29.

32. *Trodden Down Strength*, p. 6; and *Index of Chancery Proceedings* (Reynard's Division), ed. Edward Alexander Fry, 2 vols. (London, 1903), 1: xxi.

33. *Trodden Down Strength*, p. 6.

34. Ibid., pp. 6-9.

35. *Victoria History of the County of Surrey*, 4 vols. (London, 1967), 3: 447-48.

36. Ibid., pp. 8-9.

37. George Lipscomb, *The History and Antiquities of the County of Buckingham*, 4 vols. (London, 1847), 3: 154.

38. *Trodden Down Strength*, pp. 10-14.

39. Ibid., pp. 14-15, 30-31.

40. Robert Burton, *The Anatomy of Melancholy*, ed. Floyd Dell and Paul Jordan-Smith (New York, 1927), p. 384.

41. *Trodden Down Strength*, p. 12.

42. Ibid., pp. 17-18; for John Burgess, see *DNB*.

43. *Trodden Down Strength* , p. 115.

44. Ibid., pp. 70-72, 67-68, 97, 108-9, 153, 117-20; for biographical data on the clerics at Esher see G. H. Williams, "Called by Thy Name, Leave Us Not: The Case of Mrs. Joan Drake," *Harvard Library Bulletin* 16, no. 2 (April, 1968): 115-25.

45. G. H. Williams, "Called by Thy Name," *Harvard Library Bulletin* 16, nos. 2 and 3; Shuffleton, *Thomas Hooker*, pp. 65-66, and passim.

46. *Trodden Down Strength*, pp. 19-20, 22, 27.

47. Ibid., pp. 98, 24, 23.

48. Shuffleton, *Thomas Hooker*, p. 50.

49. *Trodden Down Strength*, pp. 21, 40, 34-35, 70-71, 119.

50. Ibid., pp. 23-24, 22, 28, 31; and Shuffleton, *Hooker*, p. 54.

51. *Trodden Down Strength*, pp. 41, 45-49, 50-51.

52. Ibid., pp. 70-72.

53. Shuffleton, *Hooker*, p. 36.

54. *Trodden Down Strength*, pp. 129, 72.

55. Ibid., pp. 132-35.

56. Ibid., pp. 138-52.

57. Ibid., pp. 156-57.

58. Ibid., p. 123.

59. Ibid., p. 163.

8

The Aggravation of Susanna Eyre

When Adam Eyre, yeoman possessor of a property called Haslehead in Yorkshire, kept a diary of his "Accions and Expences" in 1647-48 his vexing wife Susanna was not the only trouble on his mind. Captain Eyre, just returned from three years in General Fairfax's army, had so many problems that at his lowest points he thought himself in the "same condition with Job." He found it impossible to collect his army pay, almost £700, from a Presbyterian Parliament now deaf to the claims of such plain russet-coated fellows as he; his Haslehead property was encumbered with debt, and in part leased to a malicious joint tenant; his (or his wife's) copyhold tenants on other property would not or could not pay rent; he was ever short of cash, with obligations mounting—£250 to a neighbor, Francis Haigh, more than £100 pounds owed to "the Widow Scargell," the same amount due his sister as "residue" of her "porcion" out of Haslehead; his relations with his father-in-law were strained and unpleasant; he himself was so distracted by "continuall perturbation" and "worldly discourses" that his mind was "as a stranger from God."[1]

But Susanna Eyre, "my wife" as she invariably was in Adam's diary entries, was the closest and most inescapable of his worries: many, many days in the diary were marked with the evidence of her bad temper, her "wicked" ways. In Captain Eyre's account his wife was almost constantly angry with him because of his plan, born of desperation, for Haslehead: he wanted to sell it, and apparently use what proceeds he could get to buy land in another parish; she refused her consent to the sale. So much is clear in the pages of the diary; there was more to the warfare between husband and wife, but since Adam was the note keeper and had no reason to review an old and running combat, its central component in the months of 1647-48 was the property issue.[2]

In his unintentional self-portrait Adam Eyre was a youngish man of thirty-three, strong, able, god-fearing, conscientious, square with his many friends, a leader among the small farmers of his parish. He was incredibly hard-working, ever in action with a dizzying variety of projects, riding ten, twelve, twenty-two miles a day to negotiate over bits of land, to collect rents, to buy and sell stock and crops, to perform his duties as freeholder and church warden in the parish of Peniston, to consult with other former soldiers about appeals for their arrears. At Haslehead he both worked himself and hired help for routine needs, repairing the house, plowing and planting the fields, diverting streams for irrigation, shearing his sheep. Yet he made time for reading, loved collecting books, and had a "study" in which he had shelves built for his growing library; he read very seriously—the "Arguments of Independency" of John Saltmarsh and the sermons of William Dell (both parliamentary army chaplains whom he might have met), "Sir Walter Rawleigh's History of the World," and the "American Cobler," another travel book, the "History and Present State of Europe" (he one day bought himself a fine map of the world), "Erasmus of Roterdam in Praise of Folly," of course Foxe's *Book of Martyrs* and the Bible (for the plumbing of the "misteryes thereof"). He appears a likeable person, as appealing in his new year's resolution to get through the second volume of the *Book of Martyrs* as in his confessed pleasure/guilt in a gambling set of bowls or a convivial night in the tavern. He does not seem petty or mean, the sort who would provoke domestic strife. Indeed he recorded a habit of service to his wife: building her chicken houses and fixing household articles; bringing her things from markets, cheese, meats, tobacco (for medicinal purposes, evidently); accompanying her sometimes in *her* frequent journeying about, to parents' or friends' homes, to church or town or tavern.[3]

By contrast, the one focused view of Susanna Eyre was as Adam's cross. Her age is unmentioned, though by editorial notes we know that she was married in 1640. Because her father was also a problem on Adam's list we know that he was Godfrey Matthewman, a man prosperous enough to settle property on his daughter, and copyhold tenant on the manor of Wakefield which neighbored Haslehead's Peniston Parish. If Susanna had ever before traveled out of this area of the West Riding, her wider experience was no part of Adam's narrative. She did go briefly with him to London in the fall of 1647, where her one noted activity was to procure "a touch from the King for the evil" (it is clear that Adam did not join her in this). She was apparently illiterate—her mark is on Adam's will—and certainly no reader: by that will, Adam left his cherished books to the male cousin who was his executor. But Goodwife Eyre was a busy, competent woman. She collected rents, took grain to the mill, sold "strokes of meal," inspected and bought livestock, raised poultry, brewed ale, spun and sewed (the Eyres regularly bought rather than made or prepared the basics in cheese, meat, or even bread).[4]

Another certain point about Susanna Eyre is that during the months of the diary-chronical she was in physical pain. Early in 1647 Adam paid a Doctor Browneloe twenty-two shillings "to cure my wife's leg," and "promised him more." In May "One Heath of Barnsley" came to the house and "blooded my wife both in the foot and arme"; Adam continued the treatment several days later, himself blooding "her sore foot, which bled very well." Susanna's complaints about her hurting foot went on through the summer, into the fall: on 14 October "she had a very painfull night on her leg which swelled, and was angry quite up to her body"; on 17 October, "my wife was very angry all day, till night"; 20 November, "at night my wife was exceeding angry and had much payne in her leg."[5]

Susanna Eyre's ailment had no resolution in the term of the diary; she lived with it (and through it, surviving Adam, who died in 1661, by seven years), somehow carrying on her daily responsibilities. Would it be unwarranted to speculate about the messy work upon her foot (which surely caused an infection which should have killed her)? The Eyres were childless, a circumstance which in seventeenth-century medical lore was considered "from a fault in the women then the men" (for "in men there is nothing required but fruitful seed spent into a fruitful womb. . . ."). The "cure" for barrenness included, besides potions of herbs and flowers in wine and exotic broths, the blooding of the ankle and foot: instructions in the midwifery tracts were to "let blood in *Vena Saphens*, of the right foot, and take away three ounces of blood of evening."[6] If such were the case with Susanna her pain had a more complicated source than the red and swollen leg.

But Adam Eyre told his diary, his "dyurnall," that the conflict with his wife was about property. In early spring 1647 he wrote this: "I sent by my wife to her father to see if hee will give mee 350£, and I will make Haslehead to her for jointure, and release all his land but Oliver's farme." Oliver was Oliver Roberts, tenant at Scholes, a nearby village, and "all" the land referred to was copyhold property, "settled" by Godfrey Matthewman on Susanna. Adam Eyre waited anxiously for an answer, which when it came was equivocal: his father-in-law "desyred some time, and willed mee let my wife come to him, and hee would certify mee." Adam worried for a few days and reduced his request: "This morning I told my wife y^t if shee would furnish mee with 200£ I would secure her all Haslehead for her life, and she should have the half of it for the present, if Ed[ward] M.[itchell] would part with it; and shee refused, unlesse I would release her land in Scholes, which I refused." With this impasse Adam Eyre went immediately to Edward Mitchell, his former "leiftenant" and chief tenant on Haslehead; for the price of £450 he offered Mitchell "half the house," and gave him fourteen days to consider.[7]

It was in the midst of this unpleasantness that Susanna Eyre's foot was twice blooded. Her mood was apparently mercurial: two soldiers who had been formerly "quartered" at Haslehead came to call, and "my wife," wrote Adam, was "very extravagant in her old humorous way." A few days later she was summoned to a female friend, "now in labor." Upon her return she exploded: "This morne my wife began, after her old manner, to braule and revile mee for wishing her only to weare such apparell as was decent and comly, and accused mee for treading on her sore foote, with Curses and Othes; which to my knowledge, I touched not; nevertheless she continued in that extacy til noone. . . ." At dinner Adam's patience snapped: "I told her I purposed never to com in bed with her til shee tooke more notice of what I formerly had sayd to her"; and "I pray God," he added to himself, "give mee grace to observe; that the folly of myne owne corrupt nature deceive mee not to myn own damnacion." (Both the threat and the aside have the ring of repetition: Adam did not really believe he would deny himself his wife's bed, nor doubtless did she. The diary soon reads, "This night my wife was worse in words than ever.)[8]

In midsummer Adam Eyre signed the lease with Edward Mitchell, the latter now holding one-third of Haslehead. Adam had tried again to borrow from his father-in-law, and again been refused: "the stubbornesse of his resolucion," he wrote about Matthewman, "was not to help mee in anything, though I sold all I had. So much curtesy may I look for from him." He borrowed £50 from a friend, and in one week gambled three days at bowls, with a twitching conscience, losing each time. He was having to bribe his way into his house, from town brought Susanna an expensive "houreglasse" and "other things"; "I stayed home all day," he wrote next, "by reason my wife was not willing to let mee go to bowles to Bolsterstone," and instead, built her "a place for chickens."[9]

Susanna Eyre was not to be placated with hourglasses, chicken coops, or even a new "brueing table." Her foot hurt and her husband was a fool. Adam's diary was told of a dreadful bedtime argument and then this: "sleepe went from mee . . . whereupon sundry worldly thoughts came in my head, and namely, a question whether I should live with my wife or not, if shee continued so wicked as she is; whereupon I ris and prayd to God to direct mee a right." Susanna Eyre must have shared the thought, if not the pious reflection: shortly thereafter she "at night kept yᵉ gates shutt, and sayd shee would be master of the house for that night." The gates were opened the next day and Adam readmitted—with dark thoughts, "great temptacion," a "sore temptacion," to go to London to "seeke for new fortunes."[10]

Adam Eyre's troubles, like those of the biblical Job, grew more varied and maddening. He had a dispute with neighbors over his damming of a stream, a Christofer Marsh and wife using "ill language" about Adam's appropriation of water which was "the king's." He had repeatedly to whip a new maid, a "prentice" of Godfrey Matthewman, for her "foolishnesse" and "sloathfulnesse." Another buyer for Haslehead appeared, leaving Adam rueful that he had been "too hasty with Edward Mitchell." Worse, the latter turned out to be treacherous. "Yesterday Mitchell locked the house dore on my wife, and today on mee, and so kept us both out of the garden," Adam wrote about the first nasty episode in what became a battle for the Haslehead house: locks were broken, gates and doors were either locked or left open; relations came to such a pass that the Eyres took "tables, ranges, and other things in the house, kitchen, and buttry, into the over parlor," and put new locks on "chests of clothes" and the like "as were in the open house still." Adam prepared for litigation, got his "black box" with the papers proving Eyre ownership of Haslehead "from my grandfather to my father"; given his luck in this hard year Adam anticipated that he would be a "fowle looser" in the local court. And always at home there Susanna: "my wife" had "a very painfull night"; she "was exceeding angry and had much payne in her leg"; she "was very angry all day, til night. . . ."[11]

It was God's will, Adam Eyre knew, that he did not "find quiet here." But the divine message added that he himself was at fault for his "most miserable condition," in the "corruption" of his "depraved imagination," in his "yeelding" to "worldly discourses," in his omission of the "duty of a sanctified Christian." In such a mood of contrition Adam tackled his closest misery. He approached his wife with "words of persuasion": he asked her, he wrote, "to forbeare to tell mee of what is past, and promised her to become a good husband to her. . . ." To this appeal for peace Susanna promised "likwise" that "shee would doe what [he] wished her in anything, *save in setting her hand to papers*" (my emphasis). And Adam-Job yielded: "I promised her never to wish her therunto," he said. He concluded that less than loving exchange: "Now I pray God that shee and I may leave of all our old and foolish contentions, and joyne together in His service without all fraud, malice, or hypocrisie; and that Hee will for yᵗ same purpose illuminate our understandings with His Holy Spirit. Amen."[12]

By the diary entries in 1648 it seems that Adam Eyre had bought himself a domestic truce, and quiet enough—Susanna's sore foot must have been better—to attempt the management of his outside problems. The quarrel with Mitchell was resolved after January: "full of trembling and feare," presumably at the prospect of indictment before the sessions court, Mitchell himself wanted "an end of the buisinesse," and "articles" of agreement were signed by him and Eyre before witnesses. In March Adam was preparing to go alone to London, to carry the case of army arrears, for himself and a list of fellow Yorkshiremen soldiers, to the Parliament. Preparation kept him in a frenzy of activity, negotiating for the plowing, sowing, and the spreading of "lyme" in his fields, himself planting oats and "pease . . . parsnips and carrots" in the garden, cropping wood, dredging dams, laying hedges, fencing "the corne above the house," paying back wages and various small debts, even publishing his will, that is, having it witnessed by friends, and of course keeping up a steady round of business-social visiting. He did not take his Dyurnal to London, a sad omission, for in his six months there from early spring to September he must have had close contact with the radical soldiery occupying the capital.[13]

After his return in September 1648 Captain Eyre talked to his diary for only four more months. He was a man unsettled by the civil wars. He made the yeoman's entries: he had to juggle cash and crops for small debts and purchases; he was much involved in buying sheep, marking them with "fresh redle on the narr sholder" and putting them "to the moore." But his future, like the time, was uncertain. Would the national conflict continue? One of Adam Eyre's last entries was this: "Capt. Rich told mee Col. Maulyverer wanted a Capt. for his dragoones. I willed him to tell him I would accept of the command, if hee pleased; and hee came with mee to the mill, and told mee hee would let mee heare from him from Sheffeild tomorrow at night. . . ." Should he sell Haslehead, or honor his word to his wife? The whole entry for 11 October reads, "This day I rested at home all day and walked into yᵉ feilds, and I told my wife sith shee would not joyne with mee in sale, shee should keepe the house as shee would, neither would I meddle with her at all."[14]

Probably Adam Eyre did not rejoin the army, but the only certainty is that again on 26 January 1649 his "purpose" was "for London in the morne, God willing"; he may have been in the somber crowd which observed the execution of Charles Stuart. Surely, however, Susanna Eyre had in 1661 both her dowry lands and her widow's portion in Haslehead. By Adam's will she received all his "household goods and movables within the house, save apparell and bookes," her "wife's part for her life" in the "capitall messuage or tenement called Haslehead," and "all such writings . . . which belong to her or concerne any lands in Holmefrith secured by her father to her and mee. . . ."[15]

Adam and Susanna Eyre fade away—leaving what? Obviously, Adam Eyre's diary is valuable in its briefly brilliant illumination of the small producer as he went about the contracting and hiring, hedging and irrigating, improving and transforming his piece of the English countryside during the revolution of capitalist agriculture. In reality Adam Eyre was tied to a tightly intertwined community of personal dependency in exchange and servitude. At the same time his relationships were objectified, purposeful: Woodcock for meat and "shooes," Haigh for "meale," Marsden for plowing, Wainwright for "lyming," Milnes for hewing. The result was that Adam at Haslehead was an island unto himself in his consuming struggle to possess and accumulate property: not even a father-in-law would promise to save him from the ultimate disaster of land-loss and, had it come to it, the economic and social abyss of the hired hand. Adam was just as alone in his anxious self-searching, in his frequent depressed contemplation of failure in his Christian duty. In the short period of his diary-keeping at any rate, life for Adam Eyre was harsh and solitary: the only close friends, sharing friends, seem to have been ex-soldiers in Fairfax's army, especially the Colonel Rich with whom he sometimes "abused" himself with "too much drink."[16]

And Susanna Eyre, who in theory and culture should have provided Adam with domestic solace and companionship? She was not once a witness in her own behalf; everything about her life before 1647 as daughter and wife of small farmers is inferential, and her personality and behavior were probably distorted in the tension of the period of the diary. She had some long-existing grievance with Adam. Had she hated Haslehead at first sight, the house "undeserving of notice," built on a bleak, "dreary," windswept bluff high above the banks of the river Don?[17] Were she and her family loyal to king and Church of England as against Adam's commitment to Parliament and Independency? Did she blame Adam for their childlessness? (Even the physicians agreed that barrenness could result if the wife was not "pleased" with her husband.)[18]

There seem a couple of plausible conclusions about Susanna Eyre. In contrast to her self-disciplined, introspective, 'modern' husband (would his grandfather have been gentle as he?), Susanna was still tuned to the "domestic anarchy," the struggle "for the breeches" embedded in the old popular culture:[19] she had not made much progress toward the new ideal of the quietly comforting and obedient wife. She grasped neatly, however, the sense of property and power, or to rephrase it from her female and wifely position, the powerlessness of the propertyless. If it is impossible to know the details of her marriage contract concerning Haslehead, or the tangle of leases "settled upon" or "secured to" her by her father, it is sure that in these Susanna Eyre had a piece of power she would not relinquish; it was her edge of security—and equality.

NOTES

1. "The Diurnall of Adam Eyre," in *Yorkshire Diaries*, ed. H. J. Morehouse, Surtees Society, 65 (1877): 89, 105, 76, 88.

2. Ibid., p. 87.

3. Ibid., pp. 33, 102, 67-68, 43-45, 79, 100.

4. Ibid., pp. 62, 354, 50-58, 99-110. For a discussion of intermingled possession of freehold and copyhold, of yeomen holding both, scattered over several manors, see Mildred Campbell, *The English Yeoman* (New Haven, 1942), pp. 118-20; also, *The Agrarian History of England and Wales*, ed. Joan Thirsk (Cambridge, 1967), 4: 301-6. In the same volume see chapter 8, Alan Everitt, "The Marketing of Agricultural Produce."

5. "Diurnall of Adam Eyre," pp. 22, 35, 39, 68-75.

6. Nicholas Culpepper, *Directory for Midwives*, part 2 (London, 1662), pp. 134-35; *The Compleat Midwife, Rare Secrets brought to Light . . .* (London, 1696), pp. 317-18.

7. "Diurnall of Adam Eyre," pp. 29, 31-37. For insight into the possible complexities in settlement of such properties, see Campbell, *English Yeoman*, pp. 124-31.

8. "Diurnall of Adam Eyre," pp. 39, 42-46.

9. Ibid., pp. 48-51.

10. Ibid., pp. 51-55.

11. Ibid., pp. 52, 67, 59, 87, 61, 68.

12. Ibid., pp. 88-89, 84.

13. Ibid., pp. 92, 94, 102-4.

14. Ibid., pp. 113, 107, 111.

15. Ibid., p. 354.

16. Captain Eyre's "neighborliness" most impresses others: Campbell, *English Yeoman*, pp. 386-87; K. Wrightson, *English Society* (New Brunswick, N.J., 1981), p. 54.

17. "Diurnall of Adam Eyre," p. 353.

18. Culpepper, *Directory for Midwives*, part 2 (1662), pp. 135-37, and part 1 (London, 1651), p. 84.

19. H. V. Routh, "The Progress of Social Literature in Tudor Times," *Cambridge History of English Literature* (Cambridge, 1910), 3: 91-93.

9

The Pity of Alice Thornton

Alice Thornton wrote an autobiography in which she told more about her life than probably anyone would want to know. Unkind but true: an afternoon spent with her bulky volume tries the spirits of the most motivated reader. Written as rectification of what she considered an unbearable slander upon her respectability, her account of her life is a seemingly endless narrative of passive suffering, a heavy-laden tale of her being done to and done in.[1]

She was born Alice Wandesford in 1626, to a rich, well-placed gentry family with a scattering of fine estates in Yorkshire. Except for a brief childhood episode in Ireland she spent her entire life on the moors and in the dales of that beautiful country, at her mother's estate of Hipswell on the southern bank of the river Swale, and as wife and widow at the Thornton seat of East Newton in Ryedale in the North Riding. Her father, an M.P. and cousin of the Earl of Strafford, was rising in the court of Charles I under Strafford's star; sent as Lord Deputy to Ireland in the early 1630s Wandesford had a "noble position and estate" there, and might have had a title had the civil wars not ended his career (and life). Her mother was the daughter of one of the richest citizens of London, a considerable heiress and a striking personality in her own right.[2]

Alice Thornton gave both of her parents the reverential respect required in a Christian memoir. Her father was an "heroick soule," cherished for "his great endowments, his pietie, parts, knowledge in divinity and religion, his wisdome and paternall caire and prudence, his tender and deare love to his whole family and generation." The mother was a lady of exquisite breeding and education, as accomplished in the courtly arts as she was a "wise and prudentiall" governor of her seven children and her inherited fortune.[3] There are contrary currents, though, in Alice Thornton's portrayal of her parents which perhaps provide a clue to her lifelong, or at any rate, middle-aged melancholy: unmistakable resentment surfaces against the all-powerful pair above her in her adolescence; both of these strong people were unable to protect her, both in her experience let her down. The father died, of natural causes, grieving for Strafford and for Charles's kingdom, and subsequently the "succeeding rebellions in Ireland and England" destroyed the estate "he had so well built" to be Alice's large inheritance. The mother, indomitable and dominant, took over the guidance of the children's fortunes; we shall see how she arranged matters for Alice.[4]

From her early childhood bad things happened to and around Alice Thornton. At the age of three she fell against the hearth, splitting her head so deeply that the family feared her death; her mother somehow "cured" the wound, though it left a great scar. At five she was poisoned by spoiled beef, and in the midst of that retching sickness broke out with measles; again she almost died, but again her mother cured her. She had smallpox at six, and at this tender age first "knew God," prayed with "deepe feare and great awe," she remembered, "least I should offend Him." On the way to Ireland the family stopped in London, where a fire consumed the house next door to their lodgings. They were shipwrecked during their sea voyage, and in Ireland the family coach toppled into a river, the passengers barely saved. Playing in their new gardens Alice fell from a swing, was pushed by a rough boy, and seriously injured. Sickness, accident, disaster—in a dozen pages of this litany one sentence informs that Alice received the "best education that the kingdome could afford," plus instruction in French, singing, dancing, and playing on the lute.[5]

There is no denying that Alice Thornton grew up in difficult times, that she knew pain, sorrow, fear. She was fourteen when her father died. The next year her kinsman Strafford went to the block; his daughters, Lady Anne and Lady Arabella Wentworth, had been Alice's playmates, were like sisters to her. The Wandesford family flight from rebellious Ireland followed, a frightful exit because the mother delayed too long in trying to salvage household furnishings for her jointure property in Yorkshire. After landing in England Alice had another bout with smallpox. Journeying north the family was shot at by parliamentary troops, surely an unhappy reception. While they stopped in Richmond, south of their Hipswell destination, Alice once again "near died" of eating tainted lobster; her younger brother Christopher too tested the mother's curative skills with a sickness diagnosed as "fitts of the spleene."[6]

And Hipswell was not a quiet refuge. General Leslie's Scottish troops were all about the county, watching royalist youth (Alice's eldest brother George went into hiding) and demanding free quarter from royalist gentry: Alice's mother paid support for enemy troops through the war period which was three times the value of her estate. The Lady Wandesford rose to haughty assertion, however: she went to General Leslie himself to obtain an end of harassment which included an unwanted wooing of Alice by a Scottish officer, and the pilfering of "delecate cattell" of the mother's "owne breed."[7]

Invariably Alice Thornton's account of these trials was bounded by perceptions of her family and personal experience. The decade of the civil wars ended for her in three events: the death in childbirth of a much older sister, Lady Danby; the accidental drowning of her beloved brother George; and the climactic happening of her marriage.

Lady Danby's fate left upon the young Alice an indelible impression of the perils of being female. The Lady was in her sixteenth pregnancy—ten living children, six miscarried or stillborn because of the mother's frights or falls—which terminated in a labor, Alice wrote, of fourteen days, the baby at last coming "double into the world." Sister Danby suffered on for almost a month; exhorted to live, she answered, "I find my heart and vitalls all decaided and gon. . . . No I desire to be dissolved and to be with Christ, which is best of all."[8]

Brother George died crossing the Swale River in flood, a terrible tragedy and loss for the family of a good, sweet and generous youth. Alice implied that she lost in his death her one male protector, but it is not clear that had George not challenged the swollen river he could have prevented the misfortune of her marriage to William Thornton. Nevertheless: as eldest son he was heir to his father's properties in Ireland and Yorkshire; in pursuing his rights he had so provoked the local representatives of the revolutionary Commonwealth (it was 1651) that he and the family were declared traitors and Wandesford estates sequestered. With George dead, an uncle and a cousin—the latter with government contacts in York—took upon themselves responsibility as family heads. The two focused on Alice, she who was "likely to have a considerable fortune" from her mother and out of her father's Irish holdings. If Alice were to marry his nephew, William Thornton, said the cousin, he would see to it that the Wandesford estates were cleared. She had no "free choyce," lamented Alice: the bargain "was strucke betwixt them, before my deare mother and my selfe ever heard a silable of this mater . . . on which all the comfort of my life, or missery, depended."[9]

Alice Thornton at age twenty-five wished to remain a spinster. "I was not hastie," she wrote, "to change my free estate . . . wherein none could be more satisfied." Her days were spent in "great content and comfort" with her "excellent parent," and in any case she knew "too much of the caires of the world" to desire "the addition of such incident to the married estate." Who pushed her to it then? Surely the uncle and cousin could not have pursued negotiations without Dame Wandesford's consent. From her middle-aged perspective Alice Thornton picked her way carefully through the crucial betrayal. "But my dearest mother," she wrote, "willing to serve the family in what she could, with reference to some comfortable settlement for me, in her judgement could have otherwise, to have disposed of me nearer hand to herselfe, and my freinds." The mother might have wanted to do "otherwise" but she did not: "Nevertheless, such was my deare mother's affection to the family for itt's preservation, that she harkened to the proposall made for Mr. Thornton's marriage, albeit therein she disobleiged some persons of very good worth and quality which had solicitted her earnestly in my behalfe, and such as were of large and considerable estates of her neighbours about her."[10]

We may note in this central disappointment of Alice Thornton's life a double complaint. She had been sacrificed by her dearest mother in the interests of family property to a man she did not know nor care to know. William Thornton was not a bad man: after meeting him Alice thought him a "very godly, sober, and discreet person, free from all manner of vice, and of a good conversation." He was apparently socially dull and not over-bright (but then there is no evidence that Alice was celebrated for vivacity or wit). But further, the Thorntons were minor gentry 'up-north' in Yorkshire: Mr. Thornton's annual income from his estate was valued at less than a third of Alice's supposed inheritances. Obviously: upon the values of landed wealth Alice Wandesford was marrying beneath herself.

Formal resistance seems never to have occurred to Alice. She made one demand, that Thornton, who was Presbyterian, enter the Church of England, and agree that their children be raised in the Anglican service. He acquiesced entirely to "her conscience" (naturally, the cynic would add). And then her future was in the hands of the Lord: "I powred out my pettitions before the God of my life to direct, strengthen, leade, and counsell me what to doe in this conserne. . . . And to order my waies aright, so that if He saw in His wisdome that the married state was the best for me, that He would please to direct me in it, and incline my heart towards it. . . . And if it pleased God soe to dispose of me in marriage, makeing me a more publicke instrument of good . . . I thought it rather duty in me to accept my freind's desires for a joynt benefitt, then my owne single retired content." Her prayers encouraged her to consider the unwanted marital assignment as a sort of spiritual life journey: with God as "witnesse that knowes the secretts of hearts," she told herself that she married "not to fulfill the lusts of the flesh, but in chastity and singleness of heart, as marrieing in the Lord."[11]

On her wedding day Alice was suddenly ill with violent pains in her "head and stomacke," with "great vomitting" and "sicknesse at . . . heart." Her mother was sure she had taken a cold the previous night, by staying up too late and washing her feet "at that time of the yeare." Alice's interpretation of her cold feet was a garbled communication with the Lord: her untimely illness, she thought, was a sign from God that she had "offended" by altering her "resolves of a single life." Looking back from middle-age she knew that she had recognized in it an omen of coming "afflictions," so that, she said, "that which was to others accounted the happiest estate was imbittred to me at the first entrance, and was a caution of what trouble I might expect in it. . . ."[12]

Sick or no, Alice was married on the appointed day, and seven weeks later was pregnant—more confusion in the heavenly communication. In her seventh month she was taken on a visit to her husband's family in East Newton, and after a day of hiking in the dales went into labor. The result was everything that she expected of childbirth: the baby, a girl, was dead in an hour, and in an agony of afterbirth Alice had "a most tirrible shakeing ague." Her illness lasted "one quarter of a yeare," she wrote, "by fitts each day twice, in much violency, so that the sweate was great with faintings, being thereby weakened till I could not stand or goe. . . . The haire on my head came off, my nailes of my fingers and toze came of, my teeth did shake, and ready to come out and grew blacke."[13]

Alice Thornton endured a breeding period of fifteen years. In 1654 came the first live birth, a daughter who was named Alice. Baby Elizabeth followed in 1655; she died of "rickets and consumption" in her first year. Another daughter, Katherine, was born in 1656, a healthy, strong child. A boy baby died immediately in 1657, after which mother Alice went to Scarborough for rest from "excessive losse of blood and spiritts in childebed." A sixth pregnancy produced a son, named William, who died after birth, to the great sorrow of both parents: Alice's bereavement was the harder because her husband seemed "soe afflicted . . . being a son he takes it more heavily," she said, "because I have not a son to live." At last, Robert was born in 1662; Alice immediately projected for him the career of a "scoler." Baby Joyce appeared and died in 1665, with Alice so "terrified" with this her "last extremity" that she prepared for her death by willing out her children, "Robert to my lord Frechville, Alice to Aunt Norton. . . ."

A final stillborn boy was born in 1667; Alice had declared herself too weak for this pregnancy, but, she wrote, "it is not a Christian's part to chuse anything of this nature, but what shall be the will of our heavenly Father, be it never soe contrary to our own desires." She was still only forty-one, and might have gone on to a tenth, or fourteenth pregnancy, with all the attendant "dangerous pirills," had not Mr. Thornton, her "deare and tenterly-loving husband," unexpectedly in 1668 sickened and died.[14]

Besides pregnancies and childbearing Alice Thornton's large concerns were with money and property. Given her single-mindedly acquisitive age she was not unique in material obsessions. But surrounded by gentry avarice and ambition Alice Thornton was a loser; mismanaged and indebted estates, withheld payments of inheritances and annuities, missing portions for her girls, dwindling "maintenance" for her son, everything went badly, and since Alice could do nothing about it, she cast about helplessly and resentfully for someone to blame.

Her mother did what she could (to make amends). Dame Wandesford, wrote Alice, after she "disposed of me in marriage . . . extended her bounty towards me. . . . I, with my husband and children, did live with her for eight yeares [and] bring forth four of my children in her house; and had all manner of charges, expences, and houshold affaires, in sicknesses, births, christnings, and burialls, of and concerning ourselves and children, with the diett, etc., of nurses, menservantes and maides, and our friends' entertainments, all things don of her owne cost and charges all her daies while she lived, which could not be of lesse valuew to us clearely then £1600."[15]

Dame Wandesford was something of a managerial wizard. Out of her Hipswell jointure, which was "at best" £300 a year (and much less during the civil wars), she secluded son George in France in the mid-1640s, raised and educated two younger sons, one at Cambridge, and contrived to corner as much of her estate as legally possible for the futures of her daughter Alice and Thornton progeny. It was not easy: what she faced makes one quake, this record of mid-seventeenth-century gentry squabbling over their estates-pie.

The Wandesford problem, to try to summarize Alice's narrative which is confusing and perhaps purposely vague, stemmed from the indebtedness on all of the father's properties from the 1640s, and the fact that, by his will, income of various estates was to be reserved for his widow and younger children. The eldest son, George, had been betrothed to a daughter of Sir John Lowther, a Yorkshire squire (Alice has him from Westmoreland) of talent and experience in the accumulation of land; Sir John told George that he would never be "master" of his inheritance until he had "destroyed" his father's will, advice which George rejected as shockingly unfilial behavior. But with George's death his brother Christopher, a young man in step with the times, assumed his inheritance and his Lowther engagement. With the smooth direction of Sir John, Christopher began clearing his estates of debt and drawing together their assets.[16]

Sir John Lowther's entries in his "Great Book" for 1651 recorded the marriage of his favorite "Daughter Ellinnor to Christo. Wandesford of Kirkelington Esqr shee beeinge 18 yeares and a halfe." As her dowry Sir John gave £2,000 and lent "£1500 monie towards payment of detts the estate [Christopher's] was lyable unto; they beeinge very greate viz about £4000 that was chargeable upon it and £4000 more charged upon the English and Irish estate." There followed a precise tally of the legacies with which the estate was encumbered, Sir John listing them as so much future income for Christopher and Ellinnor after the deaths of the recipients, or after rearrangement that would "setle them in our way." The Irish estate "likewise to cum in," noted Lowther, "after detts and legacies paid and discharged accordinge to his fathers will which as yet is very uncertaine. . . ."[17]

Dame Wandesford was not quite a match for the shrewd partnership of Sir John and Christopher. Together they took from her, in Alice's charge, "all my father's personall estate given her by will," and her annuity out of Ireland of £300 a year, "which nineteen years a widdow" and thus owed £5,700, she "never receaved any part thereof." But Dame Wandesford had her victories. When Christopher declared his father's will lost, she countered by producing the document. She withstood Christopher's displeasure, the "harsh thoughts" in the "heire's minde, that she dealt hardly, because she did not give all her widdowe's patrimony to him." And most to the point, she protected Alice to the limits of her capacity: the "table gratis" to the Thorntons for eight years, and free living at Hipswell for two more years after her death in 1658; by will, all of her personal possessions and household goods to Alice and her children; the legacies due her from her husband's estate to be laid out "in landes in England," to "inure to Alice Thornton, my daughter, for her life, and after to the use of her younger sonnes and all her daughters equallie."[18]

With her mother's death Alice was bereft and unprotected. Transported north to East Newton in 1660 she disliked everything about her surroundings. She was far from home (several score miles) and among aliens: her father-in-law had had two wives, one a papist, the other Presbyterian; intolerable people, let alone relatives. They were, moreover, proud, unfriendly, and richer than she and Thornton. The papist daughters had portions paid by the cutting of "great and beautiful woods" at Newton, "which disfaced that land"; while William Thorton's inheritance was diminished by the two Presbyterian sisters, each receiving a portion "of about £1500, besides maintenance and education." Solitary and resentful, ever mindful that she had married only "to redeeme my deare brother's estate from the tiriny of our oppressor," Alice had all that (more than) she could manage, either to "stand my ground," as she put it, or to "defend the interest of my poore children."[19]

William Thornton seems to have provided precious little strength or comfort. In a rare remark on his personality Alice said he was "much addicted to a melancolicke humour" which since his youth "had seized him by fitts." There is no indication of how he spent his time, or what he considered important or even entertaining to do. He was not interested, Alice reported, in the new house they built at East Newton—paid for, she added, by her money. Perhaps he liked playing the squire: he regularly sold stock, the "best horses" Dame Wandesford had left Alice, and used the money for his purposes (which was, of course, his legal right). Perhaps he was thus dealing when he died in 1668 while attending a fair in the town of Malton. He had been seriously ill shortly before, to which crisis Alice had responded by going "sick to bed," unable, she said, of doing "my faithfull duty to my beloved husband." At the news of Thornton's death in Malton she was "still soe weak" that she kept to her "sorrowful bed," lamenting from afar the loss of "the joy of my heart and the delight of my eyes." Let us not doubt that Alice grieved with formal propriety for "this sweete saint of God," this man of "great pietie, peace, honesty."[20]

Widow Alice immediately learned a horrifying fact: Thornton had neglected to write a will. She was informed by his relatives that "by reason there was no will made" she was to be her husband's administrator, "and to pay debts, etc." She was told further that the deceased had heavily indebted both his small estates, the one East Newton, the other close by at Laistrop. Alice was now to meet these debts with the only money she had, her mother's legacy. A brother-in-law reminded her that in any case the inheritance was not hers, that all she had brought to marriage belonged "by the law" to Thornton: "for the property was in him, and not in the wife, being under covert barr." With relief and gratitude, however, Alice could score another for her mother: Dame Wandesford had expected William Thornton to burden his properties; her will had been explicitly formed to secure

Alice's legacy so that it could not be "made liable to any other use as debts. . . ."[21]

But Dame Wandesford could not reach from the grave to check her son Christopher. Calculating that Alice had had enough from family resources Christopher (Sir Christopher by this time) denied her her portion from the father's Irish estates: thus, wrote Alice, "was I striped of all the great riches and honorable enjoyments I had right unto." When all had settled she and her children were reduced to the living of the rents of East Newton, with "great difficulty" adjusting their expectations. Daughters Alice, age sixteen, and Katherine, age twelve, when their father died, were to have their portions from Alice's maternal legacy, and Robert, age six (he to be the "scoler") was to have Laistrop. The only certainty-in-hand that Alice had was still her mother's money. It might have been different, she did not fail to add, "if it might have bin rightly mannaged in my husband's lifetime."[22]

One almost forgets to include the episode that prompted Alice Thornton to write her autobiography. It seems a sad little tale, were that judgment not a mockery of Alice's "torment" within it. The truly pathetic aspect of her involvement with a young Anglican minister named Thomas Comber was that it began as one of the few genuinely pleasurable moments of her married life. That it turned out badly will not surprise; one does not expect many things to have been otherwise for Alice Thornton.

From the start of her resettlement at East Newton Alice had wanted an Anglican minister to help her 'stand her ground.' At length, in 1666, a parish living was arranged, mostly Wandesford reserves paying for the services of Mr. Thomas Comber. Alice was delighted with him, and apparently had early thoughts of his suitability as a future husband for her namesake elder daughter. Somehow—the details are unclear—because of the pique of Comber's former female patrons, rumors circulated, "horrid lyes," that he and Alice Thornton were more to one another than minister and parishioner. "By these lyes I was ruined and brought to a public scorne," mourned Alice, "I and my poore child accused and condemed . . . and all my chaste life and conversation most wickedly traduced." It was not quite as bad as that: the accusation was not made publicly, but in a bedchamber in the Thorntons' own house, with four people present, Alice and her daughter, a Mrs. Danby, friend (and relative?) who had been living there, and Mrs. Danby's female servant. Still it was a dreadful scene in which Alice, the daughter of gentry wealth and status, was attacked by a maid—with the latter's mistress standing silent behind her. In expressing her horror and shame Alice's prose for once shakes with emotion: "with a brasen face she impudently cryed out against me, and saide 'I was naught, and my parents was naught, and all that I came on was naught,' which, when I heard these blasphemous speeches against the unspotted honnor and holy life of my parents, it more wounded me then my owne. . . ." There must have been a great row: Mr. Thornton (who never had "the least shadow of suspition" of Alice's "vertue and chastity," surely a believable aside) heard the commotion, grabbed the maid and "did kike that wench downe staires, and turne her out in great rage for soe wickedly doeing this against us." Unexpectedly decisive in this moment he would have done the same to Mrs. Danby, had Alice not prevented it out of Christian charity, "which few would have done," she added. But then Alice was mostly behaving predictably, weeping "extreamly," and falling "downe before the mistres and her maide," in a "swound" for her "great calamity."[23]

This affair had a curious twist of resolution. In November 1668, two months after William Thornton died, teenage daughter Alice was married to Thomas Comber. That it was done swiftly, and moreover, in private at East Newton, with only four female witnesses (not even Thornton's brother to give the bride away), naturally caused the tongues to wag: more "fallse and abominable" lies, wrote Alice, "which said I was forced to marry my childe to hide my own blame or dishonour." The in-house version was that Thomas Comber had declared to Alice his love for her daughter, said that he had turned down a rich "proposall" for her, and wanted to marry soon in light of mother Alice's precarious health. He "did believe," Alice explained, "if I should be taken away by death, which God forbid, that her seeming freinds would strip him of her, and he never should obteine his soe long desired happiness." A marriage contract had been quickly arranged, with Comber accepting Alice's provisions: his "full performances," to be "drawne in forme of law," to "establish all her fortune upon my daughter and her issue male or female, with other clauses for the benifitt of my deare sone Robert, her brother." Thomas Comber even had a session with Sir Christopher Wandesford to be told what that sharp brother/uncle "did expect of him," in a reiterated warning to leave young Alice's inheritance untouched (so careful was Sir Christopher to rid himself of the Thornton burden).

The wedding ceremony "was performed in a very decent and a religious manner," with bride Alice conducting herself "most virteusly and modestly, with chastity in this holy action into which she did come." Mother Alice "shed many tears," considering how she "was left," and her daughter "forelorne" of all relatives "who should have bin our comfort in this great time of change." Thus "begging a blessing of God to His holy ordinance," Alice Thornton did "hope He gave a gracious return of our prayers," to which her readers over the centuries have doubtless added, Amen.[24]

Who could say that Alice Thornton was a weak woman? There is great and stubborn strength in the eternally suffering, as narrated in fact and fiction since the seventeenth century. Alice lived on in her resentful genteel poverty to 1706; when thirty-eight years a widow she was portrayed an old woman in black, "not a striking picture," according to her editor-descendant.[25] Female victim of institutionalized family and property, helplessly perpetuating herself into subsequent generations, she posed the problem herself: when did she ever have a "free choyce"?

NOTES

1. *The Autobiography of Mrs. Alice Thornton of East Newton, County York* (Durham, 1875), Surtees Society, vol. 65.

2. Ibid., Preface. Lawrence Stone calls the Wandesfords "a moderately successful upper gentry family" (*The Family, Sex and Marriage*, p. 74).

3. *Autobiography of Alice Thornton*, pp. 101-2.

4. Ibid., pp. 191-93.

5. Ibid., pp. 4-12. She received "what was then the current ideal education for upper-class women," English, reading, writing, and both spoken and written French (Stone, *Family, Sex and Marriage*, p. 205). See also, Rosemary O'Day, *Education and Society* (London, 1982), chapter 10; and Antonia Fraser, *The Weaker Vessel* (New York, 1984), chapter 7.

6. *Autobiography of Alice Thornton*, pp. 15-40.

7. Ibid., pp. 40-45.

8. Ibid., pp. 50-52. Stone, *Family, Sex and Marriage*, p. 75, notes "the exceptional fertility of the Wandesford girls," and, p. 115, the remarkable though not unusual closeness between sister and brother in this upper-class family.

9. *Autobiography of Alice Thornton*, pp. 65-66, 61-62.

10. Ibid., pp. 75-76, 62n, 76. For a good discussion of marital matters from the experience of the Verney family, see Miriam Slater, *Family Life in the Seventeenth Century* (London, 1984), chapters 3 and 4.

11. *Autobiography of Alice Thornton*, p. 77, and Preface.

12. Ibid., p. 83.

13. Ibid., pp. 87-88. For some comparative experiences, Fraser, *Weaker Vessel*, chapter 4, "The Pain and the Peril."

14. *Autobiography of Alice Thornton*, pp. 87-93, 97, 126, 143, 151, 165, 145, 172-73. See R. Houlbrooke, *The English Family, 1450-1700* (London, 1984), p. 136, for the observation that the death of babies was "intensely

painful" to Alice Thornton. In my reading the intensely painful loss was that of the male baby.

15. *Autobiography of Alice Thornton*, p. 104.

16. Ibid., pp. 195-97.

17. *Lowther Family Estate Book, 1617-1675*, ed. C. B. Phillips (Durham, 1979), Surtees Society, vol. 191: 65.

18. *Autobiography of Alice Thornton*, pp. 198-204, 105, 121, 114n.

19. Ibid., pp. 214-17.

20. Ibid., pp. 250, 149, 172-73. See Houlbrooke, *English Family*, p. 58, for an assessment of Alice Thornton as "generous, impulsive and affectionate."

21. *Autobiography of Alice Thornton*, pp. 240, 248.

22. Ibid., pp. 269, 244.

23. Ibid., pp. 222n, 236.

24. Ibid., pp. 229, 228-31. The comment in Houlbrooke, *English Family*, p. 87, is that Alice Thornton was "glad to see her daughter decently bedded."

25. *Autobiography of Alice Thornton*, Preface.

10

The Education of Elizabeth Freke

The Widow Elizabeth Freke, lord of the manor of West Bilney in Norfolk, was a cold woman in a harsh world. By gentry standards she was very well off, which gave her considerable power in her circle of relatives, tenants, and servants (she had no visible friends). She expected people to be false and conniving, and they did not disappoint her. Almost half of the 114 printed pages of her *Diary*, that part written in her last years, was a bitter account of the selfishness and/ or villainies of those about her. She held them at bay, however: "I have seen the fall of Most of my Enemies," she wrote, "And am able to subsist withoutt the Help of my Friends."[1]

Thus her "deere sister Austen" deserted her, Elizabeth Freke noted in an entry of 1710, "Munday Morning, September the eleventh. . . . Leftt Bilney, & me very Ill Inn Itt, and went for London her selfe & Maide; she hired A Whole Coach to her self att Linn unknown to me tho' I offered her Mine, soe when I saw Goe she would, I gave her Twenty pound to pay for Itt, [that] I might Receive noe Further pitty or obligation on thatt Accounte." The ingratitude of Sister Austen was what rankled: "I had pinched myselfe for these several yeares In these several sums to serve her & hers by these guifts. . . ." And then Widow Freke made a list that must have occupied her for hours of the things she had given her sister since 1675, to the cumulative value, she reckoned, of one thousand six hundred and ninety-three pounds.[2]

Thus her only son, Ralph, his wife and three children, on a visit from Ireland to Bilney, irritated, grieved, and cost Elizabeth Freke. In church one morning she watched her son "sett Frowning on me there for an howr," for what reason, she wrote, "I know nott. . . . except Itt were his feare of my Coming A Live home Againe. . . . This his Cruell usage of me. . . ." She was ready for unpleasantness from her daughter-in-law, a young woman with whom she had tangled before, once vowing she would "never see her more," and sure enough was treated "Rudely"; this despite the fact that during the visit the youngest grandchild "Lay sick heer with me (and att my Charge) all most A Month given over of the small pox. . . . [and] Infectted Fowre of my servants, of Which one of Them dyed." From "such another Time," Elizabeth Freke concluded, "Good Lord deliver mee." She toted up the toll of the year-long visit of this "Rude family," this "disorderly familly," at thousands of pounds, including loans to son Ralph; and as finale, he and his wife "both desirous of more Quality," she purchased the "patentts of A Barronett from the Queen," paying for "the Ingroseing of Itt. . . . above Five Hundred pounds."[3]

Thus her "Cosin John Frek" one day came "very Early In the Morning very Angry" that the Widow Freke had instructed him to take her "mony outt of the East Indy Company, and to place Itt in the bank of England," that she "might command Itt, being 3100£." With Cousin John Freke she had yet another long history of acrimony and distrust. A few years before he had "Ruined" her in signing over Irish rents, hers for life from her husband's estate, Elizabeth Freke thought, to her son; she had observed then that her experience was a "Warning to trust Friends with Letters of ATurney." Now Cousin John was disturbed that 3000-odd pounds was to be taken from his care. "I told him," wrote Elizabeth Freke, "My Reputation was all I had to Live on, & I had Nothing to show for this my mony butt his Memorandum, and thatt Hee had Refused me his Bond, wch I vallued nott att sixpence. . . . It would be beyound all discretion for me to have three thousand two hundred pound In his hand Thatt Had nott A foott of Land for the security of—Eliza Frek."[4]

Within Bilney manor Elizabeth Freke had had a long strained relationship with a stubbornly resident peer. She knew before she came as lord of Bilney that she could not live in the manor Hall. She had tried, continued to try, to rent this central mansion from one Lady Richardson, whose home it was "for the Third of her Dowre Given her by my deer Father," as Elizabeth Freke explained it; that is, when her father bought Bilney from Lord Richardson he had validated "frely" the existing dower-right willed to the wife. Elizabeth Freke had not a shred of sympathy for the widowed Lady Richardson; she pressured and pushed, and impatiently waited twelve years for the aging Lady to die. (Meanwhile she lived in what she called "my poore thacht house," in its pictures a charming large cottage.) At last, fulfillment came in 1698: poor old Lady Richardson "In her Closett Burntt to Death"; and over her charred remains Elizabeth Freke unsorrowfully claimed her gentry right. With great satisfaction she proceeded to furnish the manor hall with fine pieces of chairs, tables, beds, hangings, linen, and plate, bought, she noted, with money given her by her father years earlier "to buy Pins with"—"neear 1000£. . . . with 8 or 9 years' Intrist."[5]

Widow Freke quarreled intermittently for the last three years of her life with the Bishop of Norwich about her donative rights in the church at Bilney (actually the church of Pentney, copyhold lands which she also owned). She had turned out a "Drunken Debauched" curate from the church and replaced him with a Mr. Buck, in whom she saw "noe Greatt faultt," this done prior to any communication with the Norwich bishopric. She was annoyed when the bishop's office questioned, mildly and as a matter of form, Mr. Buck's license to preach: this she saw as unquestionable violation of her prerogatives and privacy. She had entered Mr. Buck as curate, she instructed the Norwich office, "Butt I except of him noe longer then his Good Behaivour to the Church, And During my pleasure. . . ." Further she informed the bishopric that the Pentney curate's "Maintenance" would have to be provided from Norwich since *she* would not pay it: "I should think Itt as prodygall in me," she wrote, "that have Little more than two Hundred pound a year Cleer" even to "give the Minester Twenty." The upshot of this altercation was that shortly before her death Widow Freke was excommunicated from her own church. But if she now trembled for her eternal soul she did not confess it to her diary. Anticipating the (frustrated) bishop's order she hustled to the church and took away her "plate" and "Whatt Elce" she had "Given Itt": one "Large sillver Flagon Cost me above fiffteen pound, one Large silver Cupp to Itt and Itts Bread plate or Cover"; one "New Common prayer Book in Turky Leather Imbrost and Gilded"; one "New Vellum book for Xings & Buriall"; one "Imbrodered Table Cloth pullpitt Cloth & Couchen of my own Worke; With one fine Damask Table Cloth. . . ." Lesser items she left there: little cups and a pewter "Flagon," a chest and "Two Long Seats, a new Bible and prayer book, one old book of Erasmus" (she thought), "3 silk Couchens" in her pew, doors from her house (!), various altar cloths, and "one old Communion Table Railed In by me"; of these things she made an inventory. And leaving the church "Tite & Whole, & not soe much as A quary in the Windows broke or the Least Breach in the Church yard," she hoped she was "Rid of all the spirituall Black Coats"—"Butt," she added, "the Key of the Church I keep to my selfe."[6]

From the moment of her arrival in 1686 as the new (and unwanted) mistress of the manor of Bilney, Elizabeth Freke had been in combat with her tenants. The essential relationship had been set back then: her manor tenants she judged a "pack of Bruite beasts." They let her know, she wrote, "that iff I thought to Nest my selfe att Billny they would starve mee outt, saying I should wash my dishes my selfe & milke my Cows too. . . . Butt when I gott footing, I soon evidenced my Right to Itt, and as fast as I could, removed those that thretned to Turne me out of doores & Billny too." Consequently she was in endless litigation with tenants—who, to be sure, obviously tried to take advantage of a solitary and female manor lord. Regularly they would "Run Away" with her rents, stealing out at night with their goods (and some of hers too); others cut down and stole her trees, "sixteen Great Elmes" and "Five and Twenty Growing Oakes In pryers Close," and concealed the theft in "A hundred of Boards for Pails & Rails"; they "ploughed up" the "Moyre," deliberately, she knew, "to wrong me off Itt"; they disputed hedges and streams and "Akers of Grass & Hay." Wretched me, "Thus am I used," Elizabeth Freke lamented, as she haled them to court. She may not have been upset that an ex-tenant swore before a Norwich judge that, in her words, "I never sued any one butt I Ruyened them & made there femillyes Begars."[7]

All servants the Widow Freke considered rogues, thieves, and potential murderers. Certainly her evidence was convincing. In her last years, weak, half-crippled, she was particularly vulnerable, needing a faithful household staff. Accidents happened: "sitting in my Chamber All A Lone Reading some partt of my Will. . . . my head Catchtt All A Fire, and In three minits Time burntt all my head Cloths Close to my haire. . . ."; she fell rather frequently, once down the main stairs, and it was a long while before she was attended to, back wrenched, knee broken, teeth knocked out, "a sad prospectt to behold." Doors of the manor house were carelessly left open—or perhaps carefully. "Munday the 16th of November," read an entry of 1713, "my kiching doore being open, Came up into my Chamber Two Ruffians. . . . and brought me A peice of paper to Insertt my Name to, Which I Absolutely refused to doe. . . . thus these two Rogues stood pulling and pinching of me for Above two howrs. . . . and Towre me by my Arms and shoulders; and when I said they would kill mee they said that they Cared nott. . . . all the while Calling me the worst names thatt there Mouthes Could utter; att Last they concluded to throw me down the staires, and by thatt way to stopp my breath. . . ." She conceded finally after "A bove three howrs' Contest," no servant appearing at any time, and signed the paper; at issue had been the disputed sum of twenty pounds. Most chilling was her fear that four of her oldest servants were "Conspireing" to murder her, her coachman, a "Cook Maid" and *her* "Rogue," and the "Divell sarah," her personal maid of many years who had "Command" of all the "Mony

& goods" in the house (including odd sums "In my Trunke In a sillver Chamber pott"). The four of them fled with loot before the Widow Freke could have them arrested, but let there be no doubt that she would have relished a fearful punishment. She brought for theft to the "Justice sitting" a pair of sometime-servants and Bilney rebels, "Goode Kneeve & Diana Davy": the two were ordered "A Good Whiping and What further I pleased," she wrote, "which I saw done to them both outt of my window Att the Carts Taile. . . . Till the Bloud spun, for examples sake. And Iff Further Complaintt to be sent to Bridwell."[8]

The editor of Elizabeth Freke's *Diary* discovered the curious fact that into the early twentieth century a legend persisted among the locals of West Bilney that the Widow's ghost haunted the countryside, restlessly irascible, punitive. 'Quiet, children—or the ugly witch-Freke will get you!'

The editor of the *Diary* also prefaced its text with an image of the young Elizabeth Freke as a sort of golden girl, rich, secure, pampered. Since Elizabeth Freke only began her diary-keeping with her marriage there is no direct evidence of this. It can be surmised, however, from the special relationship she had with her father: the eldest of his four daughters Elizabeth was his favorite. The father was Raufe Freke of Hannington, Wiltshire, a gentleman educated at All Souls and the Middle Temple, who married in 1636, he at age fifty, a daughter of Sir Thomas Culpeper of Kent. Raufe Freke was probably royalist but apolitical, passing the 1640s in discreet seclusion at his and his wife's estates in Wiltshire, Dorset, and Kent. Elizabeth's childhood was barely clouded by the death of her mother in 1650: a little girl of nine she probably became closer to her father; moreover, her mother's sister had married her father's brother, and aunt and uncle lived at Hannington too, stand-in parents for Elizabeth and her sisters, Cecily, Frances, and Judith. Protectiveness, warmth and tenderness, such in the editorial frame described the family life at Hannington.[9]

The girls were educated for marriage, appropriately trained to their gentle status in exquisite skills of upper-class housewifery: the "gorgeous embossed embroidery in which Culpeper ladies excelled," the arts of making cakes, jellies, and cordial waters, "botany," as befitting relatives of the famous physician Nicholas Culpepper, as the fundament of herbal medicine. Thus the younger sisters were married carefully, early, and well to knighted and/or prosperous gentlemen— Sir George Chout, Sir George Norton, Colonel Robert Austen. Elizabeth, though, went a different and wilfull way: she fell in love with a handsome young cousin, Percy Freke of County Cork, Ireland, a man whom her family judged from the start as "impecunious" and "thriftless." Raufe Freke argued long against the match, six or seven years, until Elizabeth was thirty, but the headstrong (or rather, amazingly patient) pair finally married secretly in London in 1671. With that Father Raufe did the loving and civilized thing: he hosted an elaborate second ceremony and bestowed upon his favored daughter a marriage portion of £6,764, to be held for her (Raufe Freke was law-trained as well as a suspicious father-in-law) by five trustees.[10]

What romantic dreams Elizabeth nourished through her long commitment to Percy Freke, why she was so enthralled with him as to defy her beloved father, we do not know. Nor do we know why her marriage brought so swift a disillusioned change, especially a too-late contrition that she had married without her "deere Fathers consentt or knowledge." The *Diary* began with the 1671 wedding but the entries were brief summaries, written later probably after Elizabeth Freke had settled in Bilney. By then Percy (as we must differentiate him; she referred to him always as "Mr. Freke") had for her a fixed character: he was an unprincipled adventurer who had set his sights on the plunder of her fortune.

Percy Freke never had a good word in the *Diary*, until, that is, he was a physical wreck, old and dying at Bilney. He might have made a case for himself. In 1671 he had some family prospects in Ireland but no estate of his own, nothing to take his new wife to, let alone dower her with. The money she brought to the marriage was his by law and custom; his assumed responsibility was to buy jointure property, or in any case to use the money to build a base of security for his coming family. Perhaps that was what he was trying to do. Elizabeth's version denied it: self-interested speculation was Percy's game.

For example: as a part of Elizabeth's portion of 6,000-odd pounds there was, in her words, "A mortgage on Sr. Robert Brooks Estate of 5000£ A year in Epping Forrest," and this, "unknown" to Elizabeth, Percy sold to "Sr. Josias Child [*the* Josiah Child, bourgeois merchant of East India Company fame], A great Bruer In London." Percy got for this deal over £5,000, or "there A boutts," Elizabeth said, "wch nither my deer Father or my self or any of my 5 Trustees knew anything off. . . . soe off Itt was sould."[11]

Elizabeth's assessment of this initial episode was that she had been swindled out of a dower property: "by Itt I were Turned outt of door, & nott A place to putt my unfortunate head In, & my Mony in a Bankers hand." Meanwhile the honeymoon couple were living in London lodgings, or Elizabeth was, while Percy busily tried to spend "the Remaineing part" of her portion, investing in this or that, being somehow cheated over an estate in Hampshire and losing thereby between 1,500 and 2,000 pounds in legal fees. Elizabeth tallied her first three years with him: "I twice Misscarryed, and . . . I Lost Two thousand and five Hundred & sixty pounds." It is interesting, though, that her sense of the romantic jostled the material loss: "I Never had to My Remembrance Fife pounds of Itt & Very Little of my husbands Company, wch was Noe small Griefe to me I Being Governed In this my Marriag wholly by My affections."[12]

Was it with Father Raufe Elizabeth Freke learned to expect nothing in the outside world but selfishness, avarice, and cunning? She returned often to the haven of Hannington, even after Percy took her to Ireland (in order, she said, to "Try my Fortune there"). Raufe Freke wanted her to separate from Percy, urged her and in fact made her promise, after her first visit to Ireland, to live with him at Hannington "for his life." But Father Raufe had raised his daughters to their marital destiny; like it or not, he had put them into the legal and customary power of their husbands. Clearly he set for Elizabeth a dilemma, between father and husband, though in the crunch when Percy ordered her obedience she *almost* always obeyed; perhaps she was compelled by the hard-dying love dream, or more likely, by helpless conformism, "that nothing Might Lye att my door," as she put it.

But certainly Raufe Freke riveted Elizabeth's attention upon propertied and financial security against a hostile, thieving world. During her first stay in Ireland he kept her baby son, namesake Ralph who was born in 1675, and thus had an excellent excuse to call her home for lessons in practical survival. At Hannington she had only to look "A Little Malloncally on some past Reflection" to get gifts from Raufe's "Closett," over the years "A Bove Twenty thousand pounds," to be used for "Needles and Pins," he told her, that is, kept from Percy's grasp. And Father Raufe provided her with the English dower which would give her a place for her "unfortunate head." (Involved in this was the only dark area between father and daughter: Hannington she could not have; it was willed to the male heirs of a younger brother, he "who now enjoys Itt," the old Widow Elizabeth was still noting with some bitterness.) Raufe's £1,000 purchase of the manor of West Bilney in Norfolk was concluded, of course, with Percy Freke's assent, the latter "Nott being strong enough with my money to pay for Itt," Elizabeth said. But it was ringed about with protective devices to make it hers, "thatt Estate," as she ever identified it, "for my selfe & my Son which my deer Father settled on me & my son." As long as he lived Raufe Freke saw to it that Bilney remained hers: when Percy was soon wanting to borrow money on "Bilney security," Raufe put the loan "on Mr. Freke's bond," rather than "Charge" Bilney with it.[13]

If selfishness, avarice, and cunning prevailed in the outside world survivors had to become selfish, avaricious, and cunning. This fundamental truth was reinforced by the Irish Frekes. Elizabeth did not at first understand the hostility of Percy's possessive mother, "My husbands Mother being very unkind to mee. . . . I never haveing had one unkind word from my Father in all my Whole Life." Presently she did: when the old woman died, "att neer Fourwre score years of age," Elizabeth observed in caustic perception, her demise was blamed on her new daughter-in-law "for Carrying Away her son." Percy's sister Bernard put that guilt at Elizabeth's "Doore," as well as the mother's burying bill of £80.

The same sister-in-law taught Elizabeth Freke that material possessions were to be jealously guarded and viciously fought for. On her second trip to Ireland Elizabeth discovered that Bernard had taken all the things she, Elizabeth, had left there: personal letters (love letters from the seven-year engagement), all her plate, "to the value of Neer Two hundred pounds," she wrote, "engraven with my own Coat of Arms in a lossenge," plus "two dozen of silver spoons of my own," and "my best Linnin." The brazen Bernard claimed that these items had belonged to her mother. "With Much A doe & high words," said Elizabeth, "I Gott A Little of my Plate A Gain."[14]

Percy Freke's behavior was a course in itself in Elizabeth's continuing education. He did not defend her against his unfriendly family, which may have been the cause of stormy scenes toward the end of her second Irish residence: perhaps after some of her "high words" he flung out a remark that "stuck deep in my stomack," Elizabeth wrote, "that he wished to never see my face more. . . ." Retreating to Hannington and sadly pondering her unhappy marriage, she had a weak moment of remembered affection—and wrote Percy of her needles and pins money, "hopeing itt might be a means of continuance with him." Indeed: Percy was there as fast as ship and coach could carry him to collect money and wife. He ordered her to return with him because he thought she had more money than he knew about, that of course true: now-cunning Elizabeth, who had "nott had Two and Twenty shillings" from him during her previous "Two and Twenty months" in Ireland, kept a secret fund, "for my own use."

Perhaps the diary-writing Elizabeth Freke was still too angry to recall details of her third stay in Ireland. She had refused "positively" to go at first, "A leadging, " she said, "my promise Made to my Deer

Father to stay with him for his Life," and citing the "unkindness" of the Irish Frekes when she was "in ther powre of Command." One last time Raufe Freke recalled her from resentful submission, to be with him at his death, he said. Percy consented and was coming too, but they were still in Cork when to Elizabeth's "gret loss, Grife and unspeakable Sorow" her father died.

Thus the journey homeward was made in mourning mixed, undoubtedly, with Elizabeth's unforgiving fury. Percy wanted to come in any case because there were encumbrances on the Irish estate he was negotiating for, and (with Father Raufe's protection gone) he thought to look at the profits of *his* West Bilney property. He dropped Elizabeth and son Ralph in London lodgings as he made a leisurely inspection, a ten-week tour, of Bilney. Finished, he merely passed through London, on his way to further Irish speculation; his departure, Elizabeth wrote, was "unknown to mee till the night before he went. . . . Which I cannott Forgett. . . . Itt was soe grieveous to me." Percy left his wife and son in London with "Butt Fifteen pounds in the world" (he must have known better, as readers of the *Diary* know better); perhaps he put a message as well as malice in his parting shot that "his estate of Billny" would not "find him in Bread and Cheese, besides the Charge of Itt."[15]

It was the year 1686, and Elizabeth Freke, matron of forty-five, came of age, a full-formed (if as yet inexperienced) member of gentry possessive society. She complained bitterly of Percy's callous leave-taking: "my unkind Husband, who never in his Life Took any Care for me, or whatt I did," who "never took Care for a Peny for my subsistance or his sons. . . ." But she decided to stand alone, to "seek my fortune for my Bread," to set up "To Farmeing," as she put it. The self-pitying dramatics were a trifle overdone: she was going to take over her property rights at Bilney, which promised to keep her in more than bread and cheese, or even needles and pins; she could expect "rentt of 526 pounds a Yeare."[16]

If a flicker of the golden girl lingered in Elizabeth Freke the experiences of being lord of Bilney manor stomped it out. From the late 1680s, though an anomaly, feme sole *and* feme covert until Percy Freke died, she was the Widow Freke, coping with tenant "Bruite beasts," murderous servants, thoughtless relatives, and false friends.

With difficulty she could even manage Percy, who appeared the first time at Bilney about a year after she had established her residence. He was furious that she was there at all, and demanded her consent in selling the manor. Elizabeth so amazed herself in refusing that, unaccustomed as she was to communicate with the deity, she put it to the intervention of His will: "God gave mee the Resolution & Courage to keep whatt I had, rather than by parting with Itt, be kept by the Charity of my Friends." Percy left "in a greatt Anger," and she heard nothing from him for almost two years. He reappeared of course, again and again, to take all that he could find of her hoarded and accumulating funds (out of "my own Industry," said Elizabeth): £600, £1,000, straight from Bilney receipts. Legally Percy was invincible: "he bought my copyhold estate att Pentney of forty six pounds A Yeare," Elizabeth fretted, "& putt his own Life In Itt for wretched me to Renew." Her small victories were apt to be private: after Percy withdrew £2,000 on her investment in the Bank of England Elizabeth closed the account; he refused to see her, she noted casually, "for Moveing that Little Remaine of my Mony. . . ." But Percy died in 1706 at Bilney, "In my Arms," wrote Elizabeth. She gave him "A Gentlemans Buriall," with hundreds of guests from neighboring gentry to lowliest tenants. This lavish entertainment cost "Above Eleven Hundred & fiffty pounds," in the Widow Freke's precise inventory (she was sure she had been "Cheated" by various suppliers); but there was nothing to "lye" at her door as she closed the books on Percy Freke.[17]

Son Ralph carried on as a troublesome problem: he turned out a replica of his father (and mother). He had a list of grievances against Elizabeth, which made him sulky and resentful. He had been "bitterly angry" that she had prevented his marriage to an aristocratic Irish heiress, somehow managing this while Percy was still in fighting form. Elizabeth's reasons for halting the negotiations of both husband and son were these: she thought the prospective bride's "quality" to be "too much for A Gentleman"; she did not approve of the large Irish family, her son "cloyed with 7 or 8 Brothers and Sisters," this somehow related to her refusal to "be a Servant to any one In my Old Age"; and "I Cared nott," she said, "to be frightened outt of my Mony, nor my son either. . . ." When Ralph later married another Irish woman he "never soe much as Asked" his mother's "Blessing or Consentt." He did ask for money, constantly demand and ungratefully receive it. A "Rude Answer" was his typical response to her gifts, which naturally were accompanied by motherly advice, it being her "Dutty to Admonish him of his Errors." The Widow Freke captured the essence of the mother-son exchange with an account of a conversation in which she chided Ralph, he the father of three sons, about his ungracious ways: "His Answer to me was I Talked to him as Iff he were butt eighteen years of Age When att this very Time hee owes mee Above Three Thousand pounds In Redy mony I can Lay him up for." The Widow Freke left Bilney and her other investments to her grandsons; judging Sir Ralph to have had enough with his father's Irish estate and her loans and gift of the baronetcy, she willed him nothing but his portrait.[18]

If the Widow Freke had pleasant, companionable associations, if she ever felt moments of simple joy in the countryside, or in music, literature, religion, if she was aroused to curiosity by the political furor of the late seventeenth century, such things were not revealed in her *Diary*. She owned several dozen books (in her careful inventory), histories, travel accounts, law codes, sermons and prayers, treatises on gardening, herbal concoctions, and "phisick," but only time spent with the last seemed worthy of mention. She did read the *London Gazette* and gleaned items of various foreign wars, deaths, and disasters among royalty and other dignitaries ("The publick News Tells mee thatt We have had Buried within this yeare three Dauphins and one Dauphiness in France, and that Sr. William Windam's house in Allbermalle strett was Burntt down to the Ground by Carelessness of Two servants. . . . His Loss Computed Att 30000. . . ."). She liked keeping the *Diary*, obviously, for personal satisfaction and perhaps as a "Dutty." Many hours must have been filled in transcribing her "secreits of cakes, Sweattmeats, etc.," in two hundred fifty recipes, and "446 prescriptions" of herbal treatments adapted for her own use "outt of Cullpeper." And her utterly absorbed periods, surely, were marked in her elaborate room-by-room tallying of her material possessions.[19]

This final Freke obsession cannot be hurried over. Before journeying to London in 1711 to take her £3,000 out of Cousin John Freke's hands, and expecting that she would "never Returne Againe Home ALive," the Widow Freke thought it "fitt & proper to make an Inventory of some of the Best Things" left at Bilney. Her list of prized articles fills in print eight tiny-type pages, a gold mine for the social historian. Things were inventoried "in the Parlor Lockt," the "parler Chamber" and "the Hall," in the "Dineing Roome," the "Kiching," the "Back house & dary," in all the "upper Garrett" chambers and all the "Closetts." There were tables enormous and small, a dozen or more, three times as many chairs, from "Rush" stools to "Great easy" recliners, "Torter shell" cabinets and chests of drawers, tapestries, pictures, "Greatt Guiltt" looking-glasses, feather beds and bolsters, "Long Turky work" carpets, draperies, curtains, valences, rods ("Iron to smooth"). Nothing was too small to itemize: "12 Little deep Cheeses of Last year," one "Old Frying pan To Rost Cofy," one "New Iron Ratt Trap. . . ." In most rooms were containers, chests, "haire" trunks, big, little, deep, and "flatt" boxes, filled with linens, blankets, sheets, books, clothes, china—the Widow Freke might have hosted a state dinner with the last. In the dining room, along with fine tapestries, a "Great Wallnut Looking Glass," assorted portraits, two tables and six "cane Chaiers," was one "Coffin for me & Itts stand Redy Fixtt, & Leaded for me with the Key of Vault."[20]

Elizabeth Freke died in 1714. She was buried in Westminster Abbey, but sadly the *Diary* was closed on how that honor was purchased by her (or perhaps by her on-the-make baronet son?). She lives, however, though not in the witch-Freke. Rather, she is marvelously fixed in the image of the rich old woman, sitting alone in her chamber reading "some part" of her will and reviewing the ABCs of her life's lessons in material accumulation: locking up, fencing in, holding on.[21]

NOTES

1. *Mrs. Elizabeth Freke, Her Diary, 1671 to 1714*, ed. Mary Carbery (Cork, 1913), p. 40. For comparative sources roughly contemporary with this oddly little-used diary, see: The Lady Newton, *The House of Lyme, From its Foundation to the end of the Eighteenth Century* (London, 1917), and *Lyme Letters, 1660-1760* (London, 1925); *The Household Book of Lady Grisell Baillie, 1692-1733*, ed. Robert Scott-Moncrieff (Edinburgh, 1911); *The Betts of Wortham in Suffolk, 1480-1905*, ed. Katherine Frances Doughty (London, 1911); *Lowther Family Estate Books, 1617-1675*, ed. C. B. Phillips, Surtees Society, vol. 191 (1979); *Some Passages in the Life and Character of a Lady Resident in Herefordshire and Worcestershire during the Civil War of the Seventeenth Century*, ed. Rev. John Webb (London, 1857); *The Early Records of the Bankes Family at Winstanley*, ed. Joyce Bankes and Eric Kerridge (Manchester, 1973). Also, Alan Simpson, *The Wealth of the Gentry, 1540-1660* (Cambridge, 1961).

2. *Mrs. Elizabeth Freke, Her Diary*, pp. 101-2.

3. Ibid., pp. 120, 59, 129, 132. It is to be noted that by Gregory King's estimates, in 1696 baronets, third in the national population in rank and wealth (behind lords temporal and spiritual), were put at the yearly income of £880.

4. Ibid., pp. 72, 118.

5. Ibid., pp. 47-48.

6. Ibid., pp. 101, 137. King's estimated income of esquires was £450, of gentlemen, £280. Mrs. Freke was not including, obviously, her "Intrist" accumulating yearly.

7. Ibid., pp. 35, 46, 74-77. If the ill will and the high turnover of personnel reported by Mrs. Freke were not unique, they do seem unusual. See Richard Gough, *The History of Myddle*, ed. David Hey (Penguin, 1981), for some "Antiquityes and Memoyres" of that Shropshire parish, or Margaret Spufford, *Contrasting Communities* (Cambridge, 1974).

8. *Mrs. Elizabeth Freke, Her Diary*, pp. 103, 55, 135, 104-6, 124.

9. Ibid., p. 1.

10. Ibid., pp. 1-3.

11. Ibid., pp. 21-22, 23.

12. Ibid., pp. 23, 24.

13. Ibid., pp. 23, 30, 53, 130, 30, 32, 26, 35, 29.

14. Ibid., pp. 25-29.

15. Ibid., pp. 30-33.

16. Ibid., pp. 35-36.

17. Ibid., pp. 34-35, 53-54, 62-71.

18. Ibid., pp. 41, 64, 129-30, 18.

19. Ibid., pp. 113-14, 121, 139-43.

20. Ibid., pp. 109-18. For an early seventeenth-century comparison, see *The Records of the Bankes Family*, "The Probate Inventory of James Bankes, 1617," pp. 43-46; and for mid-century: Joyce Jefferies's possessions, in *Some Passages . . . of a Herefordshire Lady*. For post-restoration: *The House of Lyme* living "lavishly," pp. 219, 228-34, 278, 350.

21. For the burial record: *A House of Kings, the History of Westminster Abbey*, ed. Edward Carpenter (London, 1966), pp. 248-49.

11

The Motherhood of Brilliana Harley

Brilliana Harley was that heroine of the civil wars, the deceptively delicate semi-invalid who rose from her bed to defend Brampton Bryan Castle against royalist seige in the summer of 1643. Her letters of the ordeal preserve a measure of her mettle as she refused to surrender "her house" upon the orders of the royalist governor of Herefordshire: "I thought I was bound to keep what was mine as long as I could," she wrote, "for I am persuaded if our gracious King knew my condition he would commiserate me so far that I should have liberty to stay in my own house, and enjoy what is mine."[1]

Besides her last letters (she died of "a very greate coold" days after the seige was lifted),[2] the Harley family kept a bundle of Lady Brilliana's correspondence, a few letters to her husband and many to her son, Edward or "Ned," while the latter was at Oxford between 1638 and 1641. They are revealing letters. The fifty-year-old Ned, by then Sir Edward Harley, remembered a mother who had "tenderly loved" him, who had "wisely and carefully instructed and corrected" him. The nineteenth-century editor of the *Letters* stressed the affection: the Lady had "fondly loved" her son. Did neither of them notice that Brilliana herself had worried about outsiders' judgment that she was "too fond a mother"?[3]

Lady Harley's formal biography is a minor note in the history of families advancing in the sixteenth century and markedly distinguishing themselves in the seventeenth. She was born in 1600 in Holland, where her father was lieutenant governor of the Brill. The latter, Sir Edward Conway, had commanded a troop at Cadiz in 1596 and been knighted there by the Earl of Essex; he was a secretary of state under James I, sat in Stuart parliaments until 1624, and in 1625-26 was created Baron Conway of Ragley in Warwickshire and Viscount Killultagh of Killultagh, County Antrim, Ireland. The mother was Dorothy, daughter of Sir John Tracy of Gloucestershire, a lady carrying extended 'cousinships': a sister had married Sir Horace, Baron Vere of Tilbury (like Conway a former governor of the Brill, and foremost soldier of his day in the English contribution to the Dutch wars with Spain), and had produced daughters who as contemporaries of Brilliana wedded the Earls of Clare and Westmoreland, Lord Paulet, and Thomas, to-be Lord General, Fairfax. As second daughter of Sir Edward Conway, Brilliana's marriage in 1623 to Sir Robert Harley of Brampton Bryan in Herefordshire was solid rather than glittering: Harleys had been sheriffs, knights, and members of Parliament from their county; Sir Robert, educated at Oriel College and the Inner Temple, a man of "wit, learning, and piety," had been a magistrate and deputy lieutenant in Herefordshire and an MP in the reigns of both James and Charles I.[4]

In its sober detail the Harley marriage was an upper-class set piece. Sir Robert, of "an austere and decided character," was forty-four in 1623, almost twice Brilliana's age; she was his third wife, though he had no living children from the previous marriages. In the twenty years ahead Brilliana would bear three sons and four daughters. She seldom left Brampton Bryan, while Sir Robert was away much of the time, "incessantly and zealously" occupied with county and parliamentary affairs. Though he was interested in "rural pursuits" of stock breeding and improved agriculture (and might have been a notorious encloser), most of Sir Robert's attention was upon the "business and welfare" of Herefordshire and, from 1639, of the nation. Certainly, in the 1640s, as a Presbyterian leader of the Long Parliament, he had neither time nor concern for the domestic routines of Brampton Bryan.[5]

But this situation, this marital separateness, permits a glimpse beneath the smooth Harley surface. Despite her "delicate constitution," which confined her days, weeks, to her bed, Lady Brilliana was in charge at Brampton Bryan; while she wished and tried to consult her husband, "would have him act the understanding part," on estate and family matters she was alone with problems as diverse as a schoolmaster for her younger sons and the withheld rents of royalist tenants. It is a privileged glimpse of a country-buried wife and mother competent as she was expected to be (and well enough educated to tutor her sons in translating "some things out of Latin into Inglisch," to instruct them in the events of English and continental Protestants' grappling with the papist enemy) if she could but reach out, communicate, converse.[6]

In the first eight letters of the Harley bundle, those written between 1625 and 1633, Lady Brilliana was trying to talk with her husband. Addressed to "Deare S^r," or once to "My dearest S^r," the letters are a mixture of formality and affection (and wonderful peculiarity of spelling). She celebrated always his continued good health, the "beest nwes" she could hear. She remarked upon King Charles's Parliament "dooing nothing." She reported that the "payling of the nwe park" was completed, and that his county militia company had met "to learne the use of theiare armes." She kept him informed of the health of the children, the babies coming regularly: Ned, born in 1624; Robert, 1626; Thomas, 1628; Brilliana, 1629; Dorothy, 1630; Margaret, 1631. And usually she included a sentence about her lonely self: "You see howe my thoughts goo with you," she wrote, "and as you have many of mine, so let me have some of yours." Or, "Allas! my deare S^r, I knowe you doo not to the one halfe of my desires, desire to see me, that loves you more then any earthly thinge." Again, "I much longe to heare from you, but more a thousand times to see you, which I presume you will not beleeve, because you cannot poscibilly measure my love."[7] She might have been teasing, but nothing in her subsequent letters suggests her capable of frivolous sentiment. A serious Puritan lady, Brilliana Harley was also naturally and honestly warm, her love focused in these early lines upon her austere and preoccupied middle-aged husband.

The rest of the correspondence, almost two hundred letters from 1633 to 1643, went to son Ned, first to Magdalen Hall in Oxford, where he was placed at age fourteen with a famous Puritan tutor, and after late 1641 to London or wherever he might be found with his troop of parliamentary horse. The loving warmth glows in these letters—refocused, however: Lady Brilliana had chosen a substitute object in Ned, her first-born son.

She wrote weekly to Ned, sometimes more often if a chance carrier, other than the Brampton Bryan "gardner," was bound toward Oxford. Ned was expected to reply as frequently; if he did not he felt the soft maternal pressure. "Bee not forgetful to rwit to me," she said, ". . . . I can not be very mery, tell it pleases God, to give me that comfort." And, "I rwit to Gorge that I had not hard from you (as I thought a longe time). . . . sence I can not see you, I am glad to have the contentment of a paper conversing with you, for still you are most deare to me, and I hope ever will be. . . ."[8] The boy quickly became very faithful.

The first year's letters to "my beloved child" were filled with maternal concern and admonition. Lady Brilliana worried constantly about illness: "Theare is no earthly thinge that is of more comefort to me than your being well," she wrote. "Doo exersise," she advised him, "be carefull to use exersise." She warned him "not to take medicines out of a strange hand," and sent him home remedies, "orampotabely" to be taken in "cordus watter," "bessor stone," and boiled "juce of licorich" for dosing colds. "I wisch," she cautioned, "you may not eate to much fisch. . . . I know you like it; but I thinke it is not so good for you." And "I hope," she added, "you have something over your beeds head." "Deare Ned," she assured him, "if you would have any thinge, send me word"; with or without word the "gardner" toted supplies—"turky pyes," biscuits, cakes, apples and plums, shirts, books, money—to "pleasure" the Oxford lad.[9]

A subject getting equal time was Ned's spiritual well-being. In his early months at Magdalen he had in each of Brilliana's letters a little sermon, and prayers that the Lord grant him "those choys blessings of his Spirit, which none but his deare ellect are partakers of. . . ." She recognized the continuing solidity of his education—"I beleeve, before this, you have reed some part of Mr. Calvin; send me word how you like him"—but unremitting instruction was a mother's duty: never "neglect," she told him, "that constant sarvis you owe to your God," which "the men of this world can not perseave." Thinking about the worldly and ungodly she was relieved that there were "but feawe nobellmens sonnes in Oxford," that "they send theaire sonnes into France, when they are very younge, theaire to be bred." Better to be unsullied by their "company," for "piche will not easely be tuched without leaufeing some spot."[10]

Lady Brilliana gave close attention to Ned's social development. While the Harleys were kin to most of the other leading families of their county, Ned Harley at Oxford was something of a Puritan provincial when he met his Conway-Tracy relations, members of Brilliana's more nationally dazzling family. Ned might have perceived his mother's ambivalence as she prodded him into this formidable network. "I would have you rwite a letter to my lady Conway," she told him, "I have heare inclosed sent you a coppy of the letter I would have you rwite to her." She was pleased that he was invited to her brother's home, and "not sorry" that the company thought the boy favored "my lord"—presumably her father. Of one of Ned's hostesses, Brilliana remarked that "she keepes her state, as all nobellmens daugtres doo; tho I doo not." Ned was "to submite" to his "fathers desire" that he "be contented with plaine clothes"; but he was to remember that there was "no distance" between him and any "pretty jentellman" whom he met. For "you have part in nobellness of bearth," his mother wrote, "tho some have place before you, yet you may be in theare company." She said this, she added, "not to make you proude or consaited of your self, but that you should knowe yourself, and so not to be put out of your self, when you are in better company then ordineray. . . . speeke freely, and all ways remember, that they are but men. . . ."[11]

The weekly letters with postscript "longing" to see or hear from her beloved child, the boxes of "coold pyes," dried fruit, and "violet cakes," the "littel bookes," a "leetell purs with some smale mony in it," the special something about which he was to say nothing to his father, "my ring," and "my wactch" that was his grandfather's and would "goo very well" if one did not "over winde it"—Brilliana made it very clear that Ned was never out of mind. She was bothered a little, helplessly, by the possible censorship of the Oxford tutor. Did Mr. Perkins, she quizzed the returned carrier-gardener, "not say I was too fond a mother"? And, again: "I long to see you, I will not say how much, lest your tutor call it fondnesse, and not love."[12]

Through his second year at Oxford the sixteen-year-old Ned became his mother's "great comfort," sharing her confidences as an equal. She seems to have been constantly ill, though a minor theme in all of her letters had been her poor health and confinement: "I have not been very well theas three days," was a normal entry, "and so enforsed me to keepe my beed, as I have doune many times, when you weare with me." Now she told Ned of being "extremely trubelled with a beateing at my hart," of being too feeble for "phisek" or bloodletting. Though she buried it in affirmation of the "sweetnes" of her faith in God, she was depressed: "I have had a time of siknes, and weakenes, and the loose of frinds, and as I may say, the glideing away of all thos things I tooke most comfort in, in this life." Early in 1640 she miscarried, and sank to premonition of death: "I waite upon my gratious God," she told Ned in a dictated letter. Recovering slowly and so precariously that she risked one of her "coolds" by going from her bedroom "into the parler," she discussed the pregnancy openly with Ned: "I did not thinke I had bine with Child when you weare with me" (on his fall holidays), she said.[13]

But Ned was a man by 1641, or as such his mother's letters dealt with him. He was with his father in London as the crises mounted toward civil war. Lady Brilliana wrote *to* him, and to her husband *through* him. It was Ned who was asked the whereabouts of "your fathers lodging," Ned who put his mother "in minde" to send Sir Robert "some biskets," and returned word that they were appreciated. Apologies even went through Ned: "I am sorry," Brilliana wrote, "that your father was displeased for not haveing his mony souner," this about the withheld rents of spiteful tenants. When Sir Robert was "so biussy," Brilliana bravely maintained, "I would not have him rwit": "I would have you tell your father what I thinke of your chamber and the howes. . . . I would have write to him about it meself, but that I thought it might trubell him to reade so longe a letter. . . . I thinke many letters would trubell him. . . ."[14]

In any case, it was with Ned that Brilliana wished to communicate, his letters, as she told him again and again, which brought her "more satisfaction than any other"; "I can let your thoughts run with me," she confessed. Her domestic worries and estate problems, her difficulties with her husband's "biusness"—raising the money, selling horses and plate for the parliamentary cause—were unloaded now upon Ned. His future was a central thought: out of her element and inept, perhaps, she was his unsolicited agent for the Commons seat as burgess from Hereford (apparently in this Sir Robert was also "displeased" with her efforts). Pushed to the back of the mind, but surfacing nonetheless, was the realization of a marriageable Ned: Brilliana thought it a "pitty" that "yonge men should marry," unless it were in "need of a nurs or a giude"; "I pray God," she observed, "if you ever have a wife, she may be of a meeke and quiet spirit."[15]

In the end, Ned got the burden of her Brampton Bryan peril, of her existence as a "dispised company" in the royalist midst, wife of the squire whom tenants had "growne to hate." She was stoic under her master's orders to remain: "I doo long allmost to be from Brompton," she told her son, "to come up to Loundoun . . . in a place of safety"; but "since it is not your father's will, I will lay aside that desire." As she sent for "50 waight of shot" she reported that she was "not afraide": "I cannot make a better use of my life," she wrote, "next to sarving my God, than doo what good I can for you. . . ." Somewhere in the field and trying to learn his assignment as a Captain in the parliamentary army Ned received these painful lines:

> My deare Ned, I know it will greeve you to know how I am used. It is with all the malice that can be. . . . they say they will burne my barnns . . . will not let the fowler bringe me any foule, nor . . . suffer any of my servaunts pas. They have forbid my rents to be payed. They drave away the yong horsess at Wigmore, and none of my servaunts dare goo as scarce as fare as the towne. And deare Ned, if God weare not mercyfull to me, I should be in a very miserabell condistion. I am threatened every day to be beset with soulders. My hope is, the Lord will not deliver me nor mine into theair hands; for surely they would use all cruellty towards me, for I am toold that they desire not to leave your father neather roote nor branch. . . .[16]

It may be that Ned was about to become explicitly the husband-surrogate. Lady Brilliana's next to last letter ended, "My deare Ned, let me know your mind wheather I had beest stay or remove." But it was undecided the few days later when she took her great cold, an "ill time to be sike in," she felt, and penned her final, characteristic postscript: "My deare Ned, I pray God blles you and give me the comfort of seeing you, for you are the comfort of . . . Your most affectinat mother."[17]

Obviously Brilliana Harley's revelation in her book of letters is something of an oddity by the prevailing view that seventeenth-century parents kept their distance from their children—the "interpersonal relations" which were "at best cold and at worst hostile"[18]—because of high mortality, Calvinist instruction, or their own conditioning. She is one of those exceptions Lawrence Stone grants in his forceful presentation of the sixteenth- and seventeenth-century middle- and upper-class family in its patriarchal and authoritarian "phase," the "great age of the whip," he calls it, in which the "most drastic" measures of discipline were perceived as essential to "ordered society."[19] Given the weight of this assertion she should be left on the sidelines as we register examples of major behavior: Elizabeth Jocelin's famous and forbidding *Legacie, to her unborne Childe*, say, Mrs. Jocelin almost exactly a contemporary of Brilliana Conway, her chilling puritanism "carefully" inculcated by a grandfather who was the Bishop of Lincoln;[20] or the London shopkeeper-wife telling her husband, Nehemiah Wallington, that he offended God in grieving for a dead three-year-old daughter, that he had to "consider what a deal of grief and care we are rid of, and what abundance of joy she is gone into";[21] or nine-year-old Mall Blundell, at the end of the century, reminded of how often she had been beaten because of her "rolling untidy gate" and "wild carriage" of the head (unmarriageable habits in the daughter of an impecunious squire and father of too many girls).[22]

Perhaps a special category could be designated for the Harley letters, with some title bearing upon maternal fixation with the eldest son. There are stories in this which make Lady Brilliana's a model of moderation: Mrs. Mary Bewley, who wished only to die after the death of her son and was buried in his grave; Mrs. Elizabeth Aldersey, who refused the love and marriage offer of the distinguished General Robert Venables because of her "promise" to son Samuel that she "would not do it," and accepted only after that "precious jewel . . . a child of much comfort" died just short of his eighteenth birthday.[23]

Or, and this may be preferable, Brilliana Harley and her correspondence can be incorporated with the bulk of source material as a statement that in the difficult, unsettled, emerging bourgeois society

of the seventeenth century there was a wide range of family relationship, attitude, and treatment, as in the 'modern' eighteenth, nine-
teenth, twentieth centuries: children were loved or used, neglected
or abused, raised indifferently or strictly, or even permissively. And
the case could be made that Lady Brilliana touched most of the points
of the spectrum, according to her changing circumstances and the
individuality of her children.

She was a loving, giving parent: such was her self-concept, and she
disapproved of those who were other than she. Answering Ned's opinion of a female relative she remarked, "I am sorry my lady Corbet
takes no more care of her chilederen. . . . She has a way that I should
not take, by my good will with my chillderen, without it weare to
correct some great fallt in them; but my deare Ned, as long as it
pleases God, I have it, I shall willingly give what is in my power, for
the beest advantage of you, and your brothers and sisters, as ocation
offers itself."[24] Yet her second son, Robert, might have been one of
those seventeenth-century witnesses to his stiff and critical parent.
"Robin" was one of the domestic problems which Brilliana shared
with Ned. Aged twelve when Ned left for Oxford, Robin had a history
of frightening "fittes," convulsions, possibly; he "has no fitte sence
you went," Brilliana told Ned for some months, but the remission
was not permanent. Robin was withdrawn, rude, and irritating, "cares
not," his mother wrote, "to gaine any jentile corage, comes littell to
me, but when I exacte it from him"; at the same time he was sensitive,
touchy, "apt to apprehend unkindness." As he grew "tall and very
leane" he did "exceedingly neglect himself." He was not interested
in the national scene, did not care "to know how it goos in the par-
lament." He was "angry" with his sibling, caused his brother Tom
(younger by a year and a half) to "weepe . . . in privet."[25]

Meanwhile little brother Tom was deeply concerned with the "par-
lament newes," came to his mother's room "twes or thrise a day,"
read her reports of Commons speeches ("very soleme" he was, Brilliana said) and copied out the letters she dictated when she was too
weak to write herself to Ned. "Deare Ned," she observed, "Your
brother Tom is the likest you. . . ." When Tom was ill with the "ague,"
as the Harley children so frequently were, Lady Brilliana permitted
him "to lye in the chamber by me, which pleases him very well."[26]
Inexplicable contrast it was: a comparison of sunny Tom with sullen
Robert.

Ned heard about his smaller sisters only when they were ill: of
Margaret, unwell after her maid "used somethinge to her head"; of
Dorothie, who was so sick in mid-1642 that the family for days "much

feared her." Lady Brilliana did not mention the smallest, Elizabeth, born 1634; the semi-invalid mother may not have ventured into the nursery. But news of the oldest girl, namesake Brilliana, enlivened the letters for a time. In the spring of 1641 twelve-year-old "Brill" was introduced to society, sent into the kinship network for education in the London household of "my lady Vere."[27] (Again, a country cousin Harley probably had much to learn. Apparently no foreign governess had been engaged at Brampton Bryan, nor, for that matter, a fancy tutor for Number One Son: Lady Brilliana, raised abroad, bilingual herself, was merely hoping that Ned would "not forget to spend some time to learne French" in 1642, after he had left Oxford.)[28]

Young Brilliana's exit was not forced. Your sister "much longes for this journey," her mother told Ned, "did looke much paler," as she departed, "by resen of her ernest desire." The strong impression, in fact, is that Brill was unused to being forced in anything. By "this time," her mother wrote after two weeks, "I thinke your sister has lefte wondering at Loundoun. . . . deare Ned, put her in minde to be careful of herself." Ned had immediately been made surrogate father: ". . . .take care of your sister Brill. . . . shee is yonge, thearefore, deare Ned, obsarve her carage, and let not your counsell be wanting to her." And "I hope," Lady Brilliana added, "she will have so much wisedome to take it."[29]

Clearly the mother was emotionally involved with her eldest daughter. "I longe to see your sister Brill sonn," she wrote as the royalist control was tightening in Herefordshire. The involvement was of a different quality altogether, of course, than that Lady Brilliana demonstrated with Ned. Ned was *becoming*; he was exciting male potentiality. Daughter Brill *was*, a finished or at least known female personality. Anxiously Lady Brilliana pressed Ned for news of her daughter's reception in the home of relative-strangers: let me know, she urged, "how my lady Vere likes her"; she "much" desired "to knowe how my lady Veere likes her"; she did "pray" him to tell her if sister Brill "pleases my lady Veare."[30] Rather than indifference the words suggest resignation. All she could do for a beloved daughter was to pave her gentlewoman's way into proper social circles, hoping that she would please, that the social arbiters would grant her "favor."[31] 'Modern' mothers of the next century would do it little differently.

NOTES

1. *State Papers Domestic*, 1643 (Sept. 11), pp. 486-87.

2. *The Letters of the Lady Brilliana Harley* (New York, 1968), Camden Series, p. 208. See above, Chapter 2, pp. 39-40; on Brampton Bryan see *The Victoria History of the Countries of England, Herefordshire* (London, 1975), pp. 387-92.

3. *Letters of Brilliana Harley*, pp. 248, xx, 91.

4. *DNB*; *Letters of Brilliana Harley*, pp. xii-xiii. When he died in 1631 the first Viscount Conway was succeeded by his son, Edward, Brilliana's brother, "a man of great personal charm, of amusing conversation, an epicure who preferred the delicacies of his tables to the taste of war"; he was the fond father-in-law of Anne (Finch) Conway, student of metaphysical science and friend of Henry More. See Majorie Hope Nicholson, *Conway Letters* (New Haven, 1930), p. 7. (Professor Nicholson confuses the first Viscount Conway with his father, Sir John Conway.)

5. *Letters of Brilliana Harley*, p. vii, and passim.

6. Ibid., pp. 115, 137.

7. Ibid., pp. 1-2, 3-5.

8. Ibid., pp. 8, 9, 21, and passim.

9. Ibid., pp. 39, 24, 16, 49, 46-47, 9, 29, 13.

10. Ibid., pp. 9, 7, 8, 10.

11. Ibid., pp. 32, 24, 25, 16, 21.

12. Ibid., pp. 88, 27, 20, 17, 39, 26, 91.

13. Ibid., pp. 46, 24, 42, 34, 78, 113, 80.

14. Ibid., pp. 101, 112, 133, 118, 130, 136.

15. Ibid., pp. 80, 162-63, 62-63, 85.

16. Ibid., pp. 176, 170, 180, 183, 185, 187.

17. Ibid., pp. 208-9.

18. Stone, *Family, Sex and Marriage*, p. 99.

19. Ibid., pp. 216-18.

20. Elizabeth Jocelin, *A Mothers Legacie to her unborne Childe* (London, 1624).

21. N. Wallington, *Historical Notices*, 1: xix-xx.

22. Cavalier, *Letters of William Blundell to his Friends, 1620-1689*, ed. Margaret Blundell (London, 1933), p. 45, Appendix 6.

23. For Mary Bewley, see above, Chapter 7; and *Memoranda of Mrs. Elizabeth Aldersey*, Chetham Society, 4: 25.

24. *Letters of Brilliana Harley*, pp. 34-35.

25. Ibid., pp. 11-12, 37, 120, 119.

26. Ibid., pp. 119-20, 115.

27. Ibid., pp. 110, 161, 155, and passim.

28. Ibid., pp. 13-14, 157.

29. Ibid., pp. 160, 158, 168, 156.

30. Ibid., pp. 190, 160, 157.

31. Ibid., p. 172.

PART 4

Of Sex and Swindles

12

The Enjoyment of Sex?

In a delightful study of the genial subject of chapbooks and their readers, that is, the "small books" and "merry books" peddled all over England to "humble" and "non-gentle" folk (and to connoisseurs like Samuel Pepys), historian Margaret Spufford observed that seventeenth-century women "enjoyed their own sexuality and were expected to enjoy it." Spufford was thinking of women of the rural laboring population primarily, though she adds, "cultivated" ladies of the early century liked a dirty joke, broad humor which "is still practically unquotable, even by a woman writing now."[1] G. R. Quaife's *Wanton Wenches and Wayward Wives* resurrects some memorable illustrations of this ancient axiom: one Mary Combe, for example, a Somerset innkeeper's wife who in the 1650s held drinking parties for "cuckolds and cuckold-makers only," who regularly stood—or lay—on the road "for all comers," and put her hand in men's breeches, promising "if it were ready to stand she was ready for him." And Mary Combe had a neighbor named Joan Hix, who boasted of being "occupied fifteen times in one night" and thus earning the right to call herself "a lusty wench."[2]

It is sensible and satisfying research which deals with an accessible past, Restoration biography, for instance: Nell Gwyn's gaily ingenuous record in her progress from brothel child to theater "orange-girl" to lover of stage gallants to royal mistress; or the handful of aristocratic ladies released to nymphomania in the encouraging court of the Merry Monarch.[3] But *nothing* is known for certain about the sexuality of such respectable and pious middle-class women as we have encountered in the foregoing pages. The subject, maybe not unmentionable, is at any rate unmentioned in *their* progress away from the "vulgar" teeming world of the Mary Combes; the proto-Victorians drew the shades. (In the metaphor of one of the finest phrase-makers of 'domestic' theologians, Matthew Griffith, people were to be like the elephant, a beast of "sense" and "honestie," who couples "so secretly that hee is never seene in the *Act*"; after which "he goes to a river and washes. . . ."[4]

Only in their pregnancies is there sight into the sexual activity of most middle-class married women, which is to say that sex and reproduction were united; to understate the obvious, in Lawrence Stone's words, the "pleasure principle" was not separated from the "procreative function."[5] The "carnal act," the "secret society" of man and wife in Protestant social thinking was to be performed for high purposes: the multiplying of the "holy seed" for the "enlargement of the Church,"[6] especially, the process of which sanctified the daughters of evil Eve.[7] It might be accompanied by "rejoycing and delight" in one another, granted the great William Perkins, though he immediately added that this was "more permitted to the man, then to the woman."[8] Avoiding fine distinctions medical experts taught that women were most sure to conceive healthy babies when they were "more content than ordinary" after intercourses.[9] But in any case, in Protestant culture marriage-sex-babies was the package presented; and only a witless woman could have failed to associate her sexual enjoyment with absence of control over her body, indeed of her earthly days.

In 1640 the yeoman-preacher Ralph Josselin had his "eye fixed with love" upon a "Mayde," and he said, "hers upon mee." He was twenty, she nineteen when they married; within a year she was "breeding," to the "great joy and comfort" of them both, the young couple blessing the name of the Lord for his "gift." The Lord's gifts came in profusion in the following two decades: Mrs. Josselin proved to be "a childing woman," producing ten living children and disappointing with five miscarriages. Josselin was away as an army chaplain for some months, his wife during his absence "wondrous sad and discontented." She was pregnant immediately on his return, but this time—it was her third—she was "oppressed with feares that she should not doe well in this child"; a girl-baby came safely if with "very sharpe paynes," but after it the mother was ill "as if she would have even dyed." Her convalescence was slow: "my dearest fayles somewhat in her household diligence," worried her husband, as he prayed that the Lord "preserve" and "sanctifie" her as a "choice vessel to himselfe, and comfort unto mee." Successive pregnancies found Mrs. Josselin with "sad feares of illness and death approaching"; she "droopes in her apprehension," said her husband. And he would sometimes add, "the Lord in mercy make my lusts and corruptions stoope."[10]

There is no evidence that Mrs. Josselin did not have her wits about her. She (like Lucy Hutchinson, Elizabeth Lilburne) was simply a loving and acquiescent woman who willingly met the "lusts" of her husband, and accepted her lot even unto death, though she clearly wished to postpone it, as choice and sanctified "vessel" for the Lord.

Most absolutely such women were helpless before the tyranny of Divine and Natural Law. The preachers, with their own aversion to the carnal act (even the physician of midwifery, Nicholas Culpepper, declared it disgusting that babies were conceived "between the places ordained to Cast out Excrements, the very sinks of the Body"),[11] labored to cool male sexuality with orders that it be "sanctified, seasonable, temperate, and willing."[12] But they agreed that existing as she did in subjection to the man the "wives case" was "most miserable." Only her faith could sustain her: the "yoake" laid upon her was by "Gods appointment," with no other reason. And, she would be forced to answer, "Hath thou any religion in thee, if thou see no reason in this reason?"[13]

Poor pinned Alice Thornton squirmed on the problem: so horrified by her observation of an elder sister's lingering death of puerperal fever that she wanted (1) to avoid marriage altogether; (2) to put it off as long as she could; (3) to remain chaste even though married; (4) finally having lost all along the line, to take to the abstinence of a sickbed. Was the beautiful Betty Legh another such case? The daughter of a Lancaster gentry family she was engaged in 1690 to Mr. Master, a chief representative of the East India Company and ex-governor of Madras, she twenty-four and he fifty years old. Two days before the wedding, the dowry accepted, the jointure settled, guests by the scores invited, Betty Legh wrote this astonishing letter to the bridegroom: "I must still beg of you not to insist more of this business. . . . I hope I shall end my days in a single life be it never so mean. . . . I am not strong enough to endure much trouble nor to go through a married life, if it were never so easy; I know my own constitution so well I must say nothing will ever make me happy in that life. . . . I shall always be in this minde for I could never yett bring myself into any tolerable liking for it. Sir, you cannot say that ever I have given you encouragement. . . . release my troubled heart and minde. . . ." Unhappy Betty Legh even promised to pay any "charges" incurred in jilting Mr. Master, but there was no escaping him or her family: the marriage proceeded as planned, the groom secure in his opinion that she had had but a "small indisposition of mind or body." Betty Legh might have been dismayed by the prospect of a husband twice her age. But it is interesting that her mother's one subsequent comment, in due months, was that "my daughter Master is so infinitely fond of her nursery that she cannot look off it one hour."[14]

Mrs. Ralph Josselin's five miscarriages came in a string between her seventh and final live births. "It is not yet possible to be certain," writes Alan Macfarlane, editor of the Josselin *Diary*, "whether these miscarriages were merely the result of increased age, or whether they were consciously induced as a form of birth control." On firmer ground, Macfarlane is sure that Mrs. Josselin "helped" the spacing of her pregnancies by breast-feeding her babies, since for fear of 'spoiling the milk' intercourse was supposed to wait until weaning, for Mrs. Josselin when the infant was between twelve and nineteen months. But she once thought herself pregnant, wrongly, however, even though nursing; sexual discipline had failed yet another time.[15] Almost all the preachers advocated breast-feeding by the mother (against the upper-class tradition of putting babies out to a wet nurse), but beyond that method the Reverend Josselin and his wife, he endlessly contrite for minuscule sins as a minister of God, surely would not have induced miscarriages in their own interest of family planning, nor experimented with hopes of contraception.

Practically, they *could* have done so. Echoing the theologians Nicholas Culpepper lectured that a "Christian may not cause an abortion for any cause, for it is wicked. . . . The Gentiles in Hippocrates his time never allowed it, they would not hinder conception, much less would they destroy it when made. . . ."[16] "Remedies to cause Abortion," repeated the authors of *The Compleat Midwife*, are "wicked in a high degree."[17] Which was to say that suggested means for contraception and abortion had been available since the time of Hippocrates, in an accumulation richly embellished moreover through the centuries: the ancient technique of *coitus interruptus*, though morally and medically condemned, the coming family planner of a more secularized society;[18] oral contraceptives, 'magic' potions, pessaries, purges, violent exercises.

If "to preserve the mother," Culpepper wrote, it was necessary to "purge or bleed, and the abortion follow, the fault is not the Physitian that intended it, but in the weakness of Nature and of the child. . . ."[19] Culpepper's or any standard herbal directory had lists of purging remedies: nothing simpler for the would-be abortioner who could handle her guilt. Or she could reverse the recommended regimen for the breeding female: invite sexual relations in the early weeks, eat forbidden food gluttonously, laugh and cry "immoderately," hang about places where there might be the "noise of Guns, or great Bells," sleep little and exercise furiously (confused Alice Thornton: upon what advice was she in her seventh month of pregnancy scrambling about the Yorkshire dales?)[20]

And in the sophisticated London market of information explicit means were offered to attempt to separate the pleasure principle from the procreative function: written recipes of the ages of herbs, flowers, fruits, seeds, animal parts, natural liquids, and inventive combinations thereof. *The Ladies Dispensatory*, in its subtitle, "the like never published in English" (1651), had do-it-yourself chapters, headed "To cause abortion," and "To hinder Conception." For abortion: "Castorium the weight of two drams taken with Penniroyall . . . Unwashed wool applyed in a Suppositary . . . Dung of wild she Goates taken with some sweet and aromaticall thing . . . Decoction of Lupines, fomented with myrrhe and hony . . . Pepper drunk . . . Root of Hercules Allheal cut sharp at the end, put into the naturall place of women . . . Perfume of Vultures feathers . . . Jasper stone fastened to the thigh. . . ." Contraception was promised with the use of other homely materials: "Curd of a Hare, taken three days after the womans monthly purgation . . . Pepper put into the naturall place, after a woman hath known a man carnally . . . Rust of Iron drunk . . . Scaleferne gathered in the night when the moone doth not shine, fastened unto the womans belly, with the Milt of a mule; according to the opinion of some. . . ."[21]

So who bought, studied, and experimented with the techniques suggested in *The Ladies Dispensatory*? And did users thereby find their sexuality more enjoyable? The line of inquiry is so unstable that it ought to be abandoned—or quickly shifted to the various evidence that seems to say that London women, whether of the fashionable Town or the mercantile City,[22] had more sport in sex than their provincial sisters. From the crowded experience of his Spitalfields practice Nicholas Culpepper observed that "where the desire of Children moves one to the act of Copulation, the pleasure in the act moves an hundred. . . ." Why were there more burials than christenings in the capital, asked a demographer of the 1650s? The answer, he said, was male and female "Barrenness." The environmental conditions, "Smoaky, and Stinking," and the fast pace of life in the city were partly to explain it, but additionally "Adulteries and Fornications," so "frequent" in London, did "certainly hinder breeding": for "a woman, admitting 10 Men, is so far from having ten times as many Children, that she hath none at all."[23]

For what their marketable opinions are worth, City pamphleteers never had any doubt that women enjoyed their own sexuality. The image of the happily insatiable female was untouched through the

1650s by saintly biographies: marriage made a cuckold, whether Puritan wife or no; let our husbands "goe to the warres," the citizens' wives were made to say, and then we will "live as merrily as may be, drinke, feast, and walk abroad," and "if we have a minde to it, keep and maintaine a friend, that upon occasion may doe us a pleasure . . . ."[24] And the religious ones were the most sly, playing with their 'prentices while husbands worked at statecraft, or, best, in the recall of Restoration playwright Wycherley's irreverent phrase, with "some young modest pulpit comedian to be privy to their sins in their closets" (shades of accused and shamed Alice Thornton).[25]

A unique individual, astrologer as well as "Student in Physick," Sarah Ginnor (or Jinner), communicated woman-to-woman in tracts punctuated with winking nudges and bawdy innuendoes. In her *Womans Almanack* for 1659 she told her readers to pick up the "gift of learning" they "so little set by in these days" and study astrology: knowledge in this "Art," she said, "will animate our husbands to excel us, no doubt," but it will "make them be in our studies . . . when they would be in an Alehouse"; and in any case, "we shall find the nights will be more comfortable, and the days more pleasant." Sarah Ginnor's "Astrological Observations" were mixed fun. "If Venus be in Scorpio," her readers learned, "the wantons of our Sex as well as the other sex will be pepper'd with the P___ and then wo to your Noses, for its a fatal plague to the roof of your mouth besides the downfall of Narrow-bridge and the drying up your Fish-ponds by the opperation of malignant fireworks." That medical merriment prompted her to a little jingle:

> For this my Judgement, do not take distast;
> But as I am, I wish you all, be chast.
> This is the only way, if you desire
> To be preserved from the Frenchmans fire.

The *Almanack* featured astrological symbols as explicit diagram of where "The pleasure of our Sex lies"—in the rhyming humor of a "Riddle"—and advised that "If a man be fortified strongly with the Scepter of Mars, it denotes a fit time for Venus to lye down, that mirth may be produced by the Turks entrance into Constantinople." Sarah Ginnor concluded decorously: "Yet after mirth, I wish our Sex may mend / And Vertue guide them whilst I make an End."[26]

In the late Commonwealth of Saints the London publishing market responded to female pleasure in enticement with love-tricks in apparel and appearance. The moralists, or dissembling pornographers, lectured as they would that only "Subtle Bawds" and "City-Curtesans" tried to "Insnare and beguile Youth" with "soul-destroying" cosmetics.[27] The "vice of painting" and "affectation of wearing patches" (this in imitation of Venus, who supposedly had a mole on one cheek) popped up again by the mid-1650s: parliamentary bills expressing the ministers' old wrath with such devices, and forbidding as well "immodest dresses" and foreign "fancy laces," died without legislative second reading.[28] With the Restoration pamphlets on the "Arts" of self-decoration and improvement appeared so promptly that the type must have been set and ready. *Arts Master-piece: or, The Beautifying Part of Physick*, beckoned the title page of a publication of 1660: "Whereby all Defects of Nature in both Sexes are amended, Age renewed, Youth continued and all imperfections fairly remedied. . . ." Coaxed the author in promising that his "Secrets of Nature" could be used for "profit and pleasure," "Therefore Ladies, buy these few Receipts, and make use of 'um, and if they fail, then never believe me another time. . . ."

Female possessors of cosmetic books could work on all the important parts of their anatomies. They found recipes of "Waters" for facial warts, wrinkles, "Ring-worms," and freckles, indeed "A Water that takes away all troubles whatsoever from the Face." There were "Potions that adorn the Body," to make it fat or make it lean. To dye the hair various concoctions with lye were recommended: rhubarb in lye to make "a Saffron colour"; lye with "sweet Orange pills" and herbs would turn hair "yellow, bright, and long," and also "help the Memory"; lye with Gentian Root was sure to produce hair "red and curled." Certain oils and ointments preserved, increased, blackened or restored hair, took "away faults of the Eyebrows," and "adorned" breasts, keeping them small, hardening or softening, smoothing and tightening them. Powders cleaned, whitened, and fastened the teeth, and "red Corral, pearl, Dragons blood, Bolearmenick, Frankincense, Crabs shells, each one part" mixed, marvelously strengthened the gums. Musk with complicated additives was a wonder substance which while protecting against "Poyson and Pestilence" provided perfume and soap.[29]

Incidentally: pamphlets on "Artificial Embellishments" did advise women to be clean, to avoid "sluttishness." To "curle" hair the suggested technique was to "wind it up going to bed upon a hot Tobacco pipe or iron"; but first one was to rub it well "with lye or urine, that so may be washt very clean."[30] Modern social historians so graphically aware of our ancestors' reluctance to wash any but their showing parts, and the discouragement that might be to love-making,[31] know too that fastidiousness is relative. A traveler from the south exercising the Englishman's disdain for all things Scottish remarked that the only "Monsters" across the border were the women. The "Ladies" of Scotland "naturally" abhor cleanliness, he wrote; "their breath commonly stinks of Pottage, their linen of Piss, their hands of Pigs turds, their body of sweat, and their splay-feet, never offend in Socks. . . . To be chained in marriage with one of them, were to be tied to a dead carkass, and cast into a stinking ditch. . . . I protest, I had rather be the meanest servant of the two to my Pupils Chambermaid, then to be the Master-Minion to the fairest Countess I have yet discovered . . . in Lousy Scotland."[32]

But to return to the matter of female joy in sex: Sarah Ginnor's sort of material seems mere old-fashioned sauciness in the moral climate of the post-Puritan generation. For London sophisticates of the reign of the Merry Monarch sex was the hottest business/game in town. Above and below, in the *beau* and in the *demi-monde*, female sexuality was on the block for male buyers: woman was that "sensual creature fitted for delight," in one of the Earl of Rochester's printable phrases; in John Garfield's periodically *Wandring Whore* she was, or "had," a "very good commodity."[33] In the center watched the bug-eyed bourgeois and bourgeoises, with their young perhaps chattering in the words playwright Wycherley gave to the eager little Hippolita, "'tis a pleasant-well-bred-complacent-free-frolick-good-natur'd-pretty-Age; and if you do not like it, leave it to us that do."[34] (Strange to think that behind the fictional old Aunt Caution to whom those flippant lines were addressed were the Lucy Hutchinsons, already fossilized specimens of a ridiculed period of high-minded revolutionary purpose. But: "the business of abusing the Puritans begins to grow stale," confessed the almost buried Roundhead part of Samuel Pepys in 1668, "and of no use, they being the people that, at last, will be found the wisest.")[35]

In this context confining Pepys to a parenthetical aside is akin to hiding Daniel Defoe in a footnote to a section on tradesmen. The well-worn focus needs partial adjustment, however: as a witness for the enjoyment of sex the self-revealing Pepys can here be an interpreter for the several dozen women he knew, more or less, in the period from 1660 to 1669.[36]

As any transfixed reader of the *Diary* knows, Pepys's women were a select group. For all his gregarious nature he was a shy man, sexually insecure and socially very prudent. He avoided whores, who even though beautiful might infect him with venereal disease; he was politely gallant with handsome young women he judged to be "modest," and worshipped at anonymous distance the gorgeous creatures beyond his class reach, the mistresses of courtiers and kings. His women shared the one trait of being demonstratively fond of the philandering Mr. Pepys; the most durable of them were a cut or two below him socially, and discreetly married. Pepys chose women with whom he could dally at a self-conscious midpoint—between the sexual activity of a Mary Combe (whom he would have thought disgusting) and that of the "bold merry slut" (he sneakingly admired) who entertained the circles of the Earl of Rochester or the royal master.

Still, Pepysian sex was "touse and tumble," intimate and earthy. Pepys was a kisser, a petter, a feeler: ". . . I did upon the stairs overtake three pretty mayds or women," he typically noted, "and took them up with me, and I did baiser sur mouches et toucher leur mains and necks to my great pleasure." The housemaids who combed his hair for nits and lice naturally had their breasts fondled, as did the seamen's wives visiting his naval office, or wives and daughters of colleagues riding next to him, even *en famille*, in the dark corners of coaches; in the latter case the women could expect his hand under their petticoats too, and their own hands being coyly drawn to Pepys's private parts.[37]

The female friends apparently welcomed these attentions. Their minds seem as free as their bodies—and if English women wore socks their only other accustomed undergarment was a shift "open at the breast and falling to the knees" (Mrs. Pepys was an oddity in that she wore drawers).[38] Betty Lane (Martin, after her marriage) was happy on a moment's notice to close up her haberdashery stall in Westminster Hall for an hour or two of tavern-hopping and tumble-tousing with the engaging Mr. Pepys. Mrs. Bagwell, young wife of a ship's carpenter, pursued him to his office for warm introductions to further pleasures in her home. The daughter of a neighbor, Diana Crisp, was "very loving" and "kind." A definite social equal, Margaret Penn, daughter of Pepys's associate commissioner on the Naval Board, Sir William Penn, matured under his kissing and breast caressing, and actress-singer Mary Knepp (Pepys's beloved contact with the glamorous society of the king's theater) sat hilarious on his knee as his fingers roamed and explored. Pepys's account of a fine afternoon was this: ". . . . I did give her a Lobster and do so towse her and feel her all over, making her believe how fair and good a skin she had; and endeed, she hath a very white thigh and leg, but monstrous fat."[39] He had such success that in time a small rebuff gave him hardly a twinge. Mrs. Burroughs, widow of a naval lieutenant, was one day in a coach "very averse" when he tried to pull her hand under his "manteau" to, as he put it, "mi cosa." Ah well, wrote Pepys in his pigeon-hash of romance tongues, "time can hazer-la, the same as it hath hecho others."[40]

But male and female, everybody was cautious about concluding with the "main thing," in Pepys's euphemism. Partly in him, the modeling bourgeois, it was that his (small 'p') puritanism remained in a central streak of sanctimony: promiscuous sex was bad, but less so if it were restricted to mutual masturbation (Pepys had almost forgotten the sin of Onan: "God forgive me," he sighed one Sunday after fantasizing to climax during the church service).[41] Mostly, he was simply practical: he feared the "pox" from "cunning jades"; he cherished his reputation as an upright, prospering, and important civil servant (so out of his class was the libertinism of the Stuart court); he blanched at the thought of the expense as well as scandal of a bastard child; and he was terrified that his wife would find him out (rightly so, for when she discovered just one of his amours she reduced him to quivering contrition).

If the women had any scruples behind an equal pragmatism they did not register with Pepys. "There did what I would with her," he regularly reported about the tavern maids he cultivated: probably these needy girls would have slept with him after a lobster and heavy petting had he been willing to risk it. The middle-class women were loathe to gamble their occupations and/or reputations in intercourse. As "wanton and bucksome as she is," Pepys said about Betty Lane, "she dares not adventure upon that business—in which I very much commend and like her" (he leaving all "tired with her company," and "in a great sweat" having come "so near" that he was "provoked to spend").[42] In 1664 Betty Lane became Mrs. Martin, with a husband conveniently away at sea months (but not too many months) at a time. And then she handled the problem of the main thing exactly as the playwrights mockingly portrayed it: she was "the strangest woman in talk," mused Pepys, "of love to her husband sometimes, and sometimes again she doth not care for him—and yet willing enough to allow me a liberty of doing what I would with her."[43] Her bed was Pepys's reliable retreat till almost the end of the *Diary*, a home for consummation after wrestling sessions with less protected companions. Both he and mistress Betty were undeterred by her two pregnancies and the appearance of legal baby Martins. The irony in the latter is that Pepys was probably sterile from an old operation for the "stone."[44]

Lawrence Stone thinks it "perfectly clear" that neither Pepys nor his women "had any knowledge whatever of contraceptive devices, either as protection against veneral disease or as barriers to impregnation."[45] It is perfectly clear that Pepys lacked condoms and the women diaphragms. But it is perfectly obvious that they were knowledgeable of and did the best they could with what they had. Pepys recorded one day a "great secret" told him by the surgeon, Dr. James Pierce, who was going with "some physic" to Mrs. Churchill, mistress of the Duke of York; the physic was "for the pox," Pepys commented, "or else that she is got with child."[46] Mrs. Pierce, a dallying playmate of Pepys, ran with the theater crowd—was constantly with Mary Knepp—and was so sophisticated that she painted her face (thereby shocking the prim Pepys). Would she and her friends not have taken physic when the need arose? Once after a christening Pepys attended the "gossips dinner," besides the women, he said, "ne'er a man but I"; while they were drinking "a dozen and a half bottles of wine" Pepys casually asked for advice about his "not getting of children," and the women "freely and merrily" drew up for him and Mrs. Pepys a list of ten bed-tested remedies.[47] Certainly—and if he had requested the opposite advice the odds are that they would have revealed themselves the sources behind *The Ladies Dispensatory*.

The strong message in the Pepys stories is that the women he knew enjoyed their sexuality just short of the risk of intercourse, that they had wonderfully good times during the afternoons which left Pepys "lustful as a satyr"[48] and so redfaced and sweaty that he took the longest route home. Infrequently one of them, like Mrs. Burroughs, drew a higher line: in the last meeting in his famous Deb Willet affair Pepys found that young woman "mighty coy"; he only with "great force, did hazer ella con su hand para tocar mi thing. . . ."[49] But note the initiators of a spontaneous party for Pepys in a most respectable house: ". . . to my Lady Batten's, there found a great many women with her, in her chamber merry, my Lady Pen and her daughter, among others; where my Lady Pen flung me down upon the bed, and herself and others, one after another, upon me, and very merry we were. . . ."[50]

The woman who had the least fun with Pepys was his beautiful spoilsport wife, Elizabeth. His doting, sympathetic biographers have long made Mistress Pepys the villainess in the piece: they recognize in Pepys (across three hundred years) a "normal, reasonably healthy male animal" who needed sex to ease the tensions of a most difficult career; with Elizabeth they regret the absence of any self-explanation but proceed to explain that because she was not only "frivolous, extravagant and easily aroused to anger or the sulks" but "sexually inadequate" she drove Samuel to his prowling escapades.[51] It is all very familiar.

Elizabeth St. Michel was fifteen in 1655 when she married the twenty-three-year-old Samuel Pepys (and thought of the sexual drives of the young adult Pepys gives one pause). She was lovely, so attractive that Pepys never stopped fretting that "the liquorish Flyes," in the prediction of his "father Osborne," were buzzing about to get a "lick" at his "honey-pot."[52] Idle fear: Elizabeth Pepys was quite chaste, faithful, sexually unadventurous. Her sexuality was so different from Samuel's, rather than inadequate, that despite a lively imagination she never conceived of the variety and number of his experiences. She should have been some merry somebody's flirtatious playmate. She loved a dancing, carousing party, loved adorning herself with black patches and blond artificial curls, and wearing fine gowns which displayed her white shoulders and pretty bosom, all those things for which the possessive Pepys nagged and berated her. They were angry with one another most of the time, bickering about money, and the routines of a badly kept household, and if Samuel could forget it in jaunting about in business at Whitehall or Westminster and in entertainment at the duke's theater or in the backroom of a tavern, Elizabeth had no distractions. Obediently, conventionally, she stayed at home, bored and resentful, and probably planning new ways to irritate her irritating husband. She was frequently "ill of her months," and plagued with recurring vaginal infections—or abscesses, "her old pain in the lip of her *chose*," as Pepys described it—with which he professed sympathy but chafed, "not a little impatient" in abstinence.[53] Of course, Elizabeth used sex, to punish, to push away, or to hold Pepys. And she found it, in the complications of his final Deb Willet liaison, the key to smashing victory in the marital battle of wills. Pepys, guilty, beaten, signed—as he salvaged it, "of my own accord"—a "contract" for an "allowance" to Elizabeth of £30 a year "for all expenses, clothes and everything"; the signing was done "merrily," said Pepys, and the document put in his clerk's hands "to keep."[54] In return he got apparently for the first time a passionate wife: "I have laid," he wrote, "with my moher as a husband more times since this falling-out then in I believe twelve months before—and with more pleasure to her then I think in all the time of our marriage before."[55]

But then all of the women who slept with Samuel used sex. Betty Martin's husband was appointed a consul in Algiers, probably because of the influence of Naval Commissioner Pepys. Mrs. Bagwell's husband rose steadily as a carpenter on bigger and better paying ships of the fleet, for absolutely the same reason: the wife's pleas for Mr. Bagwell accompanied every one of the sexual favors she granted. Had

Pepys not been such a careful and clever man he might well have been "treppanned," as his contemporaries named the snare, entrapment—blackmail.

NOTES

1. Margaret Spufford, *Small Books and Pleasant Histories* (Athens, Ga., 1981), pp. 62, xviii.
2. G. R. Quaife, *Wanton Wenches and Wayward Wives* (New Brunswick, N.J., 1979), pp. 156-58.
3. On the latter see *The Complete Poems of John Wilmot, Earl of Rochester*, ed. David M. Vieth (New Haven, 1968).
4. Matthew Griffith, *Bethel: or a forme for families* (London, 1633), p. 316.
5. Stone, *The Family, Sex and Marriage in England*, p. 416.
6. Griffith, *Bethel*, p. 238.
7. See the discussion of Robert V. Schnucker, "Elizabethan Birth Control and Puritan Attitudes," *Journal of Interdisciplinary History* 4 (Spring 1975): 655-67.
8. William Perkins, *Christian Oeconomie* (London, 1609), pp. 122-23.
9. *The Compleat Midwife's Practice* (London, 1656), p. 53.
10. *The Diary of Ralph Josselin, 1616-1683*, ed. Alan Macfarlane (London, 1976), pp. 7, 11, 45, 50-51, 59, 96, 122, 220.
11. Nicholas Culpepper, *Directory for Midwives* (London, 1662), p. 30.
12. William Whately, *A Bride-Bush, or A Directory for Married Persons* (London, 1623), p. 15.
13. Ibid., pp. 213, 192-93.
14. The Lady Newton, *The House of Lyme* (London, 1917), pp. 198-99.
15. Alan Macfarlane, *The Family Life of Ralph Josselin* (Cambridge, 1970), p. 83.
16. Nicholas Culpepper, *Directory for Midwives*, part 2 (London, 1662), p. 161.
17. *Compleat Midwife*, pp. 119-20.
18. Stone, *Family, Sex and Marriage*, p. 498, and passim; see J. T. Noonan, Jr., *Contraception* (Cambridge, 1965); also Orestes and Patricia Ranum, eds. *Popular Attitudes toward Birth Control in Pre-Industrial France and England* (New York, 1972).
19. Culpepper, *Directory for Midwives*, part 2, p. 161.
20. *Compleat Midwife* (1656), pp. 54-57, and of the "common error" that pregnant women should exercise or "walk much" in the seventh month, p. 103.
21. *The Ladies Dispensatory* (London, 1651), E.1258, pp. 158-63.
22. *The Poems of John Wilmot*, ed. David Vieth, p. 110n.
23. John Graunt, *Natural and Political Observations* (London, 1662-63), p. 45.

24. *The Resolution of the Women of London to the Parliament* (London, 1642), E.114(14).

25. *The Fifth and Last Part of the Wandring Whore* (London, 1661), p. 8; William Wycherley, *The Country Wife*, Act 4, Scene 3.

26. Sarah Ginnor, *The Womans Almanack* (London, 1659), E.2140(1). Sarah was Ginnor or Jinner.

27. *The Crafty Whore: or, the Mistery and iniquity of Bawdy Houses* (London, 1658), E.1927(1), title page.

28. F. A. Underwick, *The Interregnum* (London, 1891), p. 45.

29. *Arts Masterpiece, or the Beautifying Part of Physick* (London, 1660), E.2124(3), pp. 36-39, 44-45, 82, 116-37.

30. *Artificial Embellishments, or Arts Best Directions: How to Preserve Beauty or Procure it* (Oxford, 1665), p. 110.

31. See Stone, *Family, Sex and Marriage*, pp. 485-86.

32. *A Perfect Description of the People and Country of Scotland, by James Howell, Gent.* (London, 1649), E.560(7).

33. John Wilmot, Earl of Rochester, *Sodom* (North Hollywood, Calif., 1966), p. 53; *Fifth Part of the Wandring Whore*, p. 7.

34. William Wycherley, *The Gentleman Dancing-Master*, Act 1, Scene 1.

35. Samuel Pepys, *Diary*, 4 Sept. 1668.

36. Stone, in *Family, Sex and Marriage* counts "fifty-odd" of Pepys's female contacts, p. 554.

37. Pepys, *Diary*, 2 Oct. 1665; 2 Dec. 1666; 4 Jan. 1666.

38. See J. H. Wilson, *The Private Life of Mr. Pepys* (New York, 1959), p. 60.

39. Pepys, *Diary*, 2 Sept. 1660; 28 Nov. 1666; 29 June 1663.

40. Ibid., 3 Dec. 1666.

41. Ibid., 11 Nov. 1666.

42. Ibid., 5 Aug. 1663; 24 Sept. 1663.

43. Ibid., 23 July 1664.

44. Ibid., 26 July 1664; 22 Sept. 1664. J. H. Wilson, *Mr. Pepys*, pp. 4-5.

45. Stone, *Family, Sex and Marriage*, p. 554.

46. Pepys, *Diary*, 12 Jan. 1669. Mrs. Churchill was Arabella, sister to John Churchill.

47. Ibid., 26 July 1664.

48. Wilson, *Mr. Pepys*, p. 200.

49. Pepys, *Diary*, 15 Apr. 1669. Deb Willet, of course, was the Pepyses' home companion, Mrs. Pepys's live-in friend and, finally, Samuel's obsession.

50. Ibid., 12 Apr. 1665.

51. See Stone, *Family, Sex and Marriage*, p. 552; and Wilson, *Mr. Pepys*, pp. 182, 113.

52. Francis Osborne, *Advice to a Son, or Directions for your better Conduct* (Oxford, 1655), p. 46, E.1640(1), a book Pepys much admired.

53. Pepys, *Diary*, 2 Aug. 1660; 6 Aug. 1660.

54. Ibid., 4 Jan. 1669; 10 Jan. 1669.

55. Ibid., 14 Nov. 1668.

13

The Uses of Sex

Restoration playwrights' stock images were of women who were fittingly companionable with men on the make sexually. Dramatists did not need to overstretch their imaginations for material. Socially 'advanced' London of the 1640s and 1650s, even, was the scene of finely detailed real-life stories of women, midway between "Crafty Bawds" and aristocratic whores, who employed their sex for commercial and profitable ends, "treppanners" trying to parlay sex into fortune. As on the Restoration stage, some lost, some won.

Mistress Anne Swinnerton lost in her trepan, her snare or swindle, recorded in 1647 before the King's Bench Bar. She was the plaintiff in the case against man-about-town Sir Edward Mosely, Baronet, and appeared in the court of Mr. Justice (Sir Francis) Bacon to charge that Sir Edward had invaded her chamber, thrown her down in "a narrow place, betwixt the wall of the Bed," and raped her. Only her husband and her maid stood as corroborating witnesses with Mistress Swinnerton: the husband told the court that they had no counsel because "by the tampering of Sir Edward Mosely, Master Lowder, Master Ja. Winstanly, Master Blore, and Master Brownnell and twenty more, none would assist him in the maintaining of the Inditement"; furthermore, he said, these important people had pressured him and his witnesses "to stop the prosecution." The trial was shortly over, with Mosely's parade of gentleman-witnesses shredding the Swinnertons' story. Sir Edward testified that he had been invited into the room, that her husband had knocked on the door but Mistress Anne had whispered, "Let the drunken sot stay without." Asked by the court to explain that Mistress Swinnerton's clothes were "torne and rufled" when she emerged from the bedchamber, as in her maid's and husband's accounts, Mosely replied that "she always went very ill favourdly in her apparrell." His "many witnesses" swore variously that Mistress Anne regularly stood enticingly by her outside door as Mosely went by, that she had slept with him and been paid so frequently that she had "the Key of his Chamber," that the true "woundring" was that Sir Edward being "but a little Man" could have "ravisht" her who was a "lusty Woman." The clinching bit was a witness's tale of Mistress Swinnerton's presence months earlier at the Fleece Tavern in Covent Garden, where it was asserted she had gone to meet Sir Edward for dinner. She was quoted as saying "that this Roome had bin a very lucky Roome to her, for once before in this Roome, she had received three hundred pounds for the composition of a Rape"; and she had boasted that "shee would not take under two thousand pounds for a composition of Sir Edward Moseley," little enough, she had added, "hee having three thousand pounds a yeere." Mistress Swinnerton "clapt her hands" at that witness and named him "a Knave and a Rascall"; but she had "staggered at it a little," and with the court frowning upon her had to admit the assignation at the Fleece Tavern. Take "heede what company you keepe hereafter," Justice Bacon told the acquitted Mosely. Whatever the truth of the Swinnertons' evidence, they had come ill-prepared to legal battle with a baronet and his court-wise friends.[1]

In contrast to amateurish use of feminine charms there is the carefully clever campaign, both "subtil" and "stupendious," in a reporter's hyperbole, of two sisters to swindle a London tradesman, "a Dyar of Southwark," of his life's winnings. Both married, memorably named Mehetabel Jones and Elizabeth Pigeon, the sisters were a bold pair, undeterred from their plan by tongue-lashings and finally expulsion from William Kiffin's Baptist congregation, and so confident of its success that they risked the appeals of the victim's dispossessed family ultimately up to the Lord Protector, Oliver Cromwell himself.[2]

A four-man commission appointed by Cromwell—they were to examine the principals of the case, and report to the Privy Council—summarized the 'treppanning' affair. First, Mehetabel Jones had wheedled her way into the affections of the old dyer, Mr. Wessel Goodwin, even before his wife's death in 1647, and soon after that had cohabited (had "too familiar Converse") with him; admonished by the elders of their respective churches they "endeavoured to prove it lawful, notwithstanding that Mr. Jones, husband to the said Mehetabel, [was] yet alive." Mistress Jones denied the bigamy on the grounds (given her, she said, by "several learned Divines") that Mr. Jones was an evil man closed to true religion and accordingly no true husband to her: "she was free from the Law of her first Husband by the Law of God." (Mr. Kiffin and the elders nevertheless "cast her out of the Church.")

Next, the trepan: the "gaining of Mr. Goodwins estate," wrote the commissioners, was "the Design laid" by the sisters Jones and Pigeon "8. or 9. years since." That Mr. Goodwin was a "shallow weak man" did not detract from the shrewdness of the plan: the assessment of his simple character must have been the start of it all. Though his contract of marriage was with Mehetabel the old man liked living with both sisters, the two of them so flattering, warm, and loving (Mr. Pigeon too had been shunted off somewhere). So while Mehetabel soothed him domestically, Elizabeth took over the cares of Goodwin's "Dye-house-stock and Trade." The old man was apparently delighted to change his will dramatically: "in fine, by Judgments, Bills of Sale, Assignments, and such practices, to make over all his own, and his Sons Estate," to a middle-man trustee, "for the use of Elizabeth Pigeon." By this "subtile" arrangement, as the Commissioners thought it, Mistress Pigeon "got possession of that whole estate to the value of above fifteen hundred pounds," and hedged it about with "a kind of Title by colour of Law"; the Goodwin estate was "at her pleasure, defrauding thereby the Children. . . ."[3]

Finally, mission accomplished, the sisters tidied up the loose ends. Mr. Goodwin took to his bed after the examination before the Lord Protector's Commission: in the week or so that he lay dying of some undisclosed malady his two faithful nurses never left his side, or rather they were there by turns: one watching the patient, and the other their bolted front door. They simply brazened out a limp counterattack from the Goodwin children led by the eldest son whom they had ejected as partner in the trade (the son about as weak-minded as the old man). When Wessel Goodwin died the sisters refused a demand "to have the Body Dissected" until it was too late, thereby escalating family and neighborhood suspicions; but they still arranged a grand funeral procession, with "Seventy or Eighty [Gold] Rings" ordered for that many invited mourners. And they procured "Mr. John Hat, the Guild-hall Atturney," to plead Elizabeth Pigeon's "legal Title at Law" to the Goodwin estate against all challengers.[4]

The *Calendar of State Papers*, in the day's proceedings of 29 April 1656, has this entry: "Order on petition of Andrew, Thomas, and Sarah Goodwin, the children of Wesell Goodwin, of Southwark, and on a report from [Commissioners] Chris. Searle, Wm. Cooper, and Cornelius Cooke, on reference to them by the Protector of this petition, and a petition of John Pigeon, that the parties be left to seek remedy according to law in the usual way."[5]

Mistresses Jones and Pigeon seem to have enjoyed the uses of their sexuality. True, in their example Margaret Spufford's meaning has been lost, or at least badly twisted. Perhaps there is exposed here the insufficiency of individual examples: it could be surmised that lightness of heart and merry personality were simply unnatural to Mehetabel and Elizabeth; the grim sisters, they were, not much in them of the Wife of Bath on the one side, nor Moll Flanders on the other.

But highly charged themes push and shove within this subject. In a society in which relationships were so "slippery,"[6] so Hobbesian whether or no the tender-minded acknowledged it, sex was inescapably one of the closest means, brutal or subtle, by which an individual used another: with its base of massive quantities of evidence, the statement is almost embarrassingly trite. What females, beyond remote rural laborers or sheltered romantic adolescents, did not perceive that their sexuality was a weapon, had they will or cynicism enough to use it, in their formally empty armory?

The qualities which made Theodosia Stepkin/Garret/Ivie/Bryan a superb trepanner, litigant, opportunist, should have been perceptible in her youth. She was from a family of resourceful and tenacious accumulators. John Stepkin, her father, had cleared Wapping Marsh at the beginning of the seventeenth century, claimed a rich share of it "and purchased the rest"—Shadwell Park, about a mile east of London Tower, on the north side of the Thames. This he so "improved vastly," letting leases to build, that "hungerie courtiers" of James I tried to steal it from him. From 1616 two generations of Stepkins spent almost £7,000 "defending their ryte" in court; in the 1680s their cousin, Sir John Bramston, noted that it was "not quiet yet."[7] By the late date Dame Theodosia (we shall see the origin of her title) had proven her filial capabilities: in civil suits in 1673, 1675, 1676, 1679, 1683, and 1687 she had become "famous for Wit, Beauty and Cunning in the Law above any."[8]

Life seems ever to have been an adventure to Dame Theodosia, but in the decade of the 1650s, from her mid-twenties to mid-thirties, she evidently reached exhilarating peaks. Doubtless she felt it was high time. Given the demands on the Stepkin estate her father gave her husbands rather than portion. As a girl she had been "educated" in the same gentle household with the Bramston sister of cousin Sir John, and from this had been married promisingly to Mr. George Garret, "second sonn of Sir George Garret, alderman of London"; with him she lived "lovingly and virtuously" (Bramston's rather defensive line) until his death, unfortunately unexpected and quick. Widow Garret, left "nothing" by her husband but a male child, returned to her father. Stepkin this time brought her an old friend, one of his own "schoole-fellowes," Anthony Browne. Abortive affair: father and suitor fell to drinking before the introduction to the daughter, so heavily that in her presence Anthony Browne was ill, factually, "sick in her lap"; Theodosia, unaccountably fastidious, took such an "aversion" to him that she refused to see him again.[9] The time must have been 1647-48, Theodosia twenty-one or twenty-two years old. Impatiently using her as his housekeeper in Wapping John Stepkin searched the lists for a new candidate-husband, though whether he or an acquaintance of Theodosia's produced one Thomas Ivie, India merchant, is unclear. In any case, in October 1649, after intricate negotiations, the merchant's promise of gifts of fine jewels, a huge jointure and a thrown-in £1,000 to father Stepkin, the Widow Garret became Mrs. Ivie. And now her good-times decade began.

Thomas Ivie, Esquire, was a merchant of eminence and wealth when he sailed back to England in the late 1640s. He had been abroad many years: elected a Factor of the East India Company in 1632 he had last been a "chief agent," with "the Command of the persons of Thousands of People" at the Fort of St. George and the town of Madrassopotan. He was justly proud of his accomplishments in India, of having made "a Reformation of the grand Abuses which had crept into those parts, to the great Injury of the Trade," and of having constructed a town out of his "own pains and Industry, even out of the Sea itself for the better advantage and security of it." With his record he had been "often persuaded by the said Company to continue" in his post, but he had finally wanted a conclusion in that alien land, to return with his ample rewards to London investments and a long-left wife.

Landing at his Channel port Ivie was informed that his wife had died, even as she had prepared to meet him. Thus it was in "Melancholy" that rich widower Thomas Ivie re-entered London, but also in "Patience and Submission": he told himself, friends consoled him with similar words, that "as the Lord had taken one Wife from [his] Bosom, so he could bestow another."[10]

After "many severall Dayes and Months" Thomas Ivie was "persuaded" to "address" himself to Mrs. Theodosia Garret, "Widdow, and daughter of Mr. Stepkins," a young woman "represented" to him "as beautiful in mind as in person." True, his sources admitted that the Widow Garret was penniless. But Mr. Ivie was undeterred, "supposing what was wanting in *Fortune*, would be made up in *Affection* and *Sweetnesse*. . . ."[11] The wedding in October 1649 was an exciting new start for Merchant Ivie: in his forty-ninth year he had a lovely young wife, comforting piles of cash and goods (and more of both ever loading on Company ships), the expectation of power and prestige, alderman in the City, master in the Merchant Taylors Guild, later perhaps an estate in land in his native Wiltshire.

The one point upon which all parties and observers subsequently agreed in discussion of the twenty-five-year on-and-off Ivie marriage was that it was a "state of conflict." Thomas Ivie left the fullest account, out of an early desperation so great that he appealed for help, over the heads of courts and Commons, to the Lord Protector Cromwell personally; he had been, said Ivie, swindled, robbed, cuckolded, libelled as a rapist, a sodomite, a pox-spreader and a wife-beater, sued for alimony and ruined financially by decisions of Chancery Court, hounded in the streets by creditors (of his wife's debts) and so shamed before his associates that he had asked to be discharged as alderman of Langbourne Ward. The other side tended to brevity. The Stepkin cousin, Sir John Bramston, wrote that Theodosia's "storie" would "take up a volume," implying a defense had he inclination for it; Ivie was his villain, that "trade fellow" who "merited whippinge," whose published appeal to Cromwell was a "libell" not worth "labour, tyme, inke, and paper" to comment further.[12] Theodosia spoke succinctly through her brace of lawyers in *twelve* alimony suits in Chancery, in hearings before Lords Commissioners so sympathetically on the side of the wife in the Commonwealth climate of reform that, Ivie noted bitterly, she "stood there laughing" at him "in their presence."[13]

Thomas Ivie's *Alimony Arraign'd* portrays an evil Theodosia. (Members of her family were painted black too: her father, unprincipled, grasping, even incestuous; a boon companion of an aunt, who the very day after the marriage "made horns and mouths" at Ivie "behind his back," who provided a trysting place for Theodosia and lovers in her house "of ill fame in a little blind Alley," and was the fence for India goods which Theodosia stole from Ivie.)[14] It was "rather my *Fortune* than my *Person*" which was wedded, Ivie said, for "immediately after our Marriage [Mrs. Ivie] slighted me to my face, never returned, in the least measure, any reciprocal affection." She only took (and he gave: "she could no sooner propose any thing . . . but 'twas immediately provided.") In the first eighteen months Theodosia had "spent for Accommodations above 3000£ whereof 600£ was in Apparel only, 500£ in ready money"; she had "Money in her Purse . . . Coach and Horses, Saddle-Horses, and rich Furniture, rich Cloathes, Beds, Linnen, etc. . . ." Meanwhile she flaunted her adultery, and Ivie supplied the names of her partners; he added that she was "too familiar with her own Father, his hands were seen under her Coats," and he was "often in bed with her." She had gone to astrologers, Ivie claimed, seeking predictions of his death, and had been so impatient for that occurrence that she had paid her brother a hundred pounds to murder him. He accused his wife and her aunt of manufacturing evidence and bribing witnesses to sensationalize the cases brought before Chancery: medical testimonials of Theodosia beaten, Theodosia infected with his syphilis; the charge that he had seduced and impregnated a housemaid—and Ivie insisted that the poor girl had been driven to her death under their pressure for her admission of a nonexistent affair and spurious pregnancy.[15]

But we are getting the story out of proper sequence. Thomas Ivie did not initiate the court action. Rather, he made the critical error of retreating from the London scene, going alone to Wiltshire, where he bought property, the "Malmesbury Abbey House" near his old home in Hullavington.[16] He left Theodosia, he said, with five hundred pounds in cash and his permission to "pawn" some of her jewels if necessary (which he promised to redeem with the first arrival of an India shipment); and he regularly sent her imploring letters, begging his "Sweetheart," his "Most dear Heart," to join him in purifying, frugal country life. In the spring of 1651 he received his reply. It was a summons from the Court of Chancery, signed by Commissioners Richard Keeble and John Lisle, and read thusly:

> Whereas Theodosia your Wife hath on this present day preferr'd her humble Petition unto us, the Lords Commissioners of the Great Seal of England, Thereby praying Allowance of Alimony, as by her said Petition remaining with us doth appear, We do at her instance give you notice thereof, Requiring you hereby to make your personal appearance before us, on the thirtieth day of the Instant, to speak with Us about the same.[17]

From that point, as he explained it to Cromwell, Thomas Ivie's fate and fortune were controlled by the blindly prejudicial, or indifferent or capricious Court of Chancery. He spent thousands of pounds in successive hearings, hiring "very many" lawyers and "great ones." He brought in his character witnesses, "civil gentlemen" and esteemed ministers of the gospel. He put his body to clinical examination by four of the most "able and honest Physitians" in the City, who certified that he was "not onely free from the said disease but so free from it, that we cannot perceive, that he was ever tainted therewith." Money, time, assertions of piety, physical humiliation, all was totally wasted. With "grief of heart," he told Cromwell, "I found experimentally there Chancery rather a Court of oppression, than good Conscience." The Commissioners, he said, never questioned him and Theodosia together, in fact, he was certain never even read the documented rebuttals he and his sollicitors presented. The one clear communication that he had from the court was an "Injunction" upon him and "his said Counsellors, Attorneys, Agents, Sollicitors" under the "pain of 500£ to be levied" on his "Lands, Goods and Chattels" to "surcease and forbear all further Proceedings (at the common Law) against the Plaintiff." Chancery Court, Ivie charged, had exercised an "unlimited power" in decreeing "a perfect Separation and Divorce" in a way without "parallel," absolutely "contrary to the Word of God, the Law of the Nations, the Civil Law, the Law of our own Country, as well as the Practice of the Chancery itself."[18]

Always the court found for the plaintiff. Theodosia's first petition was standingly successful:

> That she being the Daughter of John Stepkins Esq. and married to the Defendant, who hath (without any cause given him) not onely deserted her company, but left her destitute of all manner of Means for her livelihood and subsistence; And that during the time she cohabited with him, she hath not only been in great danger of her life, by his cruel usage, and unjust contrivances, but by some means occasioned by the Defendant, she hath been very weak and infirm; And hath received from him such infirmities not becomming a Husband to confer on his Wife; And that by reason of his said cruelties, and the peril of receiving from his Diseases of dangerous consequences, she could not cohabit with him as his Wife, without imminent peril of her life; and the Defendant was not onely departed from her, but utterly denyed to allow her any convenient Support: And that for meer necessity she had contracted some small debts; And therefore she prayed the speedy Aid of the Court; And that they would summon the Defendant before them, that upon hearing her just complaint, she might be relieved, and have such fitting allowance by way of Alimony granted to her, as to the Court should seem meet; And that for the present, she may have some convenient Allowance for Expences in this Suite, she being otherwise unable to proceed therein.[19]

In formal decree the court observed that the Lords Commissioners were "pleased themselves to examine several Witnesses, viva voce," and that the "Cause" had taken up "many dayes in hearing" with "much Debate and Pains spent." They were "fully satisfied" that there was "good cause to give allowance for Alimony to the Plaintiff"; and so did "Order . . . that the Plaintiff have paid to her, the summe of 300£ by the year. . . ." It was "a fair sum," Ivie moaned, "enough to tempt a good Woman to be bad."[20]

Perhaps the Lords Commissioners were reminded of the hard words of another judge, "Egerton Chancellor" (Thomas Egerton, 1540-

1617), who once remarked in Chancery that "he sat not there to relieve Fools or Buzzards, who could not keep their Mony from their wives. . . ."[21] Or possibly they disliked the cut of Thomas Ivie's case, for all the great talents of his 'counsellors, attorneys, agents and sollicitors.' Someone wrote for him a long, exceedingly harsh abstract on the absolute rights of the husband over the wife, and of the absence in the law of the "Thing" called alimony. "The Civill Law . . . agrees with the Common Law," it read, "that a married Woman without leave cannot depart from her Husband . . . no more than a Servant from his Master . . . for the master may seize and carry away his Servant, if he find him . . . and recover damages for the time. . . ; so may the Husband by his Wife; which shews the propriety and interest which the Husband hath in his Wife . . . and for the losse of her society and company . . . he shall recover damages against the detainer."[22] By such conviction Ivie should have had Theodosia hauled by the hair to Malmesbury, thoroughly beaten and locked in her chamber on bread and water. But such was not Merchant Ivie's style. While he told everyone—and he petitioned Parliament over Chancery's decrees before he went to Cromwell—of Theodosia's evil behavior and desertion of him in not coming to Wiltshire, at the same time he swore that he had "perfectly forgiven her," and only wanted her "restored" to his "Bosom." To "this day," he wrote in 1654, he did "declare and protest his willingness to receive her, whensoever she will return, and give security for his well usage of her . . . [and] forget all former Passages whatsoever, that so they may for the future lead a peaceable and godly life together."[23]

Lord Protector Cromwell seems to have been moved by Thomas Ivie's sad story only enough to refer it to a committee in the Council of State. Its members reported back that "Ivy declared himself willing to withdraw his petition, and apply to the Commissioners of the Great Seal"! Good, was the official comment: "—agreed with, and Ivy's petition dismissed; if he make his application as aforesaid, the Commissioners are desired to end the same speedily."[24]

Thus round and round went Thomas Ivie. Through the next several years he must have lost more thousands of pounds in Chancery hearings, including travel expenses from Wiltshire to London. Theodosia continued to reside close to the action, her alimony keeping her, as Ivie compared it, "in a better condition, than her Father, who had but 240£ per annum, both for himselfe and his whole Family," and with her jewels and cash able to "outspend" her husband "even at Law."[25]

The Ivies reconciled in 1660. Why? Thomas's seems the large concession: he swore his old charges against his wife were "false and scandalous," and put up a ten thousand pound bond for future support and good behavior. They had a daughter, whom they named Frances. There was a possibly significant new development: Ivie was knighted by Charles II in 1661; it was Dame Theodosia, Lady Ivie, who lived at Malmesbury in Wiltshire.[26]

But the novelty and pleasure of landed gentility wore thin. In 1669 Ivie departed for London; Dame Theodosia filed a new case in Chancery and in the Ecclesiastical Court, accusing him of desertion and cruelty. The state of conflict was still an open court record when Sir Thomas died in 1674.[27]

By 1674 Dame Theodosia was already deep in her legal duels for title to Shadwell Park. She married again to a James Bryan, somewhat absentmindedly, since in 1684 (the year Bryan died) she was 'Lady Ivie' arguing at the King's Bench for her Wapping deeds. In that year's civil trial, held before Lord Chief Justice George Jeffreys, a witness testified that her husband had helped Lady Ivie forge deeds to the property, using special ink and "saffron" to age the parchment; also, said the witness, "several letters pretended to be written from Mr. Thomas Ivie to my Lady Ivie were counterfeit." Lady Ivie lost the verdict in that round, though Justice Jeffreys, in his summing-up, dropped a trace of admiration for this kindred "slippery" soul.[28] Her actual kinsman, Sir John Bramston, commented on the episode. Cousin Theodosia, he wrote, "maried a third husband, Mr. Bryan, with whom she lived well, and in good credit, which since his death hath been blasted, as if she had forged some deedes. But it is not come to issue, and I believe she will clere herselfe when matters come to an equall hearing before judges not prepossessed, as I hear some are that have had the hearinge her cause, and she must lye quiet awhile."[29]

Sir John's words suggest an emerging family legend: Theodosia, the cousin who would not lose. She was indicted on the forgery charge, and acquitted. As for those jury decisions which had denied her Shadwell Park: when she died in 1695 her will claimed it, a non-disputable part of her Wapping Marsh estate.[30]

NOTES

1. *The Arraignment and Acquittal of Sir Edward Mosely, Baronet. Indited at the Kings Bench Bar for a Rape, upon the Body of Mistris Anne Swinnerton, Jan. 28, 1647* (London, 1648), E.426(23).

2. *The Trepan: Being a True Relation, full of Stupendious variety, of the strange practices of Mehetabel the Wife of Edward Jones, and Elizabeth, Wife*

of Lieutenant John Pigeon, Sister to the said Mehetabel (London, 1656), E.884(1).

3. Ibid., pp. 15-17, 12, 2.

4. Ibid., pp. 11, 13, 14.

5. *SPD* (1655-56), 9, 302.

6. The phrase "in this slippery age we live in" was spoken by Lord Chief Justice Jeffreys in "The Lady Ivy's Trial, for great Part of Shadwell, in the County of Middlesex," *Cobbetts Complete Collection of State Trials* (London, 1811), 10: 557.

7. *The Autobiography of Sir John Bramston* (New York, 1968), Camden Series, no. 1, 32: p. 17.

8. *The Lady Ivie's Trial. For the Great Part of Shadwell in the County of Middlesex before Chief Justice Jeffreys in 1684*, ed. Sir John C. Fox (Oxford, 1929), p. xliii, the quote from Thomas Neale, lessee for lives of the Dean of St. Pauls.

9. Bramston, *Autobiography*, pp. 15, 18-19.

10. *Alimony Arraign'd; or, The remonstrance and humble Appeale of Thomas Ivie, from the High Court of Chancery, to His Highness the Lord Protect or of the Commonwealth of England* . . . (London, 1654), p. 2.

11. Ibid., pp. 2-3.

12. Bramston, *Autobiography*, p. 19.

13. Ivie, *Alimony Arraign'd*, p. 45.

14. Ibid., p. 20.

15. Ibid., pp. 4, 21, 23, 22, 27-30.

16. Fox, ed. *The Lady Ivie's Trial*, p. xxx.

17. Ivie, *Alimony Arraign'd*, pp. 5-6, 7.

18. Ibid., pp. 44, 46, 14-15, 30, 47-48.

19. Ibid., pp. 7-8.

20. Ibid., p. 31.

21. Quoted in *Baron and Feme* (London, 1700), p. 67.

22. Ivie, *Alimony Arraign'd*, pp. 38, 39.

23. Ibid., pp. 36, 40, 44.

24. *SPD*, Council of State Journals, 1649-60, 74: 67 (PRO).

25. Ivie, *Alimony Arraign'd*, p. 17.

26. Fox, ed. *The Lady Ivie's Trial*, pp. xxxvii-xxxviii.

27. Ibid., pp. xxxviii-xxxix.

28. *State Trials*, 10: 555-646.

29. Bramston, *Autobiography*, p. 19.

30. Fox, ed. *The Lady Ivie's Trial*, p. xli.

PART 5

Of Learned Ladies and Silent Signposts

14

The "Modern" Journeyers

In her *Learned Lady in England, 1650-1760* Myra Reynolds remarked upon the contrast between the "eager intellectual life of many women in the Tudor period" and the "barren half-century" of "intellectual advancement for women" during the reigns of the earlier Stuarts: the "full and rich opportunities" of the sixteenth century faded in the first decades of the seventeenth, "little or no provision at home or in schools" for girls, "practically no formulated ideals or theories" for the education of women. But it was a brief eclipse: in the restored light of the third Stuart king the educated female shone again, and with her "the real beginnings," Reynolds thought, "of the modern work of women."[1]

Myra Reynolds provided no clue of what ferment in upper-class female education she might have expected while English gentlemen and their useful ladies either defended or erased a monarch and resisted a world turning upside down—an interesting question, after all. That aside, perhaps Lucy Hutchinson *was* a freak in the 1660s as she labored alone in her closet, sustaining her stricken self in writing magnificent biography of the martyred and sweeping history of the godly's lost Cause. Mrs. Hutchinson had no published successors: even as she wrote her world-historical ambition was, like her puritanism, out of fashion. Elsewhere learned women were tending to more specialized concerns, mirroring a miniaturized world, and sometimes revealing only themselves. In comparison with the products of the "rich" Tudor opportunities they were a sizable group: a recent survey counts seventy-nine female achievers born between 1625 and 1675 listed in the *DNB*, as against forty-three born between 1550 and 1625.[2] Their individual stories began with unusual privileges or stimuli of some sort—obviously female leisure for intellectual pursuits continued a luxury of luxuries—but their backgrounds had more variety, socially and geographically, than those of the Tudor ladies of the aristocracy and courtier upper middle class. The compelling point about the seventeenth-century women, however, is this: if the educated of the Restoration were starting "the modern work of women" it was because, with *almost* no exceptions (the emphasis a bow to that unique free spirit, Aphra Behn),[3] they operated self-consciously within the separated, reduced, and disadvantaged space now 'naturally' assigned as female.

By the 1690s a few of them were saying sharp things in protest of their perceived diminished space, specifically locating the causes of female deprivation in the "usurpation of Men, and the Tyrannie of Custom."[4] Their phrases could not have occurred to Lucy Hutchinson, let alone appeared on her pages. She had surely been aware of the limitations upon female educational experience: they were there by God's design, though occasionally, for His own purpose, He might encourage a fortunate someone "beyond the customary reach of a shee wit." Male-bedazzled and Protestant-disciplined Mrs. Hutchinson certainly was, but she saw no unbridged chasm between male and female in godly society; in any case, the matter was out of human hands. Mere years are inadequate, then, to measure the distance from her to "The Lady" who published *An Essay in Defense of the Female Sex*, or to Mary Astell, the "lover" of her sex whose earthly aim was to "perswade" the "Generality" of women out of "that Meanness of Spirit" into which they were "sunk."[5]

One hundred years later a kindred mind 'recognized' these (all but forgotten) early sisters. In one of her low moments of depression and introspection that celebrated 'first' bourgeois feminist, Mary Wollstonecraft, wrote an epitaph for her (their) efforts: "All the world is a stage, thought I; and few are there in it who do not play the part they have learnt by rote; and those who do not, seem marks set up to be pelted at by fortune; or rather as signposts, which point out the road to others whilst forced to stand still themselves amidst the mud and dust."[6]

Mary Astell's *A Serious Proposal to the Ladies* was a minor *cause célèbre* in the late 1690s. Her proposal was the organization of an educational institution for women, rather obviously—that is, practically—for spinster ladies like herself. "One great end of this institution," she wrote, "shall be to expel that cloud of Ignorance, which custom has involv'd us in, to furnish our minds with a stock of solid and useful Knowledge. . . ." Though the institution was to be a "Retreat," women in it would not withdraw or be cut off from society: rather, it was to be "a Seminary to stock the Kingdom with pious and prudent Ladies"; their "good Example" would "so influence the rest of their Sex" that they would "no longer pass for those little useless and impertinent Animals, which the ill conduct of too many, has caus'd them to be mistaken for."[7] The *Serious Proposal* revived in some of its appalled male readers memories of the popish nunnery, an idea association sufficiently horrifying to bury the plan. Mary Astell, however, stoutly defended it, published an expanded and detailed *Second Part* explaining what would have been the "academical," not "monastic," learning methods and curricula of the institution.[8]

Astell's *Some Reflections upon Marriage* appeared without her name on the title page; read the "Advertisement," "Bold Truths may pass while the Speaker is Incognito." That little concealment was the only light note for readers of the book, its message steadily strengthened in four editions between 1700 and 1730. Astell's reflections on marriage as imprisonment, humiliation, and despair for wives were so unrelievedly bleak that they might have been banned by contracting parents in every shire in England; her language describing the marital trap is still harsh enough to stiffen a tender-minded adolescent. The young woman who approaches marriage with giddy romantic illusions, Astell said, is "a Fool with a Witness." In fact she was yielding her "Fortune and Person" and the "very desires of her Heart" to "a Monarch for life." She was going to be his family breeder and manager, "a House-Keeper, an upper Servant," one whom he forms "to his Will and Liking"; henceforth it would be unlawful "to Will or Desire anything but what he approves and allows," or to "quit his Service, let him treat her how he will." Men understood completely the realities of the marriage game, declared Astell. Behind his courtship face the male was saying in "plain English" to the female:

> I have a very mean Opinion both of your Understanding, and Vertue; you are Weak enough to be impos'd on, and Vain enough to snatch at the Bait I throw. . . . If for nothing else, you'll serve at least as an Exercise of my Wit; and how much soever you swell with my Breath, 'tis I deserve the Praise for talking so well on so poor a Subject. We, who make the Idols, are the greater Deities; and as we set you up, so it is in our Power to reduce you to your first Obscurity, or to somewhat worse, to Contempt; you are therefore only on your good Behaviour, and are like to be no more than what we please to make you.[9]

The Christian Religion, as Profess'd by a Daughter of the Church of England (1705) was another of Mary Astell's published essays. She was so devout a Christian that she hesitated guiltily in sharing any portion of her love of God with the earthlings of her sex.[10] She was an unquestioning Tory and royalist, so fearful of (reawakened) social unrest that "Mr. Locke" upset her with his measured advocacy of a

Whiggish right to rebellion against tyranny. Philosophically she followed the current master-guide, René Descartes. I am a "Rational Creature," she cried; she meant that all women were rational creatures, like men distinct from brute materiality in their endowment by God with an immaterial, immortal mind-soul, that the 'thinking-I' of all of them was demonstration of female possession of the "light to discern truth from falshood."[11] Reasoning toward metaphysical clarity meant as well, in Astell's words, the "entire Resignation of my Will to GOD," to "Love and Contemplation" of God, and to the rational realization of "this World [as] mere Shew, a Shadow, an emptiness."[12]

In short, Mary Astell's 'feminist' perceptions reached painful heights on one side of her mind—and slid down the smooth, worn slopes of the other. John Locke's right of rebellion against tyranny had implied meaning for unhappy wives, but Astell would not "carry it so far": "A peaceable Woman . . . will neither question her Husband's Right, nor his fitness to govern."[13] The Christian duty—and educated, "Philosophical" ladies would know it best—was silent withdrawal: "Martyrdom is the highest Pleasure a rational Creature is capable of in this present State."[14] And the Cartesian philosophy so tempting a buttress in support of female intellectual equality only accelerated the descent. The method of reasoning which cut through the barren meaninglessness of material existence to 'prove' the reality of the human mind in its divine relationship 'proved' too that marriage was both "sacred" and "venerable," the "Institution of Heaven" and the "best way that may be" for "continuing Mankind."[15] Most pertinent, Mary Astell's choice for contemplative philosophy took her directly away from the chief action, the thumping excitement of her adult environment. She even (half) mocked it: is it not "ridiculous to suppose," she wrote, "that a Woman, were she ever so improv'd, could come near the topping Genius of the Men? . . ."[16] The genius of the men, as the eulogists of their sex incessantly asserted, was in "Experimental Knowledge," in scientific investigation, in plumbing the secrets of nature; and the male geniuses came to their inquiries not with Descartes, with his dubious deductions of natural phenomena, but with the method of the English "real philosophy" of Francis, Lord Bacon.[17] So Astell, clutching her Cartesian epistemology and Christian resignation of the mind/body dualism, was left with—leading women into—a dead-end. With their mathematics and their "*Instruments*" men would master "Mistress" Nature—entering the "Beautiful Bosom" of her "Garden";[18] women could occupy themselves with philosophic "fancies."[19]

The anonymous "Lady" of *An Essay in Defense of the Female Sex* took as her proposition for debate the "Imputations" of women as "naturally defective," unqualified "for the Conversation of ingenious Men," their "Company . . . unprofitable and irksome to Men of Sense."[20] Disavowing a "religious Argument," the "Lady" (sometimes thought to be Astell, surely erroneously)[21] made her stand squarely in the material, natural, customary world, challenging the men in their claimed territory. Her philosophic sources were Hobbes and Locke, and though "Metaphysical Speculations" required "much more learning and a stronger Head" than she was "mistress of," she understood well enough what these "learned Men" were saying. They maintained that "all Souls are equal, and alike," which meant that "there is no such distinction, as Male and Female Souls." There are "no innate *Ideas*," and "all the Notions we have are deriv'd from our External Senses, either immediately, or by Reflection"; consequently, since there is "no difference in the Organisation" of male and female "Brain, and all other Parts" held to be "the immediate Instruments of Sensation," men and women were alike as feeling, thinking beings. From whence came, then, the male insistence upon the female "defect," her natural inferiority? To find the answers "The Lady" proceeded to "appeal" to "Experience," that is to say, to observation and 'experiment.'

"The Lady" saw an ascending line of female inequality. A "She Ape is as a He," she said, "a Bitch will learn as many Tricks in as short a time as a Dog, a Female Fox has as many Wiles as Male"; in "Brutes and other Animals there is no difference betwixt Male and Female in point of Sagacity. . . ." Next, the "Capacities . . . appear equal" among the "inferiour sort" of "Country People" who "subsist upon their daily Labour"; in fact, one finds in talking with such folk that the "Ballance" of intelligence falls on "our side," among the "more ready and polite" women. At any rate, while "not so equal as that of Brutes," the "Condition of the two Sexes" among the laboring poor was "more level" than among "gentlemen, City Traders, or rich Yeomen." Here "The Lady" paused for a pointed observation of the women "amongst our Neighbours the *Dutch*," in their "state of more improvement" the managers of family businesses, "keeping the Books, ballancing the Accounts, and doing all the Business, even the nicest of Merchants, with as much Dexterity and Exactness as their, or our Men can do."[22]

The prime argument that "The Lady" drew "from Nature" was aimed directly at her own educated, sophisticated urban society. Men and women were chiefly different, she began, in the "Make and Temper" of their bodies. It was clear by the simplest observation that by their size, strength, "Vigour and Hardiness" men were suited for "Action and Labour"; in contrast, women, "never design'd for Fatigue," were by the "Vivacity" of their wits and "Readiness" of "Invention" intended "for Thought and the Exercise of the Mind." But this law of nature had been overturned, declared "The Lady"; fearful of women, "Cowards" become "Tyrants"—"for none can be Tyrants but Cowards"—men had subjugated them. That assertion was developed unfalteringly:

> This is our Case; for Men being sensible as of the Abilities of Mind in our Sex, as of the strength of Body in their own, began to grow Jealous, that we, who in the Infancy of the World were their Equals and Partners in Dominion, might in process of Time, by Subtlety and Stratagem, become their Superiours; and therefore began in good time to make use of Force (the Origine of Power) to compell us to a Subjection, Nature never meant; and made use of Natures liberality to them to take the benefit of her kindness from us. From that time they have endeavour'd to train us up altogether to Ease and Ignorance; as Conquerors used to do to those, they reduce by Force that so they may disarm 'em, both of Courage and Wit; and consequently make them tamely give up their Liberty, and abjectly submit Necks to a slavish Yoke. . . .

"The Lady" cited what historical evidence she could find for her analysis; its thinness only secured the position. Since, she said, "Historians . . . as Men are Parties against us, and therefore their Evidence may justly be rejected . . . I can't tell how to prove all this from Ancient Records; for if any Histories were anciently written by Women, Time, and the Malice of Men have effectually conspir'd to suppress 'em; and it is not reasonable to think that Men shou'd transmit, or suffer to be transmitted to Posterity, any thing that might shew the weakness and illegallity of their Title to a Power they still exercise so arbitrarily, and are so fond of."[23]

An Essay in Defense of the Female Sex was mistitled. Actually it was attack and slash all the way. Wit and invention it had in abundance, its middle section of fictional character sketches (of a Beau, a Pedant, a Poetaster, a "City-Critick") a roving ridicule of male superficiality, posing, and pomposity. "The Lady" won a lot of points—before she lost the bout.

Her slip occurred in a discussion, based upon the "experience" of observation, of the social conditioning of girls and boys. It was a fact, she said, that because they were not "suffer'd to run about at liberty as Boys" little girls received books as toys, "Romances, Novels, Plays and Poems." At first they might read their books childishly, "carelessly," but all "unawares" they were learning, acquiring "a considerable Command both of Words and Sense." And rather than running about boisterously girls spent many hours 'calling' with their mothers; in such visiting rounds they had "the opportunity of imitating, conversing with, and knowing the manner, and address of elder Persons." This was why, "The Lady" thought, the girl at fifteen was "as ripe" as a male of twenty-one, why she was typically so articulate and socially precocious. On the whole "The Lady" approved of this customary recognition of the "differences"—somehow not a "disparity in Nature"—between the sexes; it was probably better, she said, than teaching girls Latin and Greek.[24]

And so in staking out the romances, novels, plays, and poems for girls "The Lady" (all unawares) conceded along with the Latin and Greek the math, physics, chemistry, the mechanical arts, and social engineering: all the male subjects. From her lonely post in the 1790s (long frustrated in her assignments of magazine reviews of 'female literature') Mary Wollstonecraft was trying to recall them, or alternately, disdaining solidarity with her unresponsive sex, trying to recreate only her own intellect as male, "asking men's questions," as she put it.[25]

Educated female 'modernizers,' late seventeenth-century "signposts," Wollstonecraft's poignant metaphor—out of a jumble of thoughts pushed a last subject for my survey. It was Celia Fiennes, a well-placed, private lady who literally traveled her chosen roads with unladylike energy and insistent curiosity, asking men's questions all the way. Astell-type feminism seems never to have struck Celia Fiennes. Her feelings about her sex were expressed in tart advice of more useful female distractions than card games and dice tables; she had a "souveraign remedy" to cure women of their "epidemick diseases of vapours," more plainly, of their "Laziness." She was artlessly uncomplaining about any "deffect" in her gentlewoman's education— no "embellishments" of Latin and Greek; she was too absorbed in the daily "studdy of those things which tends to improve the mind and makes our Lives pleasant and comfortable as well as proffitable. . . ." Yet Celia Fiennes, tourist and journalist, was as special as (maybe more special than) the avowed feminist. In one thing she was like Lucy Hutchinson: both of them cut through the marginalia in society. Mrs. Hutchinson wrote the history of the battles of God's Elect; Celia Fiennes recorded the progress of their grandsons' political economy. To each generation its magisterial activity.

The manuscript journal which in a fine modern edition (1947) became *The Journeys of Celia Fiennes* was a travelogue of a series of trips through every county in England, and touching bits of Wales and Scotland, from the late 1680s to 1700. In its brisk prefacing statement Celia Fiennes said that she began traveling to "regain" her health, indicating plainly at the same time that her fascination with her "native Land," making "observations of the pleasant prospects, good buildings, different produces and manufactures of each place," fast became purpose enough. End of self-explanation: from that point Celia Fiennes was merely the nameless reporter-on-horseback, source of streams of descriptive fact.[26]

No good editor (and Celia Fiennes had in the 1947 edition of the *Journeys* elegant and scholarly editorial attention)[27] could let the identification rest there. A luxury of evidence tells why she decided upon a hobby so significant that it resulted in "the first comprehensive survey of England since Harrison's and Camden's in Elizabeth's reign."[28] Celia Fiennes was a natural for the project; she came to it by genealogy, heritage, class, personal circumstance.

Celia Fiennes was properly A Lady, by genealogical precision both a lady and a Roundhead. Her grandfather was William, eighth Baron and first Viscount (created 1624) Saye and Sele. "Old Subtlety" he was dubbed by his enemies, the "oracle" in Clarendon's book of those "called Puritans," and a relentless critic of Stuart policies from the late reign of James I.[29] Whether true or not that the Civil War was "virtually planned" at Lord Saye's seat of Broughton Castle in Oxfordshire,[30] it is certain that with Pym, Hampden, and the handful of other Puritan notables he was central in the organization of the parliamentary confrontation with Charles I. Celia Fiennes's father was his second son, Nathaniel, who was a colonel in the parliamentary army (he was the commander-governor who surrendered Bristol to Prince Rupert's seige-force in 1643) and though one of the members of the Commons ejected from the House in Pride's Purge sat in the 1650s on the Council of State and in the Cromwellian House of Lords. Nathaniel Fiennes's second wife was Celia's mother: she was Frances, daughter of a Hampshire squire and parliamentary army officer, Richard Whitehead (the first wife was the eldest daughter of Sir John Eliot, the martyred model of parliamentary resistance to the king). At the Restoration the old Viscount made his peace with the Stuart monarchy, though he lived only until 1662, the year too of his granddaughter Celia's birth. Colonel Nathaniel quietly withdrew from public life, and lived unmolested and without penalties on his Wiltshire estate of Newton Toney, near Salisbury, to his death in 1669.

Parliamentary inbreeding and peer status: it is satisfying to the biographer that Celia Fiennes demonstrated qualities of mind and character that that background should logically have given her. Her independence and unconventionality surfaced every day that accompanied only by a couple of servants she rode out to possible hazards of rutted highways, flooding streams, unfriendly locals, and bad inns. In religion she was Nonconformist, always pleased to find sober, respectable communities of "Dessenters" in towns she visited. Her intense patriotism was centered on the England saved by Whiggish gentlemen and the blessed, "glorious," King William. In the 1630s her grandfather had rejected the idea of resettling in New England where "every man is a master and masters must not correct their servants, where wise men propose and fools deliberate."[31] Like him, she had no patience with leveling innovation: "how can those," she commented scornfully, "that are worth little or nothing be good disposers of the kingdom, treasure or priviledges, or stand up for them."[32]

And that is to say that the viscount's progressive postrevolutionary granddaughter equated mastership with accumulating wealth at least as much as with old name. Her one sibling, a younger sister, married a London "Turkey merchant" with diverse and multiplying assets; when her mother died in 1691 Celia Fiennes moved from Newton Toney to London apparently to be close to these dearest relatives. As she journeyed about the countryside she lodged with 'improving' squires, ever admiring their "good enclosures." She visited an "old acquaintance married to a tradesman," and stayed with "Mr. Foley, Tom of 10,000£," who possessed "great iron works and mines" and "6 or 10 mile" of the land surrounding his house. Appropriately, then, Celia Fiennes avoided the powerless poor, or distastefully fled the "nasty sort of people" she saw especially in Wales and Scotland; their poverty, she said, "I impute to their sloth."[33]

As a maiden lady of uncluttered leisure Celia Fiennes was perfectly situated to indulge an itch for travel. Her earliest recorded trip, made probably in the mid-1680s, was kin-visiting *cum* sightseeing. She and her mother journeyed from Newton Toney through Salisbury (inventorying the cathedral "esteemed the finest in England") south to Blandford, and proceeded to a slow looping tour of the Isle of Purbeck, west Dorsetshire, and the fringe of Devon; the itinerary was so arranged that they stayed with no less than half a dozen "relations," gentry families mostly tied to the mother's Whitehead clan. And of course there were Fiennes relatives scattered invitingly about, in and near London, Portsmouth, Chester, Derby, Leicester, Northampton, Oxford.

Editor Christopher Morris, in his elegant introduction to *The Journeys*, pointed to the larger currents, indeed the "new discovery of

England" on-going from the 1670s, enticing Celia Fiennes to her travels. She was an "authority" on spas, he noted, took the mineral waters and dipped in the medicinal springs from Epsom and Tunbridge to Bath and Knaresborough. Of the possible explanations of this preoccupation Morris thought the least likely a delicacy of health in so obviously vigorous a woman. Perhaps it was a social indisposition, a touch of the hypochondria which can accompany "the growth of wealth, comfort and leisure." Certainly it was fashionable: the spas were such a "universal" rage that the rich, the middle class, and the humble folk had their separate curative waters. Celia Fiennes "sampled" them all, egalitarian in this at least.[34]

Her beloved hot mineral baths were but one sort of 'natural wonder' being both enjoyed and investigated. Two miles from Newton Toney was Stonehenge, subject of antiquarian conjecture and 'scientific' measurement; Celia Fiennes had "told," that is, counted, its stones "often," she said, doubtless from childhood. She twice referred to the *Britannia* of William Camden, the Elizabethan topographer and antiquarian. Possibly as she transcribed her notes to manuscript form she had at her elbow its marvelous 1695 re-edition, expansive with the new scholarship of Oxford dons, county historians, and subject specialists: from John Evelyn (on Surrey) to Samuel Pepys (Navy arsenals in Kent, Portsmouth, and Harwich) to "Mr. Ray, the Great Botanist of our age" (cataloguing plants).[35] John Ogilby's *Book of Roads* might have been useful even though it charted only main routes (Celia Fiennes's adventures put her often in lanes too narrow for coaches to pass). Still Ogilby's 1675 publication was a beautiful book. Above "40000 Miles of Road" were mapped, ordinance-map style, with landscape sketched in, rivers and brooks, bridges, quarries, rills, arable and pasture land, "Fenny ground," heaths, moors or "marsh sand"; the brief text gave the tourist a little on the history, and much on the produce and manufacture, the market times, inns and "entertainment" of the towns along the "Post" and "dependent" roads, with addenda of "Turnings to be avoided," some "Backward," some "Forward," some "Acute."[36]

None of this, to repeat, Celia Fiennes thought it important to mention. In the end, neither scholarly research nor informed speculation can explain why she rode more than three thousand miles "from Land's End to Liddisdale," in singular accomplishment in her generation.[37] She did carefully calculate her mileage: "my Long Journey this summer," she noted of her last travel in 1698, "was in all above 1551 miles and many of them long miles" (the mile was still measured erratically, and tiresomely lengthened especially in northern

England).[38] Perhaps with that she expected readers to guess that she was a touring woman by her own drive and imagination, choosing her sights and planning her routes by personal criteria of essential things to see and do.

And Celia Fiennes may merely have assumed that her readers, had they her drive and imagination, would have chosen to see as she did what was progressive, productive, and profitable. With unerring discrimination through rural acres and dotting towns the Fiennes eye picked out the improvements by the hand of men.

Editor Christopher Morris researched Celia Fiennes's own investment in a piece of land in Cheshire discovered to be rich in rock salt, the first found in England.[39] She had obviously more than a passing interest in minerals and mining: in Derbyshire she observed that though the "surface of the earth looks barren" it was "impregnated with rich marbles Stones Metals Iron and Copper and Coale mines" in its "bowells." From Wales through Devonshire to Lancaster and Durham she compared kinds and uses of coal, commenting with off-hand ease, for example, about cannel coal that it was "hard and will be pollish'd like black marble, for salts or boxes or such like, the only difference it will not bear the fire as marble does else it resembles it very much"; this "Pitt Coale," she said, "burns like a candle and makes white ashes like the Scotch-Coale, the same sort is in Nottinghamshire."[40]

Mining techniques she found fascinating. In Cornish "Tinn mines" employing "a great many people . . . they blow the tin . . . take the oar [ore] and pound it in a stamping mill which resembles the paper mills, and when its fine as the finest sand, some of which I saw and took, this they fling into a furnace and with it coale to make the fire, so it burns together and makes a violent heate and fierce flame, the mettle by the fire being seperated from the coale and its own drosse, being heavy falls down to a trench made to receive it, at the furnace hole below; this liquid mettle I saw them shovel up with an iron shovel and soe pour it into molds in which it cooles and soe they take it thence in sort of wedges or piggs I think they call them; its a fine mettle thus in its first melting looks like silver, I had a piece poured out and made cold for to take with me. . . ."[41]

Indeed all manufacturing technology fascinated Celia Fiennes, the making of tin or brick or paper or Staffordshire "fine tea-potts cups and saucers of the fine red earth." She was captivated by activity in Exeter. As "Norwitch is for coapes callamanco and damaske," she wrote, Exeter is for "Serges": "the whole town and country is employ'd for at least 20 mile round in spinning, weaveing, dressing, and scouring, fulling and drying of the serges, it turns the most money in a week of anything in England, one weeke with another there is 10000 pound paid in ready money, sometymes 15000 pound. ..." Even the oat bread of Northumberland and Scotland (Celia Fiennes thought only "wheaten" bread really civilized) was interesting in production. "I saw the oat Clap bread made," she reported, "they mix their flour with water so soft as to rowle it in their hands into a ball, and then they have a board made round and something hollow in the middle riseing by degrees all round to the edge a little higher. ... this is to cast out the cake thinn as a paper, and still they clap it and drive it round, and then they have a plaite of iron same size with their clap board and so shove off the cake on it and so set it on coales and bake it." The product was, she concluded (cosmopolitan generosity) "as crisp and pleasant to eate as any thing you can imagine . . . thinn waffers as big as pancackes and drye . . . very acceptable . . . where its well made."[42]

Riding into a city or town Celia Fiennes purposefully focused on the chief features and rated them on her scale of distinction. The physical setting was a registered but minor detail: *le site* alone was never *vaut le voyage*, not even in Durham. A well-stocked market place, and a handsome market cross, if present, made the top of her charts, followed by the "pitch" and cleanliness of the streets, the style and condition of the houses (along with the status of their inhabitants), the guildhall, and the churches. She visited the cathedrals, comparing bulk of "body" and height of spire, thickness of pillars and loftiness of roof, complexity of carving, colorfulness of choirs and windows. A standing castle was an item of some attraction, or even its ruins (and a daughter of the parliamentary Fiennes knew why and when it had been destroyed).

Private architecture, however, gave Celia Fiennes her quickest measure of the worth of town. It was a simple valuation: new was good; old was bad. There were "noe fine houses" in Shrewsbury, for example, though many "large old houses," admitted to be "convenient and stately." The dismissal of wattle-and-daub Shrewsbury provides the definition of "old": in Beccles near Norwich she saw "no good building the town being old timber and plaister-work" except for the "one good house" of "Sir Robert Rich." Leicester was a town "of old timber buildings except one or two of brick" (though she was pleased that town fathers were pushing an extension into "Newark," with "stone and brick" new buildings, including a guildhall). Bedford was "an old building" where even the surrounding gentry lived "in such old houses." By contrast Nottingham was "the neatest town," of course "built of stone and delicate large and long Streetes much like London and the houses lofty and well built"; the manufacture of Nottingham was "mostly" in "weaving of Stockings," a "very ingenious art," but brick, tile, and glass were made there too, and the "strongest and best" ale. Leeds was a "large town, severall large streetes cleane and well pitch'd and good houses al! built of stone"; it was "esteemed the wealthyest town of its bigness in the Country," its people manufacturing woolen cloth, "the Yorkshire Cloth in which they are all employ'd and are esteemed very rich and very proud." In sum, the old/new, bad/good judgment presumed upon architecture: newness erased decay, fairly shouted ambition, experimentation, prosperity.[43]

As she moved outside of kinship hospitality of the south and center of England Celia Fiennes had to find commercial accommodations for herself, servants, horses. She became a pithy expert on the inns of England, not many of which equaled these offerings in Pontefract: out of "many good Inns" she stayed at the best, "the Sunn," a "very good genteel Inn" with a landlord who was also mayor of the town; she obtained satisfactory "Provisions" there too, "2 or 3 pound of Codfish" which she bought "for a small matter." Lodging was depressingly more primitive in the north. She traveled no farther into Scotland, abandoning a visit to Edinburgh, after the experience of an inn in a border market town: "I was not able to beare the roome," she said, "I rather chose to stay and see my horses eate their provender in the stable then to stand in that roome, for I could not bring my self to sit down." She had "no stomach" for the food brought to her, "noe wheaten," only "their clapt oat bread," so she bought her own, which turned out to be a happy surprise: salmon "neer a yard long" and a "very large Trout of an amber coullour," both washed down with French wine, "exceeding good Clarret," the "best and truest French wine," she said, "I have dranck this seven year and very clear . . . very fine."[44]

Celia Fiennes liked a bargain: money *was* an object. But she demanded a clean bed first, and a well-laid table; indeed good bread, cheese, bacon, and eggs could compensate for a poor inn. She searched out local products—rated beer and ale all over the kingdom—and an unexpected *specialité* touched a child-like delight: in the West Country she was served "an apply pye with a custard all on top"; "they scald their creame and milk," she said, "and so its a sort of clouted creame as we call it, with a little sugar, and soe put on the top of the apple pye," decidedly "the most acceptable entertainment that could be made me." She was something of a gourmet with seafood. In Purbeck she tasted "the best lobsters and crabs being boyled in the sea water and scarce cold, very large and sweet." North in Westmoreland she was anxious to sample the "charr fish" which a landlady reputedly did "pott up" the "best of any in the country"; unfortunately the char were out of season, though with "other fish" she got "a very good supper." To be sure, almost everywhere fish were inexpensive and probably the safest eating. Standard, excellent fare was salmon "at a pretty cheape rate," a "very large Codfish . . . very fresh and good . . . but 8 pence," and "six Crabbs" as big as "two hands" costing only three pence.[45]

There is the irresistible impulse to update the familiar personality of Celia Fiennes of the *Journeys*: to make of her the author of a pruned, one-volume *Blue Guide, Country Inns*, and *Stately Homes of England*, travel authority for middlebrow, middle-class tourists pragmatically curious and present-minded as she. With volume in hand her followers could enter, say, Canterbury, where the 'local things to see' would get equal importance and equal time: the cathedral (almost impossibly old) with "very fine" carving on the outside and within, "a fine large organ" and "most delicately painted" windows in the choir; and two flourishing trades, one in the weaving of silks, a "very ingenious art" in "fine flower'd silks," and the other a paper industry, its mills producing both brown and white paper "at a quick rate" and "so firme as it may be taken up sheete by sheete."[46]

Between towns her readers would not miss the absence of lyrical prose-appreciation of rural England. They would be remembering to look at the "Rich deep land" all "ploughed about," or "a great flatt full of good inclosures." In any case, they were anticipating the next starred sight, some gentleman's estate and "good house," occasionally a magnificent palace like Burghley House outside of Stamford (the "only fault" in which, readers were told, was "the immodesty of the Pictures especially in my Lords appartment," the subjects "all without Garments or very little"). As a properly professional travel reporter Celia Fiennes had admittance to most gentry homes, to poke about from the "kitching pastry and pantry" to the "roofe of the Staires"; she could describe items down to the "satten" stitching which "looks like painting" on the "tester" of the master's bed at Burghley House. Thus her followers vicariously explored the "finest homes," those built, naturally, of "brick and coyn'd with stone" (they were never led through half-timber antiques, the black-and-white Moreton Old Hall, for instance). They could 'know' Newby Hall, one among many, but the "finest house" in Yorkshire, know it from its splendid gates of iron and gold to its "6 or 7 Chambers," one "painted just like marble," and all with "good beds" of "crimson figured velvet . . . damaske . . . moehaire and camlet." They would 'see' its practical mechanics, the "very clear good Beer" being "well brew'd" in the cellars, or the "Landry Close with frames for drying of the cloths," even the pipes which "serv'd" water into a "Cistern" and from there to "the garden cellars and all offices"; and they would crane their necks for a glimpse of the cattle raised by the gentleman-entrepreneur of the Hall, including "one of the largest Beeves in England."[47]

Guided into London the Fiennes tour group got free time to explore the "Citty properly for trade," to admire the "London mode" of merchants' homes and noblemen's palaces, to browse in the shops and to gaze at the "sumptuous" Royal Exchange, or London Bridge—"all stone with 18 arches"—or the "Great Monument" in memory of God's "check to the rageing flame" of the papists, or to "vast" St. Paul's all newly "built up" (and possessing, in a rare change of adjective, "a sweet organ"). Before they separated, though, the tourists listened to a lecture, or rather, two lectures: the first on the Constitution, the structures of monarchy, Parliament, and courts (and "Laws" the "best in the world"); the second, an insider's account of the ceremonials of the national power elite, from coronations and royal funerals to the "Lord Mayor's Show," with shimmering depiction of props whether jeweled head-dresses or "jellys" in "pyramidyes" on the tables of the Banqueting House.[48] The tourists would appreciate, probably to the last Whiggish detail, this discursive message. Here, they were being told, was the pulsing heart and the clicking brain, the motivating center of the England which was theirs to apprehend, to use and improve.

But the imagery collapses upon Celia Fiennes's assertion that she "never signed" her manuscript for publication: it is "not likely to fall into the hands of any but my near relations," she said. True, Christopher Morris argued effectively his skepticism about that remark. Why, he asked, throughout her text did she explain family kinships that would have been perfectly plain to her near relations? Why did she refer to the manuscript as "this book," and offer it for the edification of "Ladies, much more Gentlemen"? Would someone as utilitarian as Celia Fiennes have been unaware of the contribution she had made to the new discovery of England? Morris might have added what he learned when he found her will: she needed money. She lived four decades after the turn-of-the-century "Great Journeys" (dying at age seventy-nine) on the shrinking income of small annuities, "a great diminution of the temporal estate," she testified, because of bad investments and "depredations on my lands."[49]

We are back with speculation. Could the Fiennes lady not stoop to earning money with her pen? Did she wait too long, to be out-Defoed by the smashing appearance of Daniel's *Tour of the Whole Island of Great Britain* in 1724? What, however, do such questions have to do with the only evidence, which is Celia Fiennes's journal foreword, "To the Reader"?

The foreword fills but two printed pages. A longer introduction, explained Celia Fiennes, was unnecessary: since the journal was to be filed on family shelves it required little "to be said to excuse or recommend it." To be sure, its faults were glaring, above all else the "freedom and easyness" of a literary style too crude for sophisticates of "nicer taste," and an eye for "embellishments" and "adorned" descriptive prose. And while the record of her travels might be "diverting and proffitable" to bored, homebound ladies and to schoolboys being educated for "service of their country at home or abroad," it could be of no value "to Gentlemen that have travelled more about England, staid longer in places . . . have more acquaintance and more opportunity to be inform'd." Nor would the chapter on "our Constitution, Customs, Laws, etc." interest knowledgeable gentlemen; indeed, the author could "be justly blamed" for attempting "matters farre above [her] reach or capacity. . . ."

Yet, "without vanity" Celia Fiennes insisted on the supreme significance of her travels, and urged both ladies and gentlemen to follow her in appraising the "Glory" of England. Particularly the parliamentary gentlemen needed her experience, ignorant as they were "of anything but the name of the place" they represented; with Fiennes-type travel they would learn "the nature of Land, the Genius of the inhabitants, so as to promote and improve Manufacture and Trade suitable to each and encourage all projects tending thereto, putting in practice all Laws made for each particular good. . . ."[50]

Please "studdy" my "book," and "excuse" my "erratas"—to and fro went Celia Fiennes, conscious pride jostling self-effacement. The facts tell which won out. She had the career of a "modern woman explorer," said a contemporary of Myra Reynolds.[51] Her modern work was a tour de force, mutely unpublished.

NOTES

1. Myra Reynolds, *The Learned Lady in England, 1650-1760* (Boston and New York, 1920), p. 46.

2. In Hilda L. Smith, *Reason's Disciples: Seventeenth Century English Feminists* (Urbana, 1982), p. xii.

3. And Mrs. Behn continues to fascinate, more, as Vita Sackville-West firmly established, for her personality than her pen. See, beyond Sackville-West, *Aphra Behn: the Incomparable Astrea* (London, 1927), or George Woodcock, *The Incomparable Aphra* (London, 1948), the latest work, Angeline Goreau, *Reconstructing Aphra: A Social Biography* (London, 1980.)

4. *An Essay in Defense of the Female Sex. Written by a Lady* (London, 1696), p. 3.

5. Mary Astell and John Norris, *Letters Concerning the Love of God* (London, 1695), p. 49.

6. Mary Wollstonecraft, *Letters Written during a Short Residence in Sweden, Norway, and Denmark* (London, 1796), p. 242.

7. Mary Astell, *A Serious Proposal to the Ladies, For the Advancement of their true and greatest Interest. By a lover of her Sex* (London, 1694), pp. 73-75; also, the second edition, Astell, *A Serious Proposal to the Ladies, In Two Parts* (London, 1697).

8. Ibid., see "Contents" of part 2.

9. Mary Astell, *Some Reflections upon Marriage*, 2nd edition (London 1703), pp. 32-37, 24-26.

10. Astell and Norris, *Letters Concerning God*, p. 49.

11. Ibid., p. 2; René Descartes, *A Discourse on Method* (London, 1649), part 3, p. 44.

12. Astell and Norris, *Letters Concerning God*, p. 44-46.

13. Astell, *Reflections upon Marriage*, p. 97.

14. Astell and Norris, *Letters Concerning God*, p. 46-47.

15. Astell, *Reflections upon Marriage*, p. 11.

16. Ibid., p. 91.

17. See in its marvelous entirety Thomas Sprat, *History of the Royal Society*, ed. Jackson I. Cope and Harold Whitmore Jones (St. Louis, Missouri, 1958); and Brian Easlea, *Witch-hunting, Magic and the New Philosophy* (Sussex, 1980), especially chapters 4 and 5.

18. Sprat, *The Royal Society*, pp. 246, 327.

19. "Fancies": Seventeenth-century readers would probably think of *Poems and Fancies, Written by the Right Honourable, the Lady Mary Marchoines Newcastle* (London, 1653).

20. *An Essay in Defense of the Female Sex*, pp. 8, 11-12.

21. The *Essay* has long been attributed to Mary Astell, and remains so in various card catalogues. See, however, the discussion in Smith, *Reason's Disciples*, pp. 144 and especially 150n.35; Smith's conclusion is also mine.

22. *Essay in Defense*, pp. 13-14, 15-17.

23. Ibid., pp. 18-23.

24. Ibid., pp. 56-58.

25. Wollstonecraft, *Letters*, p. 13.

26. *The Journeys of Celia Fiennes*, ed. Christopher Morris (London, 1947), pp. 1-2.

27. Christopher Morris's Introduction is so knowledgeable and thoughtful that one can only borrow from it shamelessly. Probably he would not mind;

he thought it inexplicable that Celia Fiennes, "her value to the social or economic historian . . . inestimable," has gotten so little attention.

28. *Journeys of Celia Fiennes*, p. xxxix.

29. Clarendon, *History of the Rebellion*, 3: 26.

30. *Journeys of Celia Fiennes*, p. xv; *DNB.*

31. *DNB.*

32. *Journeys of Celia Fiennes*, p. 317.

33. Ibid., pp. 335, 181, 204.

34. Ibid., pp. xxvi-xxviii.

35. *Camden's Britannia, Newly Translated into English, Publish'd by Edmund Gibson, of Queens College in Oxford* (London, 1695).

36. John Ogilby, *Britannia, or an Illustration of the Kingdom of England and Dominion of Wales* (London, 1675).

37. See Joan Parkes, *Travel in England in the 17th Century* (Oxford, 1925), pp. 301, 281. Wrote Joan Parkes, "none but Mrs. [*sic*] Fiennes could claim knowledge of every English shire."

38. *Journey of Celia Fiennes*, pp. 282, xxxix. Christopher Morris points out that it was John Ogilby who first "quite literally, put the statute mile 'on the map.' "

39. Ibid., pp. xxi, xl.

40. Ibid., pp. 96, 110.

41. Ibid., p. 257.

42. Ibid., pp. 245-46, 190-94, 188.

43. Ibid., pp. 227, 146, 162-63, 340, 71-72, 219-20.

44. Ibid., pp. 94, 204-5.

45. Ibid., pp. 256-57, 12, 191-92, 76, 83.

46. Ibid., pp. 124-25.

47. Ibid., pp. 164, 69, 84-85.

48. Ibid., pp. 284, 290, 312, 286.

49. Ibid., pp. 1, xxiv-xxv, 363.

50. Ibid., pp. 1-2.

51. Parkes, *Travel in the 17th Century*, p. 301.

Conclusion

Certainly it is as a great laboratory of social change that England of the sixteenth and seventeenth centuries has attracted a steady succession of fine historians, beginning with R. H. Tawney. They may follow so many lines of dynamic development: the concentration of land as profit-making private property; the "primitive accumulation" which transformed peasant-tenants into wage-earning poor; the explosive growth of industry and trade, overseas commerce, investment, colonialism; corporate organization, banking, capital formation; the revolutionary adaptation of political and legal institutions to the interests of individual property-owners; in L. B. Wright's sweeping arc, the formation of "middle-class culture."

In comparison in the foregoing pages there is only one line of development, scarcely dynamic, and perceived always in its distance from the frantic excitement of the seventeenth century. In its coldest, starkest statement it might be set up in staged debate, 'before and after' social commentary. For example: in the 1620s the Reverend William Gouge, speaking of God's hierarchical society, told his Blackfriars congregation that while all inferiors thought "their burden the heaviest" and were "stubborn under the yoke of subjection," women were the "most backward in yeelding subjection to their husbands"; this was the reason, Gouge said, for his harsh "domestic sermons," his repetitive order that women "subject themselves to husbands as to Christ," to the man who was "after a manner a Saviour," who had a "kinde of fellowship and copartnership with Christ." To that, all of his clerical colleagues echoed 'amen,' adding only that in Christian renunciation of the "evill" of "rebellion" yet so present in their midst, women had to learn to subject themselves willingly to their husbands, to give "voluntary" obedience, not faked for "worldly respects," but "for conscience sake."[1]

At the end of the century Mary Astell with her "bold truths" might have been making a disrespectful riposte. Of course, she said, men ordered all women to be wives, because what each of them wanted was a piece of productive property who would "breed his Children," a "Housekeeper" whose "Business and Entertainment are at home," an "upper Servant" more reliable than any he could "hire for Money." Rather than a savior Astell called the husband a "Monarch," to whom "according to some learned Casuists" the wife yielded, beyond her "Fortune and Person," the "very desires of her Heart, so as that it is not lawful to Will or Desire anything but what he approves and allows."[2]

But the main line of development of the adaptation of the female to the needs of a society of property owners was not unilinear, devoid of drama, lacking in contrast and contradiction. Indeed, here too the seventeenth century as formative age is irresistibly interesting: it was preface to the long night which lingered, Virginia Woolf thought, to the end of the eighteenth century when "middle class women began to write" (an event of "greater importance," Woolf said, "than the Crusades or the Wars of the Roses"),[3] or which stretched on, grey and gloomy, for the silent and suffering Victorians.

Thus we have Lucy Apsley, Elizabethan girl-child, educated, presumably with 'a room of her own,' writing at least one sonnet which we know was performed at a party before she locked it in a drawer. That is one answer to Virginia Woolf's "perennial puzzle" of the absence of female poets in Shakespearean England "when every other man, it seemed, was capable of song or sonnet."[4] Instructed by the ministers of God, Lucy Apsley took up her life calling as Mrs. Hutchinson, a role she filled with what seems notable individuality and initiative, strangely at variance with her self-image as dull object illuminated only by her male-sun, as at best a mirror reflecting his transcendent self. Deprived of John, Lucy Hutchinson wrote his history (so well that our generation rates her a pioneer of 'Whig history'),[5] dedicated it to his children, and locked it too in her drawer.

In the first winter of civil war London gentlewomen and tradesmen's wives came to the doors of the House of Commons to present the petition of the views of their sex, all the while trembling with their audacity, and wincing before the hoots of incredulous men. Leveller women dared to include themselves in the petitioning mass of men, and in the constitution-making majority of free citizens; but scrutinized closely, the private ambitions of one of the bravest of them reached no farther than a cottage in the country, and a husband returning each evening to its fireside. And in the popular ferment of the Commonwealth decade female sectarians searched the Bible for justification of their equal rights and duties in testifying publicly for the Lord, and put their research into activities so provocative as to endanger their liberty and their lives; in the end they would settle obediently into women's meetings, to church participation in women's 'auxiliaries.'

Some women were a triumph within the freshly redefined female domestic role, filling it creatively, embellishing it with behavior that earned not simply patronizing praise but genuine admiration from their men. Christian faith and piety helped, perhaps, as the ministers and Mrs. Hutchinson insisted, were the necessary guides; but as, for example, Dorothy Shaw's exemplary life underlined, the luck of a compatible marriage and an intelligent and loving husband were essential accompaniment.

In Mary Astell's late-century reporting love was at the bottom, after property, duty, the pressure of friends, of the list of reasons that men married: love, she said, made a "mighty Noise in the World, partly because of its Rarity." But women we have met seemed both to have hoped for and *expected* love in marriage. The lack of love, in family-arranged marriages for status and property, appears the central disappointment for all of them, the source of subsequent fixed personality traits or disorders. "I am a victim," sighed Alice Thornton; consequently she proceeded to make everyone around her as miserable as she. "Me a victim?" demanded Susanna Eyre: "I'll see about that!" In loveless marriage and consigned to her lonely castle Lady Brilliana Harley turned for solace and companionship—for a substitute husband—to her eldest son. Joan Drake, obscure, clever gentlewoman, lived out the strangest variation of marital disappointment and distress, somehow convincing godly menfolk of her saintliness at the very moment that she deserted her marriage. And victim Elizabeth Freke, the embittered, romantic Elizabeth Freke, finally secured a corner of the male propertied world from which to victimize everyone unfortunate enough to be dependent upon her.

Arguably, London middle-class women living by their wits in the marriage market reflected most faithfully, imitated most perfectly, the masters of the new society. City-wise and enterprising, why should they not have turned the trick and made their fortunes by fleecing sex-prowling, vulnerable males? We are told that an "original and lasting contribution of capitalism" was the creation, out of the massive dislocation of the laboring poor of rural England, of an "institutionalized underworld of professional crime," an underworld "of private enterprise for profit and power respond[ing] exactly, at a different social level, to bourgeois conditions for survival."[6] The women with the picturesque names, Mehetabel Jones, Elizabeth Pigeon, and Theodosia Ivie, were representative types of more or less 'genteel' female criminals, responding exactly, at their social level, to bourgeois conditions for survival.

Finally, at the century's close a few educated, privileged women described the domestication of females, their relegation to a separate, unvalued women's world; in their words are striking contrasts and contradiction. The conceptualization of the situation had changed so swiftly: scarce decades earlier Mrs. Hutchinson was explaining female subordination in unexamined acceptance of heavenly sociology; by the 1690s the author of *An Essay in Defense of the Female Sex*, her mind set in completely secular world view and unconcernedly citing her Hobbesian borrowings, asserted the *historical* process in which male "tyrants" had subjugated women. Astell's *Reflections upon Marriage* was part of this new moment of perception, inseparable from it: the situation still seemed to her fluid, possible of amendment. Thus, proposing her reforms, she wrote equally to men and to women. She presented to men the worst scenario of female bondage in marriage to shock them into understanding; she pled with them to use their unquestionable power as husbands more gently, with sensitivity and generosity. And she told women to improve themselves, to convince the "noble" male sex that they were other than "little useless and impertinent Animals"; she told them to stock their minds with "solid and useful Knowledge" (by implication, with the absorbing studies which enlivened Celia Fiennes's existence), the better to fulfill their duties as wives and mothers.

In short, outraged description of the seventeenth-century development of bourgeois women's world was affirmation of it. All of the women we have met, whether saintly models, unhappy wives, calculating criminals, contemplative intellectuals, itinerant spinsters, or even a solitary Catholic midwife, all of them affirmed the enveloping domestic sphere so effectively that in a few years it would be fixed as though in social concrete. Astell-like themes were buried; they would have to be discovered again and again by bourgeois feminists, in cycles of newly found vindications of the Rights of Women.

NOTES

1. Gouge, *Domesticall Duties*, pp. 23, 26, 345-48; Thomas Gataker, *Marriage Duties Briefly Couched Together*, p. 29.
2. Astell, *Reflections upon Marriage*, pp. 32-36.
3. Virginia Woolf, *A Room of One's Own* (New York, 1963), p. 68.
4. Ibid., p. 43.
5. MacGillivray, *Restoration Historians*, pp. 170-85.
6. C. George, "Making of the English Bourgeoisie," *Science and Society*, Winter 1971: 398-99.

Index

A Note on the Author

Margaret George is a professor of history at Northern Illinois University, DeKalb. She is the author of *The Warped Vision*, a study of British foreign policy in the 1930s, and *One Woman's "Situation": A Study of Mary Wollstonecraft*. She has published several articles in *Past and Present* and *Science and Society*. Professor George has been a Woodrow Wilson Fellow and an Andrew Mellon Fellow.